T. Hudson, Pinxt 1750.   H. B. McLellan, Sc.

HON:BLE WILLIAM SHIRLEY, ESQ.

A
Particular History
OF THE
Five Years
French and Indian War
IN
New England and Parts Adjacent

FROM
ITS DECLARATION BY THE KING OF FRANCE
MARCH 15, 1744
TO THE
TREATY WITH THE EASTERN INDIANS
OCTOBER 16, 1749

SOMETIMES CALLED
GOVERNOR SHIRLEY'S WAR

WITH A
MEMOIR OF MAJOR-GENERAL SHIRLEY, ACCOMPANIED BY
HIS PORTRAIT AND OTHER ENGRAVINGS

BY
Samuel G. Drake

HERITAGE BOOKS
2007

HERITAGE BOOKS
AN IMPRINT OF HERITAGE BOOKS, INC.

Books, CDs, and more—Worldwide

For our listing of thousands of titles see our website
at
www.HeritageBooks.com

A Facsimile Reprint
Published 2007 by
HERITAGE BOOKS, INC.
Publishing Division
65 East Main Street
Westminster, Maryland 21157-5026

Originally published

Albany:
Joel Munsell, 82 State Street.
1870.

Entered, according to Act of Congress, in the year 1870,
By Samuel G. Drake,
In the Clerk's Office of the District Court of the United States
for the district of Massachusetts.

— Publisher's Notice —

In reprints such as this, it is often not possible to remove blemishes from the original. We feel the contents of this book warrant its reissue despite these blemishes and hope you will agree and read it with pleasure.

International Standard Book Number: 978-0-7884-0294-4

TO THE

OFFICERS AND OTHER GENTLEMEN,

MEMBERS OF THE

NEW YORK HISTORICAL SOCIETY,

WITH WHOM THE AUTHOR HAS BEEN A COWORKER FOR MANY YEARS, AS AN APPRECIATION OF THEIR OFT AND REPEATED EXPRESSIONS OF ENCOURAGEMENT AND APPROVAL OF HIS LABORS,

THIS VOLUME,

EMBRACING MANY OCCURRENCES IN THE BORDER HISTORY OF THEIR STATE,

IS

MOST RESPECTFULLY DEDICATED

BY THEIR

ASSOCIATE.

History of the French and Indian War.

CHAPTER I.

PRELIMINARY.

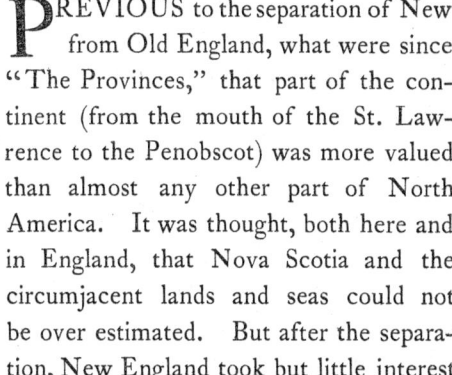

PREVIOUS to the separation of New from Old England, what were since "The Provinces," that part of the continent (from the mouth of the St. Lawrence to the Penobscot) was more valued than almost any other part of North America. It was thought, both here and in England, that Nova Scotia and the circumjacent lands and seas could not be over estimated. But after the separation, New England took but little interest in that part of the world, as it was possessed by bitter political enemies, exiled there because they had espoused and adhered to the cause of the British government. Consequently the intercourse between the sections at once nearly ceased. Hence our writers make small account of the history of the Provinces after their separation. But it is time to consider that the old political barrier has much decayed, and that in no great length of time it will entirely disappear; that the Provinces will become states, part and parcel of the great Union of States. When that day shall arrive the particular history of the early events of all that section will be sought after with as much zeal as any other. Those Provinces will one day become populous and wealthy; the great "tidal wave" of population now setting westward with such vast volume, will overwhelm the prairies, the valleys and mountains, till they can hold no more. Then the tide must turn, and the neglected coasts of Acadia, Cape Breton, and even Newfoundland, will be crowded with inhabitants in their turn.

This the reader may look upon as visionary, and too far in the distant future to be taken into consideration in scanning the history of New England; yet, with a conviction that such a result is sure, the writer has not neglected the Provinces altogether in the present compilation.

It was found impracticable to attempt a connected narrative of the body of the work; our object being a detail of events in the order of time — the events themselves having no connection — hence that part of the work is denominated a *Diary of Depredations*. This plan has been chosen as best calculated to embody the greatest amount of information naturally looked for in a work of this kind.

In former ages people were apparently satisfied with general history, and that of a kingdom or empire usually occupied far less space than that of a small town in the present age. Even up to the time within the memory of the writer, little else but general history found readers, and hence the age of particular history may be said to be of recent origin. The acts of individuals without titles seemed to have been considered of no interest, while those of kings and their courtiers were regarded little short of inspiration.

French and Indian War.

The great body of the people all over the world were ignorant, and hence easily made to believe that they had little else to do but to obey tyrannical rulers, and laud their actions; but a change has been going on, and as people became enlightened they naturally inquired of what account would kings and nobles be but for them—the People? Hence follow the other enquiries—what have been the acts of individuals in every great undertaking? who in reality have deserved the honor? And whether their privations and sufferings are not as much to be the objects of regard and commemoration as though they had by accident, and for no merit of their own, been invested with regal honors?

The following history has been undertaken specially to place upon its pages as many of the names of those who participated in the war, as well those who suffered by its ravages, as those who bore arms in it. Hence the work has been entitled a PARTICULAR HISTORY. And while we regret that our information is not so full, in some respects, as we desire, it is much further in advance, in the great objects of particulars aimed at, than anything hitherto published on the same period. Great pains have been taken to find out the names, both given and acquired, that is, christian and surnames of all parties, and generally with more success than was at first expected. Much time has been spent in endeavors to make the work as perfect in this respect as possible; because, in our view of history, that history is of value only in proportion as it makes prominent the real actors and sufferers in such history. Of what importance is it to a reader to learn that a certain officer, with a certain number of followers, on a certain time, attacked a defenceless village on a certain river, burnt the houses and carried off the inhabitants into captivity? Here is sound without sense, unless we know when and where the event took place, the names of the captives, the names of the principal depredators, as well as the incidents of the transaction. It is well known to every reader of our histories, from first to last, how lamentably deficient they are in the particulars here referred to.

It was quite a memorable saying of one of the ancient historians, that geography and chronology were the two eyes of history. That historian, or the author of that saying, ought to have added a third indispensable, and told us what the soul of history is. The reader of this preface will not require to be told what the writer considers the soul of history.

Many who have written histories of the period included in this work, scarcely notice above two events in it, and those in the most general terms. They tell us of the capture of Louisbourg and the sacking of Fort Massachusetts! And yet it was a war of about five years' duration—the entire English frontier, from Nova Scotia to the mouth of the Monongahela, was laid waste by fire and sword! At least a thousand people were killed and carried into captivity, exclusive of the losses of soldiers. The greatest sufferers were those who from necessity were obliged to make their homes in the wilderness border, and thus met the brunt of savage cruelties. To those our attention has been specially directed.

Within the last few years a very important source of information has been laid open, by the publication of documents from the French archives. The state of New York has caused to be copied from those archives whatever related to her borders, and printed them in an economical manner; thus rendering them accessible to everybody. These documents consist of minute particulars of all transactions in Canada

Materials for the Work.

during the French rule in that country; the French intercourse with and management of the Indian nations; how the Indians were employed by them in wars, and what was effected by them thus employed. All these documents were transmitted to France, have been well preserved, and through the liberality of the French government are now open for examination. The importance of those bearing on the period of this history will be observable by the reader in its perusal.

It appears from an examination of the transcripts taken from the French war office, that there was scarcely an expedition, of however small a number of men it consisted, but what was authorized by the government of Canada, and a record made of its setting out, of its return, and the success or ill success it met with. All these we now have, which is some advantage over those who have written without them.

Materials of our own are very fragmentary all along during the existence of the colonies. These had no common head, and each operated, in war and peace, on its own account. Hence there was no central point to which all matters of consequence might otherwise have been deposited, and thus have afforded the historian the means for composing a history of any particular period. Newspapers, now the great history of the world, of everybody and everything, were very few a hundred and fifty years ago, and even one hundred years ago, and those few had often slender means to arrive at the truth. Facts had to travel a great distance generally to get into type, and then it was *old* news, and if incorrect was not found out in time to make the necessary correction of any value to those immediately interested. However, notwithstanding these considerations, facts are contained in the newspapers of the times, highly valuable and indispensable, especially as they often come in as vouchers of other accounts, affording comparisons by which unmistakable truths are arrived at. There were fewer magazines than newspapers, and the accounts in these were generally copied from the former, which circumstance renders them of less historical value.

Of all the authorities useful to the historian, contemporaneous narratives are the most valuable; but these, upon the period under consideration, are very few, and some of these few are of such extreme rarity that they were unknown to most writers of history in a few years after they were published. The compiler of the ensuing work has been fortunate in his acquaintance with, and in having the use of several of this description of materials. To the author of one of these he has been much indebted; an author deserving the most honorable mention, yet almost entirely unknown, even in the section of country to which his work particularly relates; and the time has not yet arrived among the people there, in which a sense of their obligations has manifested itself, in any way, of which the writer is aware, beyond a head and foot stone in a cemetery at Northfield, with a commonplace inscription upon the former.

This neglected author was the Reverend BENJAMIN DOOLITTLE, of whom the following particulars have been obtained. He was born in Wallingford, Connecticut, July 10th, 1695; was son of John Doolittle of the same town, and grandson of Abraham Doolittle, the emigrant ancestor, who is found in New Haven about 1640. Benjamin was by a second marriage of John with Grace Blakesley, of whose early education and life no facts have been met with. It is only known that he was a graduate of Yale College in 1716, at the age of twenty-one years.* It is not material to know with whom he studied theology, but it is known that he was settled in the ministry at Northfield in 1718, in which office he continued about thirty years. His death was very sudden, occasioned, no doubt, by what in these days is termed the heart disease. A sermon was preached at his funeral by the Rev. Jonathan Ashley, of Deerfield, from the texts of Mark xiii, 37, and Rev. iii, 3, from which it appears that he died "January 9th, 1748,† in the 54th year of his age, and 30th of his ministry." The sermon was printed in Boston in 1749, making an octavo of twenty-six pages, but, as is usual with such performances, contains little information respecting the subject of it, beyond its title page. Besides the date of his death, and age, there are the following lines to his memory, upon the stone marking the place of his burial:

> Blessed with good intellectual parts,
> Well skilled in two important arts,
> Nobly he filled the double station
> Both of a preacher and physician.
> To cure men's sicknesses and sins,
> He took unwearied care and pains;
> And strove to make his patient whole
> Throughout, in body and soul.
> He lov'd his God, lov'd to do good,
> To all his friends vast kindness show'd;
> Nor could his enemies exclaim,
> And say he was not kind to them.
> His labors met a sudden close,
> Now he enjoys a sweet repose;
> And when the just to life shall rise,
> Among the first he'll mount the skies.‡

* For these few genealogical items we are indebted to the Hon. Mark Doolittle, late of Belchertown, a very distant connection of Benjamin, and a gentleman of high standing in Hampshire county.

† This date is old style, of course.

‡ Copied in Barber's *Historical Collections of Massachusetts*, 268. It seems not to have come to the knowledge of Bridgman, who collected and published what

There was also published in a Boston newspaper this brief notice of Mr. Doolittle's death: "We are informed that on the 9th instant, the Rev. Mr. Doolittle, pastor of the church in Northfield, was suddenly seized with a pain in his breast, as he was mending a fence in his yard, and died in a few minute's time, to the inexpressible grief of the town in general, as well as his own family in particular." *

Had not Mr. Doolittle been so suddenly taken away it is presumed he would have perfected and published his history of this war himself; for it is one of the most important and valuable records of it, so far as his plan extended, that can be found of any similar period in our history. His location gave him the best means of ascertaining the truth of the transactions, all of which he appears to have narrated with singular impartiality. It was doubtless well known to many that he kept a record of the events of the war, as not long after his death his manuscript was obtained and printed; but who superintended the printing, and made "the small additions to render it more perfect," no intimation is given in the work. Its title is as follows: "A short Narrative of the Mischief done by the French and Indian Enemy, on the western Frontiers of the Province of Massachusetts Bay; from the Beginning of the French War, proclaimed by the King of France, March 15th, 1743-4; and by the King of Great Britain, March 29th, 1744, to August 2d, 1748. Drawn up by the Rev. Mr. Doolittle, of Northfield, in the County of Hampshire; and found among his Manuscripts after his Death. And at the Desire of some, is now published, with some small Additions, to render it

---

he calls the *Inscriptions in the Grave Yards in Northampton and of other Towns in the Valley of the Connecticut*, 1850. This work the venerable Dr. Wm. Allen honored with *Brief Annals of Northampton*.

* *Boston Gazette and Weekly Journal*, January 24th, 1749.

more perfect. Boston: Printed and sold by S. Kneeland, in Queen Street, MDCCL." It is a small octavo pamphlet of 24 pages only.*

There is another work by the same author, but upon a different subject, which is probably the only one he ever published, and known only to the writer from an advertisement. Its title is—"An Enquiry into Enthusiasm, being an Account of what it is, the Original, Progress and Effect of it," 1743. Perhaps written on the occasion of the Whitefield excitement.

It was the original intention of the writer to publish a history of all the French and Indian wars, from the first settlement of the country to the final destruction of the French power on this continent; the number of volumes to equal the number of those wars, and he has during many years past made large collections, and extensive notes for that purpose. This volume not being in the order of time, that is, not the first in the series of those wars, but is made the first of the series, because the materials for it seemed more complete than any other; and here it may be well to give the reader an idea of the war periods to which reference is made:

The first was the Ten Years War, which followed the revolution in favor of William III, Prince of Orange, 1688 to 1698, during the administrations of Governors Phips and Stoughton, and sometimes called King William's war. Of this war Dr. Cotton Mather has given a history under the partial title of *Decennium Luctuosum*.

The second was during the governorship of Joseph Dudley, Esq., 1703 to 1713, alfo a *Decennium Luctuosum;* and called Governor Dudley's Indian War.

* See APPENDIX, A.

The third was in the term of Lieutenant-Governor Dummer's chief magistracy of Massachusetts, 1722 to 1725, and called Governor Dummer's Indian War.

The fourth was during a period of Governor Shirley's administration, 1744 to 1749, the period covered by the present volume.

The fifth extends from 1754 to the fall of Quebec, and final reduction of Canada. All of which comprehends a period of about seventy-two years, for nearly the whole of which time the entire frontiers of the English colonies were harassed by war, in the manner described in the ensuing pages; and whether other volumes will be published of the other war periods, depends on several contingencies not necessary to be mentioned.

CHAPTER II.

NOTICE OF GOVERNOR SHIRLEY.

Being a Review of a Portion of his Administration, in which an Attempt is made to correct Misstatements concerning it.

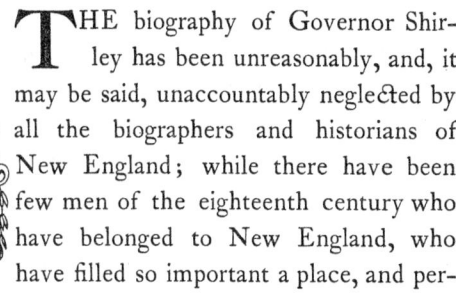

THE biography of Governor Shirley has been unreasonably, and, it may be said, unaccountably neglected by all the biographers and historians of New England; while there have been few men of the eighteenth century who have belonged to New England, who have filled so important a place, and performed such signal services as he. The reason for this neglect and injustice will be shown in the course of this notice.

The biography of Gov. Shirley here proposed is intended only as introductory to the history of the part of his administration including the Five Years Indian and French War embraced in the present work. His life is yet to be written, and will form a volume of the history of New England, if in skillful hands, inferior in interest to none, saving, perhaps, that of the Pilgrims. Therefore, in the present chapter it is only intended to review some erroneous statements which have hitherto passed for history.

Some untoward circumstances in the later war conspired to render Mr. Shirley's plans abortive. This is no uncommon fortune, and such have often happened to men of the greatest and best abilities. Whenever a man attains a position in any great undertaking, sappers and miners set busily at work to destroy his reputation. They often succeed, and pass off the stage of life undetected, except by their own consciences. They could not but know that history would expose them at some period in the future.

There does not appear the slightest grounds for questioning the patriotism of Governor Shirley. He made great sacrifices, and by his watchfulness, energy, and perseverance, the enemy were baffled in their hopes of subjecting this country and bringing it under Catholic domination. The danger was imminent when this war commenced, and Governor Shirley exerted himself to the utmost to avert such an event. No patriot of the Revolution of 1775 could have done more in asserting the rights of America than he did to avert the impending danger of falling under the rule of France. Some modern historians seem to have had no appreciation of his services, owing to a very superficial knowledge of the history of the times of which they were treating. They even bring the charge against him, that of "restoring British authority in the country!" A most extraordinary charge, considering that there was no other legal authority in the country.* Perhaps the laws may not have been so well executed before Mr. Shirley's accession as they were afterwards. If this was "restoring British authority," every good citizen had reason to rejoice. Surely nobody thought, at that early day, of independence of England, for without her aid New England would indubitably have become a province of France. Governors were not appointed to subvert the authority of the crown, but to see that the laws of the realm were faithfully

---

* See Bancroft, *History of the United States*. I hope he will not think me severe, for we have been intimate friends very hard upon forty years.

executed. Mr. Shirley did this to the entire acceptance of the country.

A contemporary historian,* an adopted citizen of Boston, generally opposed the measures of Mr. Shirley. His opposition, so far as can now be judged, arose from a fault-finding disposition, as he brings forward nothing against him except his acquiescence in the issue of paper money; but for which, as everybody knows, the Louisbourg expedition could not have been carried on. All issues of paper money are evils, and can only be warranted to prevent much greater evils. Could the Rebellion of 1861 have been put down without the aid of paper money? It was a gigantic evil, but what adjective have we that can express the magnitude of the evil if the Rebellion had not been put down?

Governor Shirley had his enemies. They are the consequence of success. To judge correctly of a man's character we must take the evidence of his cotemporaries, those known for their integrity, whose utterances have come down to us unimpeached, and whose lives are without reproach. Governor Hutchinson has spoken as highly of Mr. Shirley as one contemporary can be required to speak of another, and as his evidence must be familiar to all readers of New England history, it need not be repeated here; but we will take that of one of equally high standing, though less known, from the fact that his evidence appeared without his name, for prudential reasons. This was the Honorable William Livingston, author of the *Review of the Military Operations*,† etc., 1753 to 1756, with a full and accurate knowledge of all transactions in which Governor Shirley was engaged, thus speaks of him:

* Dr. William Douglass.
† See Sedgwick's *Life of Livingston*, page 114. That able work was first published in London, 1757, 4to, and reprinted in Boston immediately after, in the same form.

C

"Of all our plantation Governors, Mr. Shirley is most distinguished for his singular abilities. He was born in England, and bred up to the law at one of the inns of court. In that profession he afterwards practiced, for several years, in the Massachusetts Bay, and, in 1741, was advanced by his majesty to the supreme command of the colony. He is a gentleman of great political sagacity, deep penetration, and indefatigable industry. With respect to the wisdom and equity of his administration, he can boast of the universal suffrage of a wise, free, jealous and moral people."

Against this character of Gov. Shirley, drawn by an impartial and truthful contemporary, assertions to the contrary, by any at this distance of time, will hardly seduce those wishing to be well informed, into a belief of charges of the nature alluded to. "Ambitious and needy," says a modern historian. As to the first of these *crimes*, perhaps *he* (the accuser) may have *no ambition;* but the value of a man without that quality, to our apprehension, would be too small for estimation; and as to the charge of being *needy*, that was a consequence, as well as an evidence, of his integrity and honesty. This latter charge has rarely been made against public officers. Hence his enemies have never charged him with enriching himself at the expense of the province.

Another *sin* is also laid to the governor's charge — he upheld the Episcopal church! Was it not a requisite that all officers of the crown should be Protestants of that denomination? Did he ever interfere with other sects? Not at all. No such charge was ever brought against him, that has come within our knowledge. He was *ambitious* that all should have their rights, and in his account of the taking of Louisbourg,

Governor Shirley. 19

which he sent to the Duke of Newcastle,* and in his letters afterwards to men in power, he was *ambitious* that New England should not be robbed of its honors in that important service, and eventually was a principal means of obtaining for the country reimbursement for its expenses and sacrifices in that great undertaking, so long withheld through the misrepresentations of its enemies.

His letter to the Duke of Newcastle was accompanied by a journal of what transpired from the commencement of the expedition to the capture of Louisbourg. Both are written with admirable clearness, and at once discover superior literary ability, impartiality to all parties concerned, and a truthfulness unsurpassed by any writer of the time.

By the following action of the representatives of the colony, the estimation in which Governor Shirley's services were held is a noble acknowledgment of their appreciation, happily expressed, in these words: "It is with great pleasure we observe that you have once and again been the instrument in the hands of Divine Providence, of preserving the garrison of Annapolis, a province of Nova Scotia, from the French, more especially in the year 1744, when, by the forces your excellency sent from this province, it was snatched out of their hands, then just in possession of the fort; and again in the year 1745, when they were broken up in their siege of it by your surprising and successful attempt on Cape Breton; and now, again, when there was such a number of Canadians and others going against it by land and sea.

"But these things, although they have the effects of great wisdom, care, and application in your excellency, for which

---

* And "published by authority," by E. Owen, Warwick Lane, 1746, 8vo. The same was afterwards reprinted here in Boston, by Order of the General Court.

every good Englishman rejoices and is thankful, yet they have been performed at a great expense, more especially to this province, and therefore we cannot but be much concerned at the frequent return of this danger; not only because of the great difficulties in removing it from time to time, but also by reason of the doubt, whether by some surprise, impossible to be foreseen, this barrier of his majesty's dominions, of such mighty consequence, may not some time or other be lost, if it continues in its present exposed condition."

They go on and express a hope that his excellency may be able to suggest some remedy against the traitorous practices of those French subjects of Nova Scotia who, though protected by the British government, were using all means to destroy it.

After the patched up peace between England and France, in 1748, commissioners of the two governments met in Paris in 1750, to settle the boundary line between the two countries in America. The able memorial of this negotiation was written by Gov. Shirley, in which he showed that all the land between the St. Lawrence and Penobscot rivers belonged to England.* In 1753 he returned to his government in Massachusetts. The next year he explored the Kennebec river, and caused the erection of Fort Halifax and Fort Western.

While in France he married a second wife, privately it is said, at which many took umbrage, insinuating that he had taken a lady below him in social standing, and a Catholic besides; but as nothing is met with to the contrary, it is presumed that whatever of misfortune, if any, accrued from this marriage, proceeded from a spirit of detraction which soon died away.

---

* Jeremiah Dummer had many Years previous asserted the same claim. See *The Importance of Cape Breton*, page 13. London, 1746.

Governor Shirley.

In the war made memorable by its bringing George Washington into notice, and the defeat and death of General Braddock, Mr. Shirley was appointed a major-general in the British army, and he set vigorously to work to complete the conquest of Canada, fully convinced that there could be no safety for New England so long as it was under the dominion of the French. For this great object his plans were unquestionably well laid, and failed only through the inability or treachery, or both, of those on whom he was compelled to depend, to perform their parts in the undertaking. But as this cannot be discussed in a manner at all satisfactory, and does not belong to our present work, it is only necessary to remind the reader that a vindication of Maj.-Gen. Shirley has long since been triumphantly performed.*

It is a necessity in all wars to displace commanders if they do not happen to be successful in some important action, even if a misfortune happened entirely outside of their control. This was Gen. Shirley's situation, and it was enough for his enemies to seize upon, and through it ruined his prospects of future usefulness. But he lived to see a turn in that sort of tidal wave which rises far higher than it is able to maintain itself. Although for a time he was coolly treated, and met with some delay in getting his accounts through the hands of certain public officials, yet he was far from having been treated with obloquy, as some have insinuated.

Much injustice has been done Mr. Shirley by superficial writers who have not taken the pains to go to the sources of information; had they done so they would not have found him

---

* See the able and conclusive work entitled *The Conduct of Major-General Shirley in North America, briefly stated.* London, 1758, 8vo. Also, *A Review of the Military Operations in North America.* 4to, London, 1757, before cited.

claiming any honors not belonging to him, or shuffling off responsibility while an issue was doubtful, or claiming credit when such issue was to shed honors on those engaged in it.*

His extreme watchfulness while danger seemed imminent from a vast French fleet hovering on the coast during the summer of 1746, is strikingly apparent in many instances which cannot be detailed here, while they fall within the province of the historian of New England.

Claimants to the honor of an enterprise are not wanting after it has proved successful. So in the case of the Cape Breton expedition, there were no less than three noted gentlemen who, or their friends for them, laid claim to originating that of 1745. These were Col. James Gibson of Boston, Robert Auchmuty, Esq., also of Boston, and Major William Vaughan of Damariscotta.† The first named was a wealthy merchant, and is said to have advanced £500 towards setting the expedition on foot, accompanied it, and afterwards published an account of it. Respecting Mr. Auchmuty's claim, it is said that while an agent in England to adjust the boundary line between Massachusetts and Rhode Island, he published a work on *The Importance of Cape Breton, and a Plan for taking the Place*. Not having met with this performance, and its date being unknown, it must have been of small consequence, especially as secrecy was of the first importance. Besides, the capture of all and any important points from the French were common and daily topics of conversation. Mr. Auchmuty was the grandfather of the late Sir Samuel Auchmuty, a lieu-

---

* Dr. Eliot unfortunately fell into this error in his generally good biographical notices of New England men.

† He was then (1744-5) called "Capt. Vaughn," and had a block-house there with fourteen men in it which performed scout duty. See Eaton's *Thomaston*, I, page 54.

Governor Shirley. 23

tenant-general in the British army, and remembered on account of his expeditionary voyage to South America in 1806. Mr. Hutchinson, then speaker of the House of Representatives, makes no mention of Auchmuty in connection with the Louisbourg war, nor does he of Gibson, but he says (what he does not appear fully to sanction) that Vaughan "was called the projector of the expedition." That "it is probable he laid before the Governor a proposal for it, and it is certain he took great pains to induce the people to think favorably of it." A late author* says Vaughan first proposed the matter to Gov. Wentworth, who referred him to Gov. Shirley.

But the careful reader of this part of the history of New England has seen, that as early as May 14th, 1744, M. Du Vivier sailed from Louisbourg with an army of about 1000 men, captured Canso, and carried the garrison prisoners to Louisbourg. These prisoners being soon exchanged, and on returning home gave such an account of the defenceless state of the city, and of the fortifications there, that Gov. Shirley was satisfied the place might be captured, if attempted before it could be reinforced from France. Many were so zealous as to urge a winter expedition to the island, nothing doubting but that the fortifications could be carried by an escalade, by reason of the great depth of the snow, which usually lay in drifts they said, even with the tops of the walls of the fortifications.

Mr. Vaughan had traded there, and was well acquainted with the place from the reports of those he employed. In 1744 he was carrying on a fishery at Montinicus, and fitting out vessels for that purpose at Portsmouth, in New Hampshire, when the question of a secret expedition was raised, and into

---

* Judge Potter in his *History of Manchester*, 217.

which he entered with an energy and boldness very properly termed rashness. He was a son of Lieutenant-Governor Vaughan of that province. The most that he ever claimed of the honor of originating the expedition, judging from the publication probably authorized by him, was that "of having revived, at least, if not of being the original mover and projector of this grand and successful enterprise."* In another place the same writer remarks: "That Mr. Vaughan first set the expedition on foot; nay, that he revived it, when absolutely rejected by the General Assembly; that he behaved with all the gallantry and bravery as well as zeal for the service whilst it was going on, that could be expected from a person in a much higher rank, are facts which stand in need of no proof," according to certificates and original letters then in the hands of Mr. Vaughan.†

After a careful investigation of the period covered by the administration of Governor Shirley, it is confidently assumed that few, if any, of the colonial Governors of New England had more at heart the good of the country than he. His disinterested patriotism was, no doubt, a great benefit beyond his immediate administration, and was not without its influence on his able and fortunate successor, Governor Thomas Pownall.

Governor Shirley lived till the

---

* *The Importance and Advantage of Cape Breton, truly stated and impartially considered.* London, 1746, 8vo, p. 128. † *Ibidem*, 131.

commencement of the turbulent times which preceded the Revolution. He was then quite aged, and we do not find that he took any part in the political movements of that time. He was absent from the country through the most of that period, but returned, and died at his seat in Roxbury, March 24th, 1771, aged about seventy-eight years. His name is perpetuated by having been given to several places, though the compilers of gazetteers do not seem to have known the fact. Point Shirley perpetuates it in the vicinity of Boston. This place was so named with much ceremony, in 1753.*

The remains of Governor Shirley were deposited in King's Chapel, Boston.

It was so much the fashion of American writers subsequent to the Revolution, to decry those who had been in the service of the crown, that impartiality is seldom to be found in their accounts of them; and we are sorry to see the same prejudices lurking in popular works even to this day.

A circumstance which affected the reputation of Mr. Shirley immediately after he was superseded in command in America, should not be overlooked by his biographer. Two of his successors met with a fate similar to his; one, Lord Loudon, from causes which he quite satisfactorily proved he could not control, while the other, Gen. James Abercrombie, failed from causes which have not been urged in excuse or mitigation. The consequence was the three commanders were indiscriminately buried in the same grave of public opinion. Then came Wolfe, Monckton, Murray and Amherst. The British lion was at length fully aroused. Warned by the mistakes of Braddock and Abercrombie, the guidance of the pioneer woodsmen of New England was listened to, and the fall of

---

* See *New England Historical and Genealogical Register*, XIII, page 111.

Canada ensued. What Gen. Shirley, and others who labored with him, had done, was turned to the account of those they had made fortunate by their sacrifices. Hence it followed that all which had been achieved by Mr. Shirley and his companions in arms was lost sight of, and all the credit and glory were heaped upon their more fortunate successors. The saying is true, that "truth is mighty and will prevail," but it is often sunk so deep in the mire of falsehood, that it is a long time in coming to the surface.

Mr. Shirley promoted William Johnson to an important command, who, in a most treacherous manner, played false to him, and intrigued with the unscrupulous Delancy to blast the prospects of his benefactor. And it has since plainly appeared, that few men at any time ever realized greater renown on so small an amount of merit, as General, afterwards Sir William Johnson. But we leave him to his biographer.

Had circumstances favored the well-laid plans of an expedition against Canada, the enemies of Gen. Shirley would have been silenced; and, when it is well known that that expedition failed through the evil intentions and intrigues of men high in office, it ill becomes the modern historian to pronounce the plans of Gen. Shirley visionary and ill-conceived.

The vast preparations of France against New England, in 1746, have been alluded to, upon which it is proposed to be a little more explicit. Those gigantic preparations exceeded anything of the kind in magnitude since the armada of Spain for the conquest of England in 1588. Fortunately for New England, the elements and disease fought for the devoted country, which otherwise must, in all probability, have been laid waste by an embittered and relentless enemy.

In consequence of the knowledge Governor Shirley had

Governor Shirley.   27

that this French armada was hovering on the coast, he could not uncover the important points on the sea-coast until assured that the danger was past. When he had the positive intelligence that the armada was so severely handled by tempests and disease as not to be feared, the season was so far advanced that the invasion of Canada, as originally ordered by the home government, could not be prudently undertaken. And above all, the men of war from England, which were to cooperate, had not appeared. To turn the services of a great body of men, which had been raised for the Canada expedition, to some account, one against Crown Point was suggested. This was agreed to by the other colonies, Connecticut and New York; but owing to the lateness of the season, and their tardy movements, nothing was effected.

Will it any longer be alleged that the Canada expedition of 1746 was a Quixotic one, for the failure of which Governor Shirley was alone responsible? When every one can assure himself that Gov. Shirley, as did the other governors of the other provinces, received the "express commands" of his majesty, through his prime minister of course, that "men be forthwith raised" for that expedition; that owing to the failure of support in due season, as already remarked, the main design could not be entered upon; it was therefore hoped, as the New England men raised for the reduction of Canada were already in the field, something might be effected with them against Crown Point before the winter should set in. With this take into view, that every part of the frontier was beset by the enemy, now at liberty from the overthrow of their armada, to operate with which they had been kept in readiness during the summer. Now, even Albany was in such peril that no one could safely venture a quarter of a mile from its garrisons.* It was from this perilous condition of the country that Gov. Shirley, with the promised assistance of New York and Connecticut, strove night and day to relieve the people. Everybody then well understood that Crown Point was the great hive whence issued the principal war parties of the enemy; that there was their magazine of provisions, arms and ammunition; that there they retreated and replenished after every expedition against the frontiers; and therefore an effort should be at once made to break up that horde of assassins; that until it should be broken up, no relief of a substantial character could be expected. The object was manifestly worthy of an extraordinary effort, and was entered into with zeal. New Hampshire agreed to furnish 1000 men, Connecticut 600, and Rhode Island 400, to be joined with the 2000 ready in Massachusetts. Why it was not attempted to be carried into effect, has already been explained.

Detractors of Gov. Shirley's reputation, some time after the Cape Breton expedition, put in circulation a report that before the capture of Louisbourg he uniformly spoke of the undertaking, in his speeches to the General Court, as "their expedition," and after the place was taken, as "my expedition," as though he intended, in case of failure, to shirk all responsibility. We have failed to find any such expressions; and, on the other hand, we have found a straightforward man-

---

* The enemy had become so elated by success, that marauding parties, when protected by the night, had even ventured into the suburbs of the city, and there laid in wait to take prisoners. One of the enemy's Indians was peculiarly expert in enterprises of this kind, and had seldom failed in securing and carrying off his prey, even from within the confines of the city of Albany. An Indian named *Tomonwilemon* had become noted for such exploits. Smith's *New York*, Continuation, 482.

Governor Shirley.

liness in that and all other of his proceedings, of which any honorable man might be proud.*

With a few facts respecting the personal history of Governor Shirley, this notice will be closed.

The exact date of the arrival of Mr. Shirley in New England has not been met with. It is said to have been six or eight years previous to his appointment as governor of Massachusetts. Hence he came probably between the years 1733 and 1735, as he was one of the original subscribers to *Prince's Annals*, which was published in 1736. His family appears not to have come over until after his appointment as governor, in 1741. His wife, it is said, did not join him here till after the latter date, but continued in England, using her endeavors to obtain for him the office of collector of the port of Boston, which to him was preferable to the governorship; but Mr., afterwards Sir Henry, Frankland, secured that place.

We have in another work † had occasion to give a sketch of the origin of the family from which Governor Shirley descended, and will therefore not be particular on that head in this place. Suffice it to say that he was descended from a Sussex family, was son of William Shirley of London, by Elizabeth, daughter of John Goodman. Mr. Shirley died in 1701, when our William was but seven years of age. He married Frances, daughter of Francis Baker, of London, by whom he had William, mortally wounded with Gen. Braddock at the Monongahela, in 1755; John, a captain in the army, died at Oswego; Thomas, born in Boston, governor of the Leeward Islands, a major-general in the army, a baronet in 1786, died in 1800. Of the daughters, Elizabeth married Eliakim Hutchinson; Frances married William Bollan, the king's ad-

---

* See APPENDIX, A. † *History and Antiquities of Boston.*

vocate in the court of vice admiralty in Massachusetts. She died March 21st, 1744, in her 24th year, in giving birth to her first child. Harriet married Robert Temple, Esq.; Maria Catharine married John Erving, Esq., of Boston, who, at one period, resided in Milk street.*

In the midst of his great cares and anxieties Governor Shirley lost his wife, a lady held in great esteem by all classes of the community. She died on the 31st of August, 1746, and was interred in King's Chapel, September 4th following, where a monument with an elaborate inscription informs us that she was born in London in 1692, that she had four sons and five daughters, and that she was "the perfect love and delight of this province." † Dr. Colman preached a sermon on the occasion of her death, which was printed. The Rev. Mr. Commissary Price, of King's Chapel, had also preached "a sermon very suitable to the mournful occasion."

At one period, probably before he was appointed governor, Mr. Shirley lived in what was then King street. On assuming the gubernatorial chair he, as was the custom of the governors of the province, resided in the Province House, nearly opposite the head of Milk street. Some time after he became governor, he purchased a tract of land in Roxbury, adjacent to the line dividing it from Dorchester; on this he erected an elegant mansion, some twenty-five rods from the main road, which stood in all its ancient grandeur until about 1867. It then was purchased by William Elliot Woodward, Esq., and converted into several dwellings. For many years it was known as the Eustis estate, it having been owned and occupied

---

* To a descendant, Mr. SHIRLEY IRVING of Boston, I am indebted for the loan of a portrait of Governor Shirley, from which the copy accompanying the work is obtained.

† See *Bost. News Letter*, 11 Sep., 1746.

Governor Shirley.

by Governor William Eustis; from which latter circumstance the main avenue leading thence to Boston is named Eustis street, but with much greater propriety would have been called Shirley street. Unfortunately propriety is seldom considered in conferring names in and about Boston. After the death of Gov. Shirley the estate appears to have belonged to his son-in-law, Eliakim Hutchinson, who, having left the country in the time of the Revolution, it was confiscated to the state, and it was used to quarter soldiers in while the British troops held possession of Boston. After the Revolution (about 1793 or '4) one Dubuque occupied it, a refugee from the French revolution. He brought with him a cook named Julien, who afterwards became celebrated in Boston as an eating-house keeper, or *restaurateur*, at the corner of Congress and Milk streets.

W Shirley

CHAPTER III.

Character of the Warfare of the Period — Proceedings of the Governor of Canada — French Account of Expeditions against the English Frontiers — French Story of their Wrongs.

THE mode of warfare practiced in the times of which the history is now undertaken, exhibits all parties in a state of deplorable barbarism. This war was but little more than one hundred years ago. It was carried on, especially on the part of the French, as though humanity had no place in the nature of their rulers. They fitted out hundreds of parties of savages for the express purpose of proceeding to the frontiers of the English settlements, shooting down poor men while tilling their fields to raise crops to support their families, seizing their wives and children, loading them with heavy packs plundered from their own homes, then driving them before them into the wilderness. These, when faint with hunger and unable longer to stagger under their burdens, were murdered, their scalps torn off and exhibited to their *civilized* masters on their arrival at French headquarters! And for such trophies bounties were paid!

Thus, year after year this practice went on. Many read the history of these wars as they read a romance. It is no romance. It was an awful reality to thousands. It should be so far realized by every one, that all who read may have a true sense of what their homes, now so pleasant, have cost.

French Management.

It was an easy thing for Europeans to gain the confidence of savage Indians. This done, it was quite as easy a matter to impose upon them. When Europeans were at war among themselves, each party could gain to itself numbers of Indians by presents and falsehoods. The French made the Indians believe that the English had cheated them in trade, had taken their lands without giving them any equivalent, and thus made them believe that they ought to drive them out of the country. The English did the same thing, but not to so great an extent, for they never could make themselves such favorites with the Indians as the French could, for reasons not now necessary to be stated.*

As early as the 13th of October, 1743, the Governor-General of Canada, M. de Beauharnois, wrote to Count Maurepas, the French minister at Versailles: " The Lake of the Two Mountains may be regarded as the place which would be exposed to the first attack in case of rupture with our neighbors, and as that whence aid could be easily drawn for the different incursions which would be made into that colony. The nations composing the three villages, number over three hundred warriors, who to bravery conjoin a strong attachment towards the French, and whatever is connected with the service of the king in whose name all business among them is transacted. Situated as they are, at the head of the towns and rural settlements of the colony, not only are they in a position to offer the first

---

* That by the intermarrying with the Indians, they have always a great number of Jesuits and priests with them ; and by instructing them that the Saviour of the world was a Frenchman, and murdered by the English, they are excited to commit all manner of cruelties upon the English, as meritorious. Jeremiah Dumner's *Memorial to Ministry of England*. 1710, in *The Importance, etc., of Cape Breton*, pp. 18, 19. Dr. Cotton Mather has something very similar in his *Magnalia*.

resistance, but also to discover any parties of Indians in alliance with the English, and to put us on our guard against them."

Hence a comparison of the condition of the two countries is not difficult to be made, which cannot fail to show that the French of Canada had a most decided advantage over the English colonies in a war of that period. They had nearly all the Indians on their side, while the English none, or too few to be taken into the account.

The French population of Canada at this period must be considered. Ten years previous (1734) there were 8000 men able to bear arms, of which number 6600 had arms, and there were on hand then about 100,000 pounds of powder. Not only had the number of men greatly increased by the year 1744, but the quantity of warlike stores had, it is reasonable to suppose, increased proportionably; fortifications, too, had been increased in number, and old ones repaired, and their armaments augmented. On the 27th of March, 1745, Governor Clinton wrote to the Duke of Newcastle, that he had ascertained that the French forces in Canada were nearly thus: Militia, Indians, and regular troops, on the St. Lawrence, ten to thirteen thousand able to bear arms; thirty-two companies of regulars of thirty men each, these companies not being half full. The Indians numbered five hundred and seventy, exclusive of allies at a distance, namely — "Cacknawages, about two hundred and thirty; Conessetagoes, sixty; Attenkins, thirty; Neperinks, thirty; Missiquecks, forty; Abenaques at St. Francis, ninety; Obinacks at Beçancourt, fifty; Hurons at Lorette, forty."*

The population of Massachusetts was, at the same time, scarcely 200,000 souls; about equal to that of the city of

---

* The reader may find it rather difficult to identify some of these tribes.

Population of New England. 35

Boston alone at this time. The other three colonies, New Hampshire, Rhode Island, and Connecticut, did not probably contain more than Massachusetts; so that in New England, in 1744, the whole number of people may have been something under 400,000. Connecticut was next in importance to Massachusetts, containing about half as many people, and New Hampshire about 30,000, and Rhode Island about one thousand less than New Hampshire.

It is in the next place proposed to give a specimen of the French accounts of their operations in Canada for fitting and sending out parties to distress the frontiers of New England, from their headquarters at Montreal.

It should be remembered that French dates differ from the English; that is to say, the dates of the same transactions which happened on the same day, differ by eleven days, because the French dated by tne Gregorian reform of the calendar, which the English did not adopt until 1752. Therefore, when an action is said by a French writer to have happened on August 3d, 1746, an English writer would date the same event eleven days earlier, namely, July 23d.

When the great number of murdering and robbing parties sent out from time to time by the French is considered, it is not a little surprising that they did not do more mischief than they did. It is indeed surprising that anything was left undestroyed on all the frontiers, from one end of the country to the other. Those details thus commence:

"December 30th, Lieut. St. Pierre left Montreal with a detachment, consisting of two lieutenants, two ensigns, on full pay, four second ensigns, seven cadets, one surgeon, and an interpreter, three volunteers and one hundred and five colonists, making in all one hundred and twenty-six Frenchmen, and thirty-seven Iroquois and Nepissings, to encamp in the neighborhood of St. Frederick, for the purpose of opposing the enemy's attack against said fort."

Fort St. Frederic was at Crown Point, and by the English called Fort Frederick. The place had been previously called Point *de Cheveux*, by the French.

"1746, January 24, Sieur St. Luc de la Corne was sent to reinforce Sieur de St. Pierre, with a detachment of one second ensign, six cadets, two volunteers, one hundred colonists thirty Iroquois, who have remained under Mr. de St. Pierre's orders until the 1st of April, when they arrived in this town, after having made divers scouts on Lake Sacrament and in the neighborhood of the above fort.

"January 31, Capt. Desabrevois has been detached with Chevalier de Niverville, ensign and fifty-three Iroquois, to the South river, in Lake Champlain, on occasion of an alarm.

"March 16, Chevalier de Niverville, officer, and Sieur Groschesne Raimbault, cadet, left this town with some Abnaquis Indians, on their way towards Boston, and returned with some scalps and prisoners, one of whom he took with his own hand. Sieur Duplessis Jr., an officer, started at the same time with six Algonkins and Nepissings in the same direction, and joined the preceding party, with whom he returned, bringing in a prisoner who was captured at the same time.

"April 20, a party of fourteen Iroquois, belonging to the Sault St. Louis, commanded by Ontassago, the son of the grand chief of that village, who sojourned at Fort St. Frederic, and made several scouts to Sarasteau [Saratoga].

"Theganacoeiëssin, an Iroquois of the Sault, left with two Indians of that village, to go to war near Boston. They returned with two prisoners and some scalps.

French Expeditions. 37

"Thesaotin, chief of the Sault, left with twenty-two warriors belonging to that village, to make war in the direction of Boston. They returned with some scalps. One Iroquois was killed and two wounded of the party.

"Ganiengoton, chief of a party of eight Iroquois, belonging to the Sault, set out in the direction of Boston, and returned with two scalps.

"April 26, a party of thirty-five Iroquois warriors, belonging to the Sault, set out. They have been in the neighborhood of Orange [Albany] and have made some prisoners and taken some scalps.

"A party of twenty Abenakis of Missiskouy, set out towards Boston and brought in some prisoners and scalps.

"April 27, a party of six Iroquois of the Sault St. Louis struck a blow in the neighborhood of Orange.

"May 7, six Nepissings started to strike a blow in the direction of Boston, and returned with some scalps.

"May 10, Gatienoudé, an Iroquois of the Five Nations, who has been settled at the lake for two or three years, left with five Indians of that village, and Sieur St. Blein, to strike a blow in the neighborhood of Orange. This small party brought in one prisoner. Gatienoudé, the leader of the party, is killed and scalped by the English on the field of battle.

"May 12, six Iroquois Indians of the Sault set out towards Boston, and returned with some scalps.

"May 15, ten Indians, part Iroquois of the Sault, and part Abenakis, set out to strike a blow in the direction of Boston. They made an attack and brought away some scalps.

"May 17, thirty-one Iroquois, belonging to the Lake of the Two Mountains,* struck a blow in the neighborhood of Boston,

* Near the mouth of the Ottawas river, about nine miles below Montreal.

and brought back some prisoners and scalps, and laid waste several settlements on their way back.

"May 18, ten Nepissings left, who struck a blow towards Boston.

"A party of eight Iroquois belonging to the Sault has been fitted out, and has been to make an attack in the same direction.

"May 22, nineteen Iroquois belonging to Sault St. Louis, have been equipped. They have been to strike a blow in the direction of Orange.

"May 24, a party of eight Abenakis of Missiskouy, has been fitted out, who have been in the direction of Corlard, and have returned with some prisoners and scalps." By Corlard is probably meant Corlaer's kill below Albany.

"May 27, equipped a party of eight Iroquois of Sault St. Louis, which struck a blow near Orange, and brought back six scalps.

May 28, a party of twelve Nepissings, who made an attack in the neighborhood of Boston, have brought away four scalps, and one prisoner whom they killed on the road, as he became furious and refused to march.

"A party of Abenakis of Missiskouy, struck a blow near Orange and Corlard,* and brought in some prisoners and scalps.

"Equipped a party of ten Iroquois and Abenakis, who joined together to strike a blow towards Boston, and returned with some scalps.

"June 2, equipped a party of twenty-five warriors of the Sault, and three Flatheads, who joined the former in an expedition to the neighborhood of Orange, and who returned with some scalps.

* Corlaer's creek, twenty-eight miles below Albany?

French Expeditions. 39

"June 3, equipped a party of eighteen Nepissings, who struck a blow at Orange and Corlard.

"June 4, equipped a party of sixteen Iroquois of the Sault, who return to where they have already struck a blow.

"June 5, equipped a party of eleven Nepissings and Algonkins, who have struck a blow in the neighborhood of Boston, and have brought in some prisoners.

"June 6, equipped a party of seventeen Nepissings, who have struck a blow in the direction of Boston, and brought back some scalps. These Indians have had two wounded.

"June 8, equipped a party of eight Iroquois of the lake, who have struck a blow near Guerrefille.*

"June 12, equipped a party of ten Abenakis Indians, who struck a blow in the direction of Boston.

"June 13, equipped a party of six of the same Indians, who made an attack in the direction of Boston.

"Equipped a party of nine Nepissings and Algonkins, who have struck a blow in the Boston country. One of these Indians was wounded.

"June 17, equipped a party of ten Abenakis, who went to make an attack at the river Kakécoute†, and were defeated near a fort; their chief, Cadenaret, a famous warrior, has been killed; the remainder returned with some scalps, and left others which they were not able to bring away, the dead having remained too near the fort.

"June 19, equipped a party of twenty-five Indians of the Sault St. Louis, who struck a blow near Orange. One or two

---

* Perhaps a settlement at or near the mouth of Green river, then called Green's Farms. The editor of the *New York Col. Doc's*, X, 33, calls it Deerfield, but gives no reason for it.

† Probably the Dutch fort at Schaghticoke, which was on the Hoosuc river. See August 20, 1746.

of these Indians were wounded; they brought away some scalps.

"June 20, equipped a party of nineteen Iroquois of the Sault St. Louis, who went to Orange to strike a blow.

"June 21, equipped a party of twenty-seven Iroquois of the same village to go to Orange; Sieur Carqueville, an officer, and Sieur Blein, a cadet, have been of this party, which has brought in a prisoner that was on the scout to Sarasteau [Saratoga], and some scalps.

"July 16, Lieutenant Demuy left this town with a detachment under his orders, consisting of five ensigns, six officers of militia, ten cadets, forty-eight settlers, and about four hundred Indians, partly our domiciled Indians, and partly some from the upper country. This party tarried at Fort St. Frederic, and has been employed scouting, and working on the river au Chicot, where they have felled the trees on both sides to render its navigation impracticable to our enemies. Several of these Indians have formed parties and been out on excursions, Mr. Demuy having been ordered to wait for the party commanded by Mr. de Rigaud, whom he joined.

"August 3, Mr. de Rigaud de Vaudreuil set out [on his expedition which resulted in the capture of Fort Massachusetts, extracted in that account further on].

"August 31, equipped a party of Iroquois of the Sault, consisting of six men. Also a party of eight warriors from the same tribe, from whom no report was had when the dispatch was made up."

Such is a sample of the manner pursued towards the people of the frontiers, and this was called making war for the interest of the French nation! Retaliation in the same kind was expected, and would have been justified as honorable warfare;

Indians with the French. 41

but, as will be seen, the people of New England were not prepared for retaliation, and never effected but very little in that kind of service.

The following minutes accompany the French record of expeditions for the years 1745 and 1746: "June 30, thirty-eight Iroquois of the Five Nations came to speak in council. July 23, thirty-one Outawois of Detroit, some of whom returned home, being unwilling to go to war; sixteen Wild Rice (Folles Avoines); fourteen Kiskakons of Detroit, who gave proofs of their fidelity to the French, and who have all been to war; four Sioux came to the council to demand a commandant, who could not be granted them. August 2, fifty Poutewatamies; fifteen Puans and ten Illinois came to go to war; five Outawois of Michilimakinac, and forty Outawois of the Forks who have been on the war path. Aug. 10, sixty-five Mississaguez from the head of Lake Ontario; eighty Algonkins and Nepissings from Lake Nepissing, near Lake Huron, who have been to war; fourteen Sauteurs came with the Outawois from Michilimakinak, to go to war. 22 Aug., thirty-eight Outawois of Detroit, seventeen Sauteurs, twenty-four Hurons, and fourteen Poutewatamis; a portion of all these who came on the last date were of Mr. Rigaud's detachment" [at the taking of Fort Massachusetts].

It is true the French had their story of wrongs, and their complaints should be heard and their accounts brought to the same test as our own. Therefore a few of their charges have been selected, and will now be introduced.

Towards the end of December, 1744, the English committed the following treacherous acts and barbarities. M. Ganon, having the command of a detachment of English troops, was sent to observe the retreat of the French and savages before

F

Port Royal in Acadia, where he found two lonely cottages of the Mikmaks. In them were five women and three children, and two of the women were big with child; but, regardless of these things, they plundered the cottages and inhumanly butchered the five women and two children, committing acts upon the murdered women too revolting for recital.

No act corresponding to this is found in the English annals; nor have we found, among those engaged on the side of the English, any one of the name of Ganon. The only name approaching it is that of *Gorham;* but though Capt. Gorham was employed in expeditions to Nova Scotia, at the head of a body of Cape Cod Indians, we do not meet with him there till some time after this.

The next count in the French charges (though they say it happened five months before the other) is against "one David," captain of an English privateer, who having artfully set up French colors in the strait of Frcusac, or Frowsack,* where, by means of a renegade who served under him as interpreter, inveigled the chief of the Indians of Cape Breton, and his family, to come on board his ship. The name of the chief was James Padenuque. They confined him in a dungeon, carried him to Boston, and in the end stifled him in a vessel on board of which he was put under pretence of sending him back to his own country. With this chief his son was taken, eight years of age. Him they kept, and would not restore, perfidiously refusing to do so, notwithstanding his ransom had been paid by the restoration of several prisoners.

All this may be true, though nothing like it has found its way into authentic records, that we can recognize. As to "one

---

* Called on Charlevoix's Map, *Passage as the Gut of Canso,* separating Nova *du Canceau.* By the English it is known Scotia from Cape Breton.

French Complaints.

David," it possibly has reference to Capt. David Donahew, with whom we shall presently meet.

In the month of July, 1745, "the same David" got by stratagem an Indian family into his hands, but they escaped "the very night they were taken." At the same time they took the Indian interpreter, named Bartholomew Petitpas, and carried him prisoner to Boston, refused all offers of ransom, and finally put him to death.

In the same year (1745) a priest, missionary among the Indians, was invited to Louisbourg by some of the principal English officers to confer upon public matters. He had their letters guaranteeing his safe return; but, when he was in the power of the English, they took him and sent him to England.

Also, in the same year, at Port Toulouse,* they dug up the dead bodies of several Indians and burnt them. They likewise desecrated places of burial, by breaking down all the crosses. This was the work of some inhabitants of Boston.

"The horrid affair of 1746," of selling the Indians woolen goods, "all poisoned," so that, in the basin of Mejagonche,† upwards of two hundred of them died, is probably wholly an invention, and has reference to the clothes of dead mariners distributed amongst the Cape Sable Indians by French naval officers, of which mention will be found elsewhere in this history.

The next and last charge to be noticed here, is, that in 1749, towards the end of the month of July, when the inhabitants of New France were strangers to the suspension of arms, the

---

* Formerly called Port St. Peter, on the coast of Cape Breton, just at the entrance of the Strait of Frousac. *Amer. Gaz.*, 12mo, 1776.

† Perhaps the same as that called on Charlevoix's Map, *Maganchinche*, and on some English maps, *Merlignash*, on the southern coast of Acadia.

Indians had taken some prisoners on Newfoundland. These prisoners informed their captors of the peace, and were at once liberated, treated as brethren, and entertained in their wigwams. Yet, on the first opportunity, these perfidious guests, at midnight, murdered five and twenty of these innocent and unsuspecting people!

These accusations or charges are the substance of speeches delivered to the eastern Indians by the Count de Raymond, to inflame them to prosecute the war.

CHAPTER IV.

Condition of the Inhabitants on the Frontiers — Declaration of War by France and England — Line of Forts ordered — Canada little known to the English — No Security for the English but in its Conquest — Causes of War — French Right to Canada — Jesuits at Penobscot — Nova Scotia — The English Colonies not united — Question of Boundaries — Fort Oswego built — The Six Nations — Assure the English of their Support — The French seize Canso — Attempt Annapolis — Siege raised — The Mohawks — A Council at Stockbridge — Attempt to secure the Eastern Indians — War declared against them — Their Murders — Reward offered for Scalps and Indians — Indian Council at Albany — Attempt to secure the Penobscots.

ALWAYS when war existed between England and France, nothing was expected by the North American colonists but that their frontiers were to be a scene of blood, and those who contemplate the circumstances of the settlers at this distance of time, will, without much reflection, wonder that people could be found who would thrust themselves several miles into the wilderness, and take up an abode, knowing the perils to which a war exposed them. To understand this state of things we have only to reflect that almost the whole population were poor, and, as families increased, the young men must provide for themselves and their families. Their means would not allow them to purchase land already taken up, and thus settle down with those previously located, and of course in more security. Hence, young men from old families, and others from abroad, in times of peace located themselves often far in advance of earlier settlers. In such situations these found themselves on the breaking out of

war. Then the question recurs—why did not such settlers retire to the older settled places when war existed? Here again a little reflection teaches that families thus isolated, in a short space of time become quite strangers to those from whom they were separated, and hence have no place of refuge in that direction; or very likely the families from which they separated are poor like themselves, and unable to provide for fugitives, however near of kin they may be to them. And then, parents and other kindred are swept off by death, often times, or have removed to other places. Thus it is easy to see how a poor frontier family is exposed in a time of Indian wars. Such families have made homes, and they have no others; children are multiplying among them; to abandon those homes was to abandon all means of living, and to throw themselves upon the charities of strangers. These will feel little compassion before a disaster strikes those flying before it; and yet may overflow with sympathy when such sympathy can be of no benefit.

Another consideration is to be kept in view in estimating the liability of the frontier settlers to the horrors of a savage warfare. It must be borne in mind that in those days this people was nearly cut off from a knowledge of the politics of their time; that their means of knowing what was passing in European courts, and even but a few miles distant, and in their own country, were not only extremely scanty, but such as they did receive was very dubious and uncertain; and hence they often knew nothing of war until a deadly blow was struck in their very midst. Thus it cannot fail to be apparent to every reader of the history of the times included in this treatise, how important it is that the above considerations be kept in mind to enable them to have even a small appreciation of the hardships and sufferings of our immediate ancestors.

The war which began in 1744 took the frontiers by surprise, although such an event had not only been feared by the officers of the colonial governments, but was anticipated, yet with a faint hope it might be averted by the negotiations then going on between the agents of George the II, and those of Louis XV, the occupants of the respective thrones of England and France. The French monarch was encouraged by that of Spain, Philip V, who had been feebly fighting England for about five years. The Spanish war did not, however, immediately affect New England, and General Oglethorp was successfully opposing the aggressions of Spain at the south.

Thus stood the political atmosphere, when suddenly proceeded from Versailles the formal declaration of war by France against England. This was done on March 15th, 1744, and on the 29th of the same month England accepted the challenge, declaring war against France in return.*

It was about two months before the news of the declaration of war reached New England, while the French and Indians of Canada had the intelligence near a month earlier, and immediately commenced the work of destruction. Governor Shirley was alive to the condition of things, and at once raised five hundred men to be stationed at points where attacks were expected; three hundred of them were for the service on the eastern border, and the other two hundred for the upper valley of the Connecticut river.

There had arrived in Boston harbor, some time before the news of the declaration of war, most opportunely it is certain, twenty cannon of forty two pound caliber, and two thirteen inch mortars, which had been forwarded by the home govern-

---

* These declarations may be seen at *Memoirs*, I, 44-47. *American Maga-*
large in Beatson's *Naval and Military* *zine*, I, 381, 384.

ment for Castle William. All necessary equipments came with them, as mortar beds, carriages, shells, shot, etc. The ships in which they came arrived on the last day of the year (1743) and the war materials were landed on Long Wharf, and thence in sloops taken to the castle, the last on January 21st, 1744.*

Soon after the news that war had been declared was received, the General Court of Massachusetts ordered a line of forts to be constructed, to extend from the Connecticut river to the boundary of New York, and ninety-six barrels of powder were sent to supply the inhabitants. This was not a gift, but was dealt out to them at cost.

Few of the people of New England knew anything about the frontier of Canada, while every point of the border of New England was well known to the Indians. Many of these had constantly traded with the English at their houses, and consequently knew minutely their situation, and hence became sure guides to the French in their expeditions. Indeed, some of the Indians had lived in the immediate vicinity of many of the towns, and the people had become so accustomed to them, that they looked upon them as friends, and flattered themselves with the hope, that in the event of another war they would be friends, and side with them rather than with their enemies. But no sooner was it known to them that war had been resolved upon, than all these Indians withdrew to Canada, and at all times acted as guides to the French soldiers. They would have done the same thing for the English under like circumstances, because plunder was the chief, if not the sole cause which always governed their conduct. It is doubtless true, as the writer has stated in another work,† that, in some instances,

---

* *American Magazine*, I, 176, 219. † The *Old Indian Chronicle*, p. 2.

Importance of Canada.

the settlers had wronged them in various ways; perhaps insulted and abused them, and treated them as inferiors, without reflecting that "Indians never forget injuries." The Indians often had too much reason to complain of being over-reached in trade, by those authorized by the government to traffic with them.*

It is easy to discern how deplorable was the condition of the scattered settlers thus circumstanced. It was likewise easy to discern that so long as the French were masters of Canada, a liability of war between France and England would always exist. To live in a continual state of suspense in times of peace, and fear of the tomahawk and scalping-knife in times of war, could only be endured in the hope that the time would come when they could triumph over their enemies. This could only be expected by the reduction of Canada.

The conquest of Canada had long been contemplated, and several times attempted, but hitherto those attempts had all proved abortive; another war had commenced, and with prospects not at all improved. Nothing remained for New England but to make the best defence it could, and this under the certain prospect of a bloody contest.

For any one to take a different view of the relation between the French of Canada and the English of New England, that is, to suppose those peoples could ever live as distinct nations, without collisions, was an absurdity too palpable not to be seen by every individual of the latter; and yet there were many able men in England using all their influence against dispossessing the French of Canada; and even after the fall of Quebec,

* See *Journals of the Gen. Court*, 7 July, 1739.

Secretary Pitt was urged in a publication,* addressed to him, written with much power and great ability, to give up all thoughts of insisting upon a treaty with France in which Canada should be given up to England! The arguments made use of were in the interest of those who thought more of an income from sugar plantations in the West Indies than the lives of thousands of their countrymen on the borders of New England, and are therefore not worth a refutation or a repetition here.

People may become so familiar with hardships and dangers as to regard them less than may be imagined by those at a distance from them. Were it not so, few could be found to face them again and again, and year after year, and from generation to generation.

It has been said that the English and French are natural enemies. This will be conceded only by those who consider men as wild animals. The real cause of the contentions among men is the ambition to take what does not belong to them. There can be no question but that Canada belonged to the French rather than the English, if prior occupancy gave right. The French claimed also by prior discovery. But the English claimed by the same right, though they claimed no further north than forty-five degrees of north latitude. By the year 1613, the French had extended their settlements from the Gulf of Saint Lawrence to the mouth of the Penobscot.†

---

* An octavo of 148 pages, in bourgeois type, entitled, *A Letter to a Great Minister, wherein the Demolition of the Fortifications of Louisbourg is shown to be absurd, and the Importance of Canada fully refuted.* London, 1761.

† According to the relations of the Jesuits, two of their number commenced a settlement at the mouth of the Penobscot in 1611; "et ils furent les pierres fondamentales de ces missions dans cette partie de l'Amerique Septentrionale." Argall carried them off, upon which event they remark: "Ils furent sur le point d'être mis à mort par des corsaires anglais qui les avient pris."

Their settlements were declared to be encroachments, and in this year one Capt. Argall was sent from Virginia to dispossess them, which he performed in the ruthless manner of the times. This was the commencement of hostilities between subjects of the two crowns on any part of North America. No permanent settlement by Englishmen had then been made here. From this time, 1613, to the treaty of Paris in 1763, one hundred and fifty years, numerous wars occurred between these two nations, during the existence of which the settlements in New England were disturbed by frequent alarms, and the horrors of savage cruelties.

Nova Scotia* being considered the key to the eastern colonies of New England, Oliver Cromwell, in his time well understood the importance of that country. He accordingly sent an expedition and reduced it to the rule of England. This was in 1654, but by the treaty of Breda, in 1667, it was restored to France.

For a long time it was extremely doubtful which nation would ultimately possess the North American provinces. The contest was surely to be revived so long as both parties laid claim to it, or portions of it, because both fully understood its vast importance, in a commercial point of view.† But the great difficulty with the English colonists was their own contests amongst themselves, chiefly about their boundaries, in which contests they spent more money than it would have cost

---

* The *Acadia* of the French; so called by them in allusion to *Arcadia* in the Grecian Peloponnesus, but with what propriety I cannot determine. *Genuine Accounts of Nova Scotia*, p. 3. London, 1750, 8vo. It was granted to De Monts, in 1603, by Henry IV, of France. By the treaty of Utrecht, 1713, it was conceded to belong to France, and to extend from the Gulf of the St. Lawrence to the Penobscot.

† *The Contest in America, by an Impartial Hand,* p. [x] 800. London, 1757. An able and valuable work.

them to have kept the French within the bounds allotted to them. Thus, a judicious writer of the time remarks, that while the colonies were wasting their substance contending for the bone, the French ran away with it.*

At this comparatively early day the colonies seem not to have learned the value of union, which they so well understood about twenty years later, when oppression came from the mother country. And yet they had seen that it was by a want of union among the Indian tribes that they had been able to establish themselves in the country. They did not need the instructions of Cæsar, who said of the conquest of the Britons, that "while everyone fought for himself they were all easily overcome."

Thus it was, that while New Hampshire and Massachusetts were contending about their boundaries, and New Jersey and New York were at bitter feuds about theirs, the master key to all of them, Crown Point, was seized upon by the French, who there built Fort St. Frederic in the year 1731.

Aware of the great importance of the avenues by water from the lakes of Canada to the English settlements on the Atlantic coast, Mr. Burnet, when governor of New York, in 1727, built, at his own expense, Fort Oswego, as a counter movement to the French proceeding in erecting Fort Niagara, at the entrance into Lake Ontario of the Niagara river, on the New York or eastern side, a point commanding more communications, over a vast country, easterly and westerly, than any other point in North America at that time, and for many years after.

Having little to fear from any but the New England colonies, the French had been slow to complete their cordon of fortresses

* *The Contest in America*, etc., p. 22.

Counteraction of Mercenaries. 53

towards the south; and it was not till the year 1754 that they commenced one at that very important point, the confluence of the Alleghany and Monongahela rivers.

It was well known that great opposition was exerted by certain English merchants and traders of New York, to prevent their own government from securing the important posts of Crown Point and Oswego, because it was for the pecuniary interest of those traders that those places should remain in the hands of the French. And thus it was they got easy possession of those places, and for years quietly possessed them. Even the Indians of the Five Nations saw how, that through the avarice of the few the honest were plundered, and did not fail to protest against this state of things, at the same time shrewdly remarking, that "the French built their forts with English strouds."

So reckless do men become when their private interests are in anticipation. With such indifference and disregard of the public welfare, a few years more and all would have been lost; for, as to the respective claims of the French and English to territory in North America, that of the former, to say the least, was as good as that of the latter. Indeed, neither had any rights here further than they had acquired them by actual settlement and permission from the aborigines where any claim was set up by them. But these premises have been fully discussed elsewhere.*

On the 18th of June, 1744, agreeably to the request of the governor of New York, a great number of the Indians of the Six Nations, consisting of the "Mohawks, Oneydes, Onondagas, Tuskaroroes, Cayeuges, and Sennekes," assembled at Albany and held a conference with Commissioners of Indian

* See *Old Indian Chronicle*, edition of 1867, 4to, Chap. I.

Affairs, "in order to renew, strengthen, and brighten the covenant chain that had so long tied them and the subjects of His Majesty the Great King their Father in mutual ties of friendship." After the governor had recounted to the Indians the intentions of the French to make them subservient, and to draw them off from their allegiance to the English king, and requesting a promise from them to stand by and defend their allies the English, they made answer in the strongest terms, that nothing should cause them to abandon their friends; "that it should not be in the power of the devil himself" to divert them to the French; that though they did not think it just that they should seize any of the French that came among them and deliver them to the English, as the Indians should not be the aggressors, yet the English might come and take them; but they inclined to peace, until some of His Majesty's subjects were attacked. In short, their reply was full of good sense.

As already remarked, the French of Canada having the news of the declaration of war above a month earlier than the English of New England, and having been in expectation of the rupture, had prepared themselves to act with promptness; so that in three days after receiving the news from France, Gov. Duquesnel,* of Nova Scotia, dispatched M. Duvivier from Louisbourg with an armament against Canso, about twenty leagues distant, which he entered in the night of the 13th of May, surprised the garrison, consisting of about eighty men, burnt the fort† and other buildings, and returned to Louisbourg with his captives.

---

* He died on the following September (1744), and was succeeded by M. Duchambon. *Memoirs of the War*, p. 32. "Du Quesnel was a good old soldier, while Du Chambon was an old poltroon."

† Douglass says "it was an insignificant place, and did not deserve the name of fort." *Ibid.*, I, 339. True of many English places nominally held by them.

Attack on Annapolis.

The first news the English had of the event was brought to Boston by a fisherman, who happened to be on the neighboring fishing-ground, and saw the smoke of the burning fort and other buildings, upon which he made all sail for Boston.

But a little while before the declaration of war, the French instigated the Indians upon the river Saint John to send a deputation of their head men to Lieut.-Gov. Paul Mascarene, the English commander at Annapolis Royal,* who were instructed to pretend a renewal of former treaties; by which device they were to ascertain the actual state of the place for defence. Having succeeded to their wishes in this, they at once invested it with about six hundred Marechite and Mickmack Indians, on the 30th of June, with a few Frenchmen, the whole under the command of a Frenchman named Le Loutre, a priest, and one Clermont; but Mascarene successfully defended the place.

The news of the fate of Canso having reached Boston as just mentioned, Governor Shirley rightly judged that Annapolis Royal would next be attempted. He therefore, with the utmost expedition, dispatched away a messenger for that place to advise Governor Mascarene of the fate of Canso, and to urge him to hold out until he could send men to reinforce him, which he would exert himself to do with the utmost of his power. The bearer of this important dispatch fell into the hands of the enemy, which was very fortunate for him, otherwise the force immediately sent by Shirley would have fallen upon the enemy's fleet † which had intercepted the messenger. Thus the wise precaution of the governor was a misfortune to the English; for had he dispatched an armed force without the

---

* The name *Annapolis Royal* and *Annapolis* without the *Royal*, are indiscriminately used in the different accounts.

† "A banker of about four hundred ton, with a brigantine and sloop." Shirley's *Memoirs*, p. 20.

precaution, it would surely have hemmed in Du Quesnel and his fleet before the beleaguered town, and they would have become an easy prey. But in wars, as in other affairs, errors and mischances on the one side often balance those on the other. It was a sad mistake of the governor of Louisbourg, in that he did not first secure Annapolis Royal, because that could have been easily effected, and then Canso would have fallen almost without a blow, and thus the whole of Nova Scotia, with its sixteen thousand inhabitants, would have been under the control of the metropolis.

It was not an error that Governor Shirley sent a messenger to warn Governor Mascarene of his danger, but it was a misfortune that threw the messenger into the hands of the enemy; while, on the other hand, it was a serious error that the French governor committed in wasting time on Canso instead of Annapolis Royal. This error sent his fleet, under Du Quesnel, up the Bay of Fundy, where it intercepted Shirley's messenger, and afforded it time to cut its cables and make good an escape. For in two days after that messenger left Boston, namely, on July 2d, Capt. Edward Tyng, with about eighty men, in the Province Snow, sailed for Annapolis Royal, and in two days more arrived before the place.

On the arrival of the English forces before Annapolis Royal, they found it invested by about seven hundred Indians, with a few French mixed with them disguised as Indians, with the priest before mentioned at their head. The fort was in no condition to stand a siege, being nothing but a ruin.* It had been besieged eleven days when the English arrived, but the besiegers

---

* It had been entirely neglected for about twenty years, its garrison resting "in supine indolence, hogs and sheep from without, passing fosses and ditches, and mounting the ramparts at pleasure." *Douglass*, I, 318.

Capt. Tyng's Expedition.

had no cannon, and their attacks were chiefly in the night; so that the garrison were nearly worn out when relief arrived. The fear of falling into the hands of the Indians nerved the defenders almost to superhuman efforts. The garrison was now reinforced and the fort put into repair, and before the end of the year (1744), besides other reinforcements, Massachusetts sent to the place a company of Indian rangers which rendered great service in scouting and guarding the garrison.

When the account of the capture of Canso was carried to France, it caused great rejoicing, and *Te Deum* was sung at Notre Dame in Paris, and pompous details of the affair were trumped up and published in the French journals.

The result of the expedition for the relief of Annapolis was immediately published at Boston in the following strain:

"On the 13th of July (1744) Capt. Tyng in our province snow, Prince of Orange, arrived here from Annapolis Royal. He sailed from this port on the 2d instant, with between seventy and eighty new raised volunteers for reinforcing His Majesty's garrison there (for the encouragement of which levies, and one hundred more now raising under proper officers, this government has lately granted an handsome bounty) and arrived safe at Annapolis about one o'clock on the 4th instant, to the inexpressible joy of the whole garrison, the fort being besieged by a large body of Indians, who came before it on the 30th of June, with a French priest, and one Clermont, another Frenchman who had been lately employed as a spy in the fort, and in daily expectation of receiving assistance in two vessels from Louisbourg. They had the insolence to send a flag of truce to Gov. Mascarene to demand the surrender of the fort, promising good quarters to the garrison if he complied, and threatened to destroy them all if they took it by storm.

They had killed two soldiers whom they surprised without the fort, burnt several of the English houses, and destroyed many cattle, and had lost three of their own number by the great artillery of the garrison. Upon Capt. Tyng's arrival and the transport under his convoy, for the French ships, which they expected, and were coming to the shore to meet him; but on finding their mistake betook themselves to a precipitate flight, the priest leaving behind him his crucifix and other superstitious trumpery."*

From another source the following amusing particular is taken: "Upon Capt. Tyng's arrival, the Indians seeing the hammocks in the netting of the ship, took them for Indians; and being informed by a French woman that he had a great number of Mohawks on board, and had landed several hundreds of men to cut them off, they ran into the woods with the utmost speed," their priest being so panic stricken, that he left his baubles as before mentioned.†

Pains were taken, when war was looked upon as imminent, to secure as many of the Indians as possible in the interest of the respective parties. The small belt along the Atlantic shore of English settlers was situated, as it were, between two fires. The enemy on their back had every advantage. They could always approach the English undiscovered, and when they had committed murders and depredations could bury themselves in the wilderness, and pursuit oftentimes only aggravated the mischief already done, as the pursuers frequently fell into ambushes and were cut off.

The Mohawks, a formidable part of the Six Nations, were

---

* *American Magazine*, I, 483.
† *Boston Evening Post*, of 16 July, 1744. There was a company of Indians on board, under Capt. Gorham, called Indian Rangers. See *Douglass*, I, 319. These Rangers will be further noticed.

Conference at Stockbridge.   59

held in great dread, as they were the most cruel and warlike of all the tribes known when the war of 1744 broke forth. This tribe or nation was divided. Part of them were called French Mohawks, because they were under the influence of the Jesuits, and could be relied upon to take up the tomahawk for that nation in the event of war; while those dwelling nearest the English had embraced protestantism. All the English asked of these was to remain neuter, and let the English and French settle their own quarrel, and to use their best endeavors with the French Mohawks to remain neutral also.

To secure so desirable an object, the English, through the agency of their missionary among the Stockbridge or Mohekanuk Indians, the Rev. John Sergeant, were able to induce a deputation of the Mohawks to come to Stockbridge and confer upon the subject. A conference was accordingly held, and on the 5th of June, 1744, Mr. Sergeant made a report of the result of it; but does not give the names of those who took part in it. The Mohekanuk speaker addressed the Mohawk chief as Uncle, and the Mohawk chief addressed the Mohekanuk as Cousin. They are both rather poor specimens of Indian eloquence.

A report had gone abroad that the French Mohawks had agreed with those living on the borders of the English to remain neutral. The Mohekanuk chief put the question to his Uncle in these words: "I ask you a question. I hear you have agreed with the French Mohawks to sit still in case of a war between their friends and ours. You well know how that matter is. I desire you to tell me what we are to do in that affair. If you say we must sit still, we will sit still. If we see those Indians help their friends, we must help ours." To which the Mohawk speaker replied: "Cousin, the information you have received of our engaging with the French Mohawks to stand neuter in case of a war between the French and English, is very true. Those Indians have promised us, that they will not meddle with the war; but set still in peace, and let the white people determine their dispute themselves. We have promised them the same, and desire you to join with us in the same peaceable disposition."

Notwithstanding these engagements, and even if they were fully adhered to, the French had vastly the advantage, as they had access to all the Indian nations of Canada, of whom they always found enough ready to espouse their cause against the English settlers.

The eastern Indians were next to be secured, if possible, and prevented from joining the French. To this end several Indians of the Five Nations had, at much expense, been procured in their country and brought to Boston, and accompanied commissioners to Penobscot,* and there had a talk with such Indians of that region as they could meet with. All that is known of this undertaking is contained in a publication of the time, and is in these words: "July 24, 1744. This day the Commissioners appointed by this Government to accompany the Delegates from the Six Nations of Indians to the Eastward, in order to confer with the heads of the tribes in those parts, returned hither in good health; and so far as we can learn, the Eastern Indians are sincerely desirous to continue at peace with us."

That these hopes of peace proved entirely delusive, is certain, as will appear from a declaration of war against these Indians not long after, by the governor of Massachusetts, an

---

* They sailed from Boston July 7th. Penobscots, as will be seen further along. There were other attempts to secure the They caused great expense, and no benefit.

Declaration of War.

abstract of which is here given for the facts it contains. It is drawn with due formality, and with Gov. Shirley's well known ability; headed: "A Declaration of War against the Cape-Sable's and St. John's Indians," and dated "at the Council Chamber in Boston, the 19th day of October, 1744." The reasons for the *declaration* are set forth in the preamble as follows: "Whereas the Indians inhabiting his Majesty's Province of Nova Scotia, commonly called the Cape Sables Indians, who have submitted themselves to his Majesty's government by solemn treaty with the governor of the province of Massachusetts, did some time in the winter last past, in the port of Jedoure, in a treacherous and cruel manner, murder divers of his Majesty's English subjects, belonging to a fishing vessel* owned and fitted out by his Majesty's subjects of this province, and did seize the said vessel with the goods and effects belonging thereto: And, whereas the said Cape-Sable's Indians, with the Indians of the St. John's tribe, who have likewise submitted to his Majesty's government, by solemn treaty with the commander of this province, have in a hostile manner joined with the French king's subjects, his Majesty's declared enemies, in assaulting his Majesty's fort at Annapolis-Royal, and the garrison posted there, divers of whom they have slain; and have likewise killed a master of a sloop belonging to this province, while he was assisting that garrison in providing fuel for them; and the said Indians have also for divers

---

* This doubtless has reference to the following, published in the *Boston Evening Post* of April 30th, 1744: "Some time in the fall of 1743, a schooner belonging to Marblehead, in which were six men and a boy, put into a harbor at or near Cape Sable, where they were all murdered except the boy; him they reserved and sold to the French. He is lately returned and gives this account. The vessel they plundered of everything." The names of the murdered are unknown.

months past, in an hostile manner, blocked up the said fort, and kept the garrison upon continual alarms," etc.

The Declaration goes on to warn all the Indians to the west, or this side of the St. John's river, not to hold correspondence with those of St. John's and Cape Sable's, or Nova Scotia Indians; particularly the Penobscots, Norridgewalks, and Pigwackets.

On the 26th of October, the General Court offered a reward for the killing and scalps of the St. John's and Cape Sable Indians, in these terms: "To any company, party, or person singly, of his Majesty's subjects to or residing within this Province, who shall voluntarily, and at their own proper cost and charge go out and kill a male Indian of the age of twelve years or upwards, of the Indians above named, after the 26th day of October last past, and before the last day of June, 1745, (if the war lasts so long) anywhere to the east of the Penobscot beyond a fixed line, the sum of £100* in bills of credit, new tenor; and £105 for a male Indian captive of the like age; and the sum of £50 for women; and the like sum for children under the age of twelve years killed in fight; and £55 for such of them as shall be taken prisoners."

And on the 2d of November, the line beyond, or to the east of which Indians might be killed and scalps taken, was published, namely: "to begin on the sea-shore three leagues from the most easterly part of Passamaquady river, and thence run north into the country through the province of Nova Scotia to the river St. Lawrence."

Quite early in the year Gov. George Clinton† took unwearied

---

* " Whereof, at present, 1748, fifty shillings is equal to twenty shillings sterling. *Old Tenor* is only one quarter of the *New Tenor.*" *Douglass,* I, 320.

† This Governor Clinton should not be confounded with that of the patriot governor of the same name, conspicuous in the Revolution. DeWitt Clinton was of this family, and a nephew of the patriot governor.

Conference at Albany.

pains to keep the Six Nations to their allegiance. Having procured deputations from the Mohawks, Oneydes, Onondagas, Tuskaroras, Cayeuges, and Senekes, to come to Albany, a conference was begun on the 18th of June. To this conference Massachusetts sent John Stoddard, Jacob Wendell, Thomas Berry, John Choate, and Thomas Hutchinson. Before leaving Albany the Massachusetts men submitted certain conditions for the observance of both colonies. These were in substance similar to the articles of union between the New England colonies, formed in 1642. And here it may be well to state that the Six Nations generally adhered to the English throughout the war, and parties of Mohawks retaliated, though to a small extent, the depredations of the French and Canada Indians on the English frontier, by expeditions against the Canadian settlers.

In the late conference at Albany several of the Indians of the Mohawk tribe were engaged to accompany agents of Massachusetts to the Eastern Indians, especially the Penobscots, and to use their influence with them to assist the English against the St. John and Cape Sable Indians. Col. Pepperrell and some others of Massachusetts, met the Penobscot Indians at *Georges* in the beginning of July. The meeting was friendly, and the English flattered themselves that those Indians would not only remain at peace with them, but that they would send a number of their warriors to aid them in the war lately declared against the tribes before mentioned; and it appears that the Penobscots actually agreed to furnish a number of their warriors for this purpose, who, according to the terms of Gov. Dummer's treaty (which they always regarded), were to have their men ready in forty days; yet, up to the middle of November, there had been no compliance, and Col. Pepperrell was again sent to demand the men as agreed upon. The result was a further time was asked for, under the pretence that their young men were away on hunting expeditions. However, about the middle of January, 1745, it was ascertained that the young Penobscots declared they would not take up arms against the St. John's Indians.* This doubtless satisfied the English that the French Jesuit influence was greater than any they could exert.

* It may be worthy of note that all the historians of this period knew nothing, at least say nothing, respecting the important transactions above sketched, although they were brought about at great cost to the country, and individual sacrifice. It should be minutely detailed in a history of Maine, and a life of Sir William Pepperrell should not be without it. Materials are not wanting.

CHAPTER V.

DIARY OF DEPREDATIONS.

Strength of the French — Donahew's Expedition — Surrender of Louisbourg — Incidents of the Capture — Prudence of Gov. Shirley — The Effect of the Capture in England — Donahew's Expedition and Death — His Steward's Escape and Narrative — Other Facts respecting Donahew — William Phips's Exploit and Death — People killed at Ashuelot — War commences with the Penobscot Indians — Trouble at Louisbourg — Gov. Shirley proceeds thence — Gov. Clinton and the Six Nations — Another Declaration of War — Indians killed — Another Conference at Albany — Depredations at Sheepscott — Nehemiah How's Captivity — Indians surprise Saratoga — New York offers a Reward for Scalps — Depredation at Bedford, N. H.

NEWS from Canada having been recently obtained, in writing to the Duke of Newcastle, on March 27, Gov. Clinton makes the following statement respecting the condition of the French: "They have considerably increased their settlements on our backs, and almost inhanced the Indian trade to themselves, by means of the lake Cadaraqui [Ontario] whereon they have two or three vessels of fifty or sixty tons, with six or eight swivel guns each, and manned with twelve or fifteen men, with which they carry on their trade. They have also built forts, and trading houses ranging along the lake (contrary to the faith of treaties), whereby they hold their power over all the Indian nations, except those dependent on our provinces, and even among those they have, and do daily gain too great an influence." *

* *New York Colonial Documents*, VI, 275.

Donahew's Expedition.

May 14, 1745. Governor Clinton, in a speech dissolving the general assembly of New York, severely censures the members for neglecting to provide protection for the frontiers of the colony against the incursions of the Indians and French.*

May 15. Capt. David Donahew, in the sloop Resolution, with two other armed vessels, meets a French armament of some nine hundred men on their way from Annapolis to Louisbourg to strengthen that place. The following is Captain Donahew's account of the fight he had with them: "On the 15th instant, in Askmacourse † harbor, up the bay [of Fundy], my luck was to meet with two sloops and two schooners, and an unaccountable number of Indian canoes. At six the same morning, the Captains Becket and Jones, who were connected with me, and being to leeward, saw some smoke, which they pursued, and soon lost sight of me. I pursued my chase, and at ten o'clock came up with and fired on them. They strove to decoy me into shoal water, which I avoided, they being a thousand in number, and I but forty odd. We spoke to each other for two hours and a half; they knowing my name, desiring me to prepare my fast for them, and I telling the cowards they were afraid to row up, the weather stark calm. As they came to hand I killed, but the number I know not. I fired two hundred four-pounders, double round and partridge, fifty three-pounders; besides my swivels and small arms continually playing on them. My stern, by force of firing, is down to the water edge, roundhouse all to pieces, but bold hearted. Had it not been so calm I should have done as I would; but not one breath of wind, and they rowing all around

---

* The reader will find the opposition to Governor Clinton fully explained in *Livingston's Review*, elsewhere cited.

† Asmacouse. *Douglass*. Not laid down on the maps under this name. Perhaps that since called Advocates Harbor.

me, both head and stern; but Capt. Becket and Capt. Jones appearing in sight, they retreated and run into shoal water. I followed them within pistol shot, till I run on ground, but, blessed be God, have got safe off. This was the army that besieged Annapolis, and was on its way to assist Louisbourg, but their design is prevented."

This force, so opportunely defeated by Donahew, had retired to Minas,* after being driven from Annapolis, as previously related. They were on their way from Minas intermediately. Douglass says they were nine hundred strong, or "about nine hundred ragamuffins." One "Mr. Marin, a lieutenant from Canada, was a captain of a company of savages, or Indian rangers," and composed a part of the force. The brave Capt. Donahew at a little later period, on another expedition, fell into the hands of the enemy, and, with many others, was massacred, as will be seen hereafter.

June 17. Louisbourg was surrendered to the English, which was the great event of this war.† The expedition was planned by Gov. Shirley, and met with the full approbation of nearly all of those then composing the government. The governors of nearly all the colonies favored it, and it was carried into successful execution. A few knowing ones of that time, to exhibit their superior sagacity, said the expedition would be a failure; but when they learned that it had completely succeeded, they attributed its success to accident, or good luck. Dr. Douglass, the historian, then living in Boston, and writing

---

* In that part of the township of Horton which borders on the basin. No traces of it are now to be seen, except the cellars of the houses, a few aged orchards, and groups of willows, the never-failing appendages of an ancient settlement. *Haliburton*, II, 115.

† It is worthy of remark that this was just thirty years before the battle of Bunker Hill.

his history, was opposed to Gov. Shirley. He generally disagreed with his measures, and when he could not deny that their effect was beneficial, he was careful not to admit that he had misjudged, but that it was a chance circumstance. Thus by an ingenious use of language he, in the minds of many, has caused some, even able historians, to give a wrong tone to their relations of the taking of Louisbourg. Dr. Douglass will always be a valuable authority for the events of this period, because he wrote at the time, and was acquainted personally with some of the principal actors. Hence his bias is not sufficiently guarded against. The following insidious, and at the same time ingenious passage in his history is recollected. Upon the capture of Louisbourg he says: "If every circumstance had not turned in favor of the expedition, and if every circumstance had not turned against the French, the expedition would have failed." Now this is a sort of taking assertion, but it is far from being a just one. The French were in the strongest fortress in America, had, or should have had, the best means of defence known to warfare, while the assailants were exposed to every annoyance; and as to their circumstances, they were as untoward as to any army whatever; being exposed to all the vicissitudes of a voyage by sea, and a landing upon a coast dangerous in the extreme from natural causes, and this in the face of an enemy on their own ground. Surely it does not appear as though "all the circumstances" were in favor of the expedition. Now the expedition succeeded because it was conducted with secrecy and energy. The governor left the least chance to accident. As early as February he had dispatched a messenger to England requesting a naval force to be sent him, and another to Admiral Warren in the West Indies.

It is not the purpose of this narrative to detail the particulars

Louisbourg Expedition.

of the taking of Louisbourg, because it has been so often done by all the historians of this period.* A few important facts, generally unnoticed in the common accounts, will be given.

In seven weeks from the time Gov. Shirley issued his proclamation for raising troops for the expedition, three thousand two hundred and fifty men were enrolled in Massachusetts, three hundred and four in New Hampshire, and five hundred and sixteen in Connecticut. The Massachusetts men were embarked the 24th of March, and sailed under the convoy of the Shirley *Galley*, afterwards called the Shirley *Frigate*. The whole naval force of the colony of Massachusetts consisted of three frigates of twenty guns each; a snow of sixteen; a brigantine of twelve; and five armed sloops mounting from eight to twelve carriage guns. A sloop from Rhode Island, and one from Connecticut, had ten or twelve guns each.†

The train of artillery consisted of eight twenty-two-pounders, twelve nine-pounders, two mortars of twelve-inch, one of eleven, and one of nine-inch. These were taken from Castle William. Also ten cannon borrowed of Governor Clinton of New York. These were eighteen-pounders.‡ Brigadier-General Samuel Waldo commanded the land forces. Colonel Samuel Moore commanded those of New Hampshire, Lieut.-Col. Simon Lothrop those of Connecticut; Lieut.-Col. Gridley commanded the artillery. Over the whole was Lieut.-Gen. Wm. Pepperrell.

Such was the ambition of the people of New England to participate in the expedition, that more men volunteered for it than could be received, and two companies were discharged and a month's pay given them. All the transportation at the command of the government had been already taken up.

---

* See APPENDIX, B.   † Shirley's *Memoirs*, 40.   ‡ *Ibidem*.

August 8. Rear-Admiral Peter Warren wrote from Louisbourg, giving the following account of his successes at that place: "The Charmante, a French East India ship of five hundred or six hundred tons, twenty-eight guns and ninety-nine men, very rich; the Heron, another French East India ship from Bengal, pretty rich; the Notre Dame de la Deliverance, a French ship of twenty-two guns, and about sixty men, from Lima in the South Seas, for which place she sailed from Cadiz in the year 1741, are brought into this harbor. This last had on board, in gold and silver, upwards of £300,000."

Louisbourg had fallen after a determined and bloody siege, but the importance of the conquest soon lost much of its consequence by the course given to events which restored it again to the French, as though it had cost nothing. This was particularly unfavorable to New England, which had lost so heavily in its active men, so much needed in a new country, to say nothing of the honor in a measure lost by the restoration of the costly acquisition. The suffering of the troops was incredible; often without shoes to their feet, or clothes, beyond a few rags, to shield their bodies from the weather, they toiled day and night, doing the labor of beasts of burthen and men as well, week after week, until more than a thousand lay sick at one time, and yet it is said, that up to the time of the capitulation, but about thirty had died of sickness, and that but one hundred and one had been killed by the enemy and other accidents, while, of the French, about three hundred had been killed within the walls of the city, and six hundred and fifty regular troops were surrendered. There were besides about thirteen hundred effective men belonging to the place, in all of which, together with the women and children, there were above four thousand to be transported to France.

Louisbourg Expedition.

With the place there fell into the hands of the victors immense material of war and other property, among which were seventy-six cannon and mortars, and provisions for five or six months. Many rich merchant ships, during and after the siege, were taken by the fleet. Admiral Warren kept the French flag flying long after the capture, and thus several were decoyed under his guns before they were aware that the place was taken. The value of these prizes was estimated at over a million pounds sterling, half of which went to the naval captors, and the other half to the Crown; and thus the New England men, who had been the means of this great acquisition, got no part of it!

In his account of the capture, General Pepperrell said, that when he marched into the city, he believed such ruins were never seen before, which was not to be wondered at, as nine thousand cannon balls and six hundred bombs had been thrown into it before it surrendered; which we may believe, as he says, "sorely distressed them, especially the day before they sent out a flag of truce, when our incessant fire prevented their showing their heads, or stirring from their covert ways, and some of them ran into the sea for shelter."

At the time of the surrender there remained but one house in the town which had not been shot through and through; such breaches had been made in the walls, and our batteries so advanced, that the enemy could stand to their guns no longer. Out of nineteen shell thrown from the light-house battery, seventeen fell within the Island battery, one of which fell upon the magazine, causing great consternation.

Care was taken to send off the inhabitants with all possible dispatch after the English were in possession of Louisbourg. Fourteen transports were got ready in an incredibly short time;

so that by the fourth of July (since a more noted day in American annals), only thirteen days after the capture, the unfortunate prisoners of war sailed for France, under the convoy of the Launceston man of war, Capt. Robert Man commander. They arrived at the port of Brest after a short passage, but here they met with treatment from the French Admiral on that station, which is characterized as cruel and brutal in the extreme. Such was the report of Col. James Gibson, who accompanied the prisoners as agent of the cartel transports on the part of the commander-in-chief.

There were many other prisoners to be transported besides those at Louisbourg, which are " summaried "* as follows: "The French people transported from Louisbourg to France (including the Vigilant's † men) preceding July 17, 1745, were four thousand one hundred and thirty, whereof one thousand eight hundred and twenty-two via Boston, and seventy-six via New Hampshire. The French, while in Boston, were allowed in old tenor per week, namely: an inhabitant from Cape Breton, twenty shillings; a sailor, fifteen shillings; captain of the Vigilant, five pounds; second captain, three pounds, and each officer forty shillings."

After we have seen the origin of the expedition against Louisbourg, and its progress and ultimate success, all brought about, so far as the former was concerned, by New England, it will seem very singular that a reimbursement to this country was a long time withheld by the government at home, through the false representations of influential bad men. This state of the case is so well set forth in a speech of Governor Shirley to

---

* *Douglass*, I, 568.
† " A sixty-four gun ship, with near six hundred men," taken by Commodore Warren, May 21. See APPENDIX, C.

Speech of Gov. Shirley. 73

the General Court, on the 29th of May, 1746, that it shall be given in his own words:

"As you may be solicitous to know what success your application for a reimbursement of your expenses in the late expedition against Cape Breton has met with, I think it proper to inform you, that though I have received several letters from one of your agents upon that subject, yet as all of them till my last (which I shall communicate to you) contained only accounts of the disadvantages which the Province lay under as to their demand, for want of the services of the New England troops in the reduction of Louisbourg, being fully known, whereby it happened that the merit of them (upon which the merit likewise of the colonies concerned in that expedition, it is reasonable to think, will be chiefly estimated by the ministry) has been most surprisingly diminished, disguised and concealed, and the laying before you these accounts could have had no other effect than to give you a fruitless concern and uneasiness, I forbore doing it, and chose to wait for more agreeable ones, which I have the pleasure to acquaint you I received by the last ship from London, and find that since the arrival in England of the representation of the behavior of the land forces, and the share which they had in making the late valuable acquisition to the British dominions, which I sent from Louisbourg, to be laid before His Majesty, your demand has taken a more favorable turn, and there is now a most promising prospect of your succeeding in it, and of our retrieving the honor of the New England land forces, and the opinion of the merit of the colonies concerned in the late expedition, which is justly due to them."

In the same speech he says: "It is a particular satisfaction to me, to consider that by the method which I have pursued for reinforcing that garrison [Louisbourg] instead of that proposed by the late Assembly and Council, I have saved £17,000 sterling, greatly promoted the levies for the two regiments [Pepperrell's and his own], strengthened the garrison more than otherwise it would have been, and made way for the discharging of such of the New England forces as are desirous to return to their homes."

It was as well known in England as in this country, that the principal credit of the capture of Louisbourg belonged to New England; and yet there were those in Old England ready to appropriate all the honor of the enterprise to that country. But there were some there who had honesty enough to place the credit where it belonged, and to ridicule the authors of the claims to all the glory. A writer in the *Westminster Journal* of August 3d, expresses the opinion that a secret expedition against Louisbourg, or any other point, could hardly have been put in practice in England without a discovery. In another article in the same journal, but of a few days earlier date, there appeared a dialogue, in the course of which the following homely though very just cut is given: "Well, Mr. B.," said one, "Cape Breton is taken; sure that must stop your mouth for a while at least." "Really," said the other, "I think it is a very fine acquisition; but I remember a story of a certain lord, whom his companions used to joke, and whose wife being brought to bed, his lordship says to one of them, 'Now I hope I shall have no more of your impertinence, for my wife has a fine boy.' 'Indeed, my lord,' answered the joker, 'I never questioned your wife's abilities in that respect!'"

The same article then goes on, broadly intimating that the whole undertaking was of New England origin, and all that

Donahew's Expeditions.

the English administration could claim was the honor of firing the Park and Tower guns in honor of the acquisition.

June 29. The gallant Capt. Donahew is surprised by the French and Indians, and himself, with many of his men, slain.* His loss was deeply lamented, as he had rendered very important services on various occasions, especially in the capture of Louisbourg, in the siege of which he was in command of one of the ships of the squadron.

For a considerable time the fate of Capt Donahew was unknown, but on the 27th of July a vessel came into Boston from Annapolis Royal, having on board Mr. Picket, who was steward to Capt. Donahew, from whom the facts of the affair in which himself, his commander and several others fell into the hands of the Indians, were obtained. Picket further relates, that Capt. Donahew, with eleven men, went on shore in the Gut of Canso, and were at once nearly surrounded by two hundred and fifty-three French and Indians. Donahew and his men being at once cut off from retreating to their vessel, defended themselves for above a quarter of an hour, in which time the captain, his brother, and three others were killed. The rest, six in number, all being wounded, were taken prisoners. The enemy had but two killed in the fight, but many were wounded. The Indians cut open the body of the captain's brother, sucked his blood, cut, hacked and mangled it in the most barbarous and brutal manner, and then eat a part of the flesh. They then proceeded to do the same

---

* Dr. Douglass says Donahew was dispatched from Boston to remove the French from St. John's Island, and on his way landed in the Gut of Canceau. Douglass may have confounded the last expedition with an earlier one, mentioned in our text. St. John's Island, so named by the French, is that now known as Prince Edward's. Lescarbot gave it the name *St. John*, also *Codfish Island*.

by the bodies of the other slain. After this exploit they set off for Minas with the seven that remained alive, the relator himself being one. Him they decided to kill and eat, but some of the French interceded and persuaded his captors to sell him, which they finally did for an amount of money. From Minas he got to Annapolis Royal, and thence to Boston, as above narrated. The other prisoners were taken to Canada. One of these, John Bradshaw by name, died there on the 24th of November following. He had recovered from the wound which he received when he was taken, but his constitution was broken, and he pined and died, of consumption as was supposed. Where he belonged is not known. Another was William Prindle. He died on the 4th of July, 1747; was a New England man, but his residence is not given. Another was James Owen of Brookfield, in Massachusetts. He was killed after quarter had been given.

It is to this affair, perhaps, that the French writers at Quebec refer in the following passage: "Lately, a boat belonging to an English merchantman having landed at La Hêve for wood and water, the Micmac Indians killed seven of the crew and brought their scalps to Sieur Marin; they [the Micmacs] can be depended on to pursue the same course as long as means will be found to furnish them with arms, powder and ball."*

While the siege of Louisbourg was progressing, Capt. Donahew had been dispatched to Bay Verte to destroy the place. In passing the strait of Canso he met with a party of Indians. These were attacked by a company of his men, contrary to orders, who went on shore under Captains Jaques and Hannaford. They were overpowered, Capt. Jaques killed, and Hannaford wounded; the rest escaped. Donahew was early

---

* Letter from Messrs. de Beauharnois and Hocquart to Count de Maurepas, dated Quebec, 12 Sept., 1745. In *N. Y. Col. Documents*, X, 11.

engaged in this war. We find him putting out from Newbury in a privateer on the 7th of November, 1744, manned with sixty men. The vessel belonged to Boston, and hence it appears the English were not much behind the French in early acts of hostility. Donahew sailed directly to the eastern fishing ground, and made several captures of French fishing vessels. Taking notice of his enterprising spirit, the General Court voted (on the 7th of February) that, with his vessel, he should be taken into the service of the Province. His vessel was the sloop Resolution. Andrew Hall and Samuel Gerrish of Boston were his agents. These agents preferred a claim on the government in September of the next year, in favor of Capt. Donahew's estate. From which claim it is shown, that early in this war the captain had captured eleven Cape Sable or St. John's Indians, brought them to Boston and delivered them here in compliance with Gov. Shirley's order. The claim of the agents was not allowed, but the reason for not allowing it is not given. Perhaps the Indians were captured before they had commenced the war.

He had been extremely active against the enemy. In April, 1745, he took and carried into Chapeaurouge Bay a French brigantine with a cargo of molasses, for which the war committee allowed him £1525 15s.

July 5. William Phips having but recently settled at Great Meadow* fort, some sixteen miles above Fort Dummer, is surprised, while hoeing corn, by two Indians. They seized him and led him away about half a mile, when they stopped, and one of them went down a steep hill to get something he

* There were other *Great Meadows;* one occupied by the Housatunnuk Indians, "above the mountains," 1736; called by them *Wnahktukook.* *Hopkins,* 46, 47. This is in Westmoreland, N. H., formerly Narraganset No. 2.

had left. On his return Phips seized one of their guns and shot him down, and then fell upon the other with his hoe, which it seems he had carried with him, or perhaps was carried along by the other Indian. With this he knocked him down, and after chopping him till he thought he had killed him, started to run; but at that instant three Indians appeared and shot down Phips, killed and scalped him, and treated his body in a shocking manner. The Indian that was *hoed* so severely, died of his wounds, according to the information given by the Indians after the war.

Some time after the death of Mr. Phips, his widow married Mr. Caleb Howe. She afterwards suffered a doleful captivity, as will be seen by a reference to her well known Narrative.

Great Meadow Fort was in what is now Putney, Vermont, in the eastern part of the county of Windham, on the westerly side of Connecticut river. Putney is ten miles from Brattleborough. It was chartered by New Hampshire in 1753, and in 1766 rechartered by New York, and finally fell within the jurisdiction of Vermont. The Great Meadow was in a bend of the river, comprising about four hundred acres of excellent land.

July 10. "The same, or some other party of Indians,"* who did the mischief at Great Meadow, came to Upper Ashuelot, now the town of Keene, New Hampshire, waylaid the road, and shot and scalped Deacon Josiah Fisher,† as he was driving his cows to pasture. He was among the early proprietors of the town, ten years before he was slain. His body

---

* *Doolittle's Narrative*, p. 2.
† We find nothing in the *Annals of Keene* to throw any light on this affair, excepting that the author points out the locality of the murder. See *Collections of N. H. Historical Society*, II, 87.

Surprise near George's Fort.

was found soon after he was killed, about half a mile from the garrison.

July 18. The Thanksgiving which had been appointed to celebrate the taking of Louisbourg, took place and was heartily entered into all over New England. Sermons were preached on the occasion, among which was one by the Rev. Thomas Prince of the Old South church in Boston; in which is detailed the proceedings of that remarkable expedition with an accuracy and ability which has rendered it one of the very best accounts anywhere to be met with. It was dedicated to Governor Shirley, whom he denominated "the principal former and promoter" of the enterprise.*

Your most vehement/full humble servant T Prince

July 19. War begins in the eastern country. An express arrived at Falmouth from Capt. Jabez Bradbury, stationed at George's Fort, that a man and forty cattle had been killed, and a garrison and saw-mill burnt, which is the first mischief done about the Penobscot. They took one prisoner as they approached the fort, and fired on a woman, whom they wounded in the shoulder. The report of the gun and the shrieks of the woman alarmed the garrison, a fire from which afforded the wounded woman an opportunity to reach the gate and enter it without farther injury. Capt. Bradbury, in his dispatch to

* See APPENDIX, B.

Indian Murders at Brunswick.

Gov. Shirley, represented that the Indians were about seventy strong, and that they killed fifty or sixty head of cattle, besides hogs and horses. Upon this news the governor ordered Capt. Thomas Sanders, of the Massachusetts frigate, to sail forthwith to the invaded territory;* and Capt. Bradbury believing some of the Penobscots were among those who had attacked his fort, notified the tribe to give up such as participated in it, in fourteen days, but they took no notice of the demand.

July 30. On the third of August an express from the eastward arrived at Boston with the intelligence that the Indians had surprised two men a little above Brunswick, one of whom they killed and scalped, the other they scalped and left for dead, but being soon after found by his neighbors, hopes were entertained of his recovery. The men were not shot, but knocked down and beat with clubs.

The same day a man was killed at Topsham, and a boy was scalped. The same event, probably, recorded in the last paragraph.

Insubordination began to break forth among the soldiers soon after the capture of Louisbourg. It arose from various causes; a principal, perhaps, was that the men generally supposed they would be at liberty to return home as soon as the city was taken; another was the unequal distribution of plunder, or rather the disappointment which arose from the inhabitants being allowed by the capitulation to retain their effects unmolested; but, above all, sickness was making terrible havoc among them. Their officers could only appeal to the commander-in-chief at Boston for relief. Hence the clamor for the governor became so pressing upon Gen. Pepperrell, that

---

* There is given a thrilling incident connected with the career of Captain Sanders the younger, by Mr. Eaton in his *History of Thomaston*, I, 56.

Gov. Shirley at Louisbourg.

through his and the other officers' urgency, Gov. Shirley consented to proceed to Cape Breton.

August 3. Gov. Shirley, with his lady, sails for Louisbourg, where he remained until near December following, returning in Boston Dec. 8th, after a tedious passage of eleven days. He returned in the Massachusetts frigate, Capt. Edward Tyng. On leaving the ship, near Castle William, she fired a salute of seventeen guns, and, on landing at the fort, it fired twenty-one guns. He lodged at the castle that night. The next day he was rowed up to Boston in a barge, the Shirley frigate and other vessels firing salutes. He debarked at the end of Long Wharf amid the acclamations of crowds of enthusiastic citizens, and under a military escort proceeded to his residence in the Province House.

While at Louisbourg the governor labored diligently in collecting an accurate detail of all the proceedings of the siege and capture of the place, a copy of which he transmitted to the Duke of Newcastle.* All the principal New England officers attested its accuracy by their signatures.

David Creighton and his companion, venturing a short distance from the garrison at St. Georges (or Georges as the English generally wrote it), were killed and scalped. Boyce Cooper and Reuben Pitcher, proceeding down the river for rock-weed, fell into the hands of the enemy and were carried to Canada. Cooper was naturally jovial, appeared contented, and made himself familiar with the Indians; gave them all the information they desired about the English, their forts, cattle and men, and thus secured good usage. His fellow prisoner seems to have possessed a violin, and dying, left it to Cooper, which he was able to use, and thus enhanced his importance,

---

* This valuable and authentic document will be found entire in APPENDIX, D.

and eventually secured him an early release. He was a native of Ireland.*

Aug. 20. In a message from Gov. Clinton of New York to the General Assembly of that province, he charges the Six Nations with having broken their treaty of neutrality; that from their apprehensions of having been wronged by the white people, they had visited the governor of Canada the last summer. He (the governor), recommends the Assembly to provide for holding a conference with them this fall, that their grievances may be redressed and their friendship secured. He had heard of two other nations of Indians to whom he desired to send invitations to come to the conference; namely, the *Chonondado* and *Attowas*. The since well known tribes, Onondagos and the Ottowas.

August 23. Lieut.-Gov. Spencer Phips, now acting governor in the absence of Gov. Shirley, declares war "against the Eastern and Canada Indians;" for that the "Norridgewack and Penobscot tribes, and other Indians of the eastern parts," contrary to treaty, "are now broke out into open rebellion," and committed divers acts of hostility, entertained and harbored Cape Sable's and St. John's Indians, joining with them in perpetrating the most cruel murders upon persons in those parts, burning their houses, and killing great numbers of cattle,† attacking the fort at St. George's river, and, when a flag was sent to them, justified their perfidy and cruelty, and bid defiance to the government. Also, in the western parts of the province, had already killed two and scalped them; others were driven from their estates, their substance destroyed, and in constant

---

* The above is from Williamson, who gives no date. *Hist. Maine*, II, 238.

† Having reference, doubtless, to the murder of Captain Donahew and some of his men before mentioned, and the affair of July 30th last.

Indians Massacred. 83

peril of their lives in getting their harvests; that the Six Nations, who undertook for the performance of neutrality, had failed to prevent what is complained of. And it was ordered that well disposed Indians who had not joined the enemy, should, in fourteen days, repair to the forts of the English, and live amongst His Majesty's subjects, in places assigned them, and there be protected.

Sept. 5. In the vicinity of George's fort, one Lieutenant Proctor and nineteen men had a fight with a number of Indians, in which two noted chiefs are killed; namely, Col. Morris and Capt. Samuel. Another, called Col. Job, is taken prisoner and carried to Boston, where he died in prison. The following is Lieut. Proctor's narrative of the whole affair. With his captive, Col. Job, the lieutenant arrived in Boston Sept. 8th, in a small schooner: "On the first instant, being at Georges, and understanding that a number of Indians had been lately seen near the fort, he mustered up sixteen men and boys from the block-house, and went in quest of the enemy. About twelve o'clock at night, and three miles from the fort, they discovered four Indians about a fire, upon whom they discharged their guns, and killed Col. Sam and Lieut.-Gov. Moxas (as he was called), and took Col. Job prisoner, but the other fellow made his escape. Those three Indians were principal men of the Penobscot tribe, and all well known in Boston."

The scalps of the other two were brought, and the bounty demanded on them according to the governor's proclamation; but Lieut.-Gov. Phips, in his speech at the opening of the General Assembly, remarked that the circumstances were such as to render it necessary to defer granting the bounty. The governor had good grounds for his delaying the bounty, no doubt, for, from other sources of information, it seems that these Indians had been to the fort, not knowing of the attack of the 19th of the last month, or before the fourteen days had expired, to trade, and had departed for their own place, but had encamped for the night not far off, and in this condition (perhaps drunk with liquor obtained at the fort) were fallen upon as above related. That no bounty was paid is inferred from the fact, that after the war a present was made to the wife of Job on account of the loss of her husband. If his value was accurately estimated by the government, her loss was not great — a seven-eighth blanket!

Sept. 15. A son of Col. Cushing is killed by some unseen Indians at Sheepscott, and two lads, James and Samuel Anderson, are taken captive and carried to Canada. Their father was killed, probably at the same time. The Indians kept the two boys with them all winter, and the following May they were sent to prison at Quebec.

Sept. 27. James Kinlade is taken at Sheepscott, carried to Canada, and imprisoned at Quebec. On Nov. 19th one man is delivered to the prison in Quebec, who says James Anderson's father was killed and his uncle was taken at the time he was. Another man, Jotham Williamson, taken on Sheepscott river, was imprisoned at Quebec at a later date.

Oct. 5. In pursuance of Gov. Clinton's urgent request, the Indians came to Albany to hold a conference from many of the tribes of the Six Nations, some five hundred in number. The governor having notified Massachusetts, Rhode Island, Connecticut, New Jersey and Pennsylvania, they send the following gentlemen, namely: Massachusetts, John Stoddard, Jacob Wendell, Samuel Wells, and Thomas Hutchinson;

Conference at Albany.

Connecticut, Roger Wolcot, Nathaniel Stanley;* Pennsylvania, Thos. Lawrence, John Kinsey, and Isaac Norris. Arent Stevens and Coenradt Weiser, interpreters.

The commissioners on the part of Massachusetts returned to Boston on the 20th of October, and as a result of their conference with the Indians it was published, that "the Six Nations readily renewed their covenant with the several governments; that they had taken the hatchet against the French and Indian enemy, and only wait till the governor of New York shall order them to make use of it."

Oct. 8. A company of thirteen Indians surprise some Englishmen while gathering corn at Sheepscott, killing two and wounding a third.

Oct. 11. An attempt was made to surprise the fort at Great Meadow. As the enemy approached it they came upon Mr. Nehemiah How, and took him prisoner. He had been cutting wood some forty rods from the fort, and was returning to it when he was overtaken by twelve Indians, who hurried him away into a swamp, and there pinioned him. When he saw the Indians he hallooed so as to alarm the fort, and the men inside fired upon them, killing one and mortally wounding another. A third, who had hold of Mr. How, barely escaped, a bullet passing through his powder-horn. How was carried to Canada, and from one prison to another, and finally to Quebec, where he died a prisoner, May 25th, 1747, after a year and upwards of seven months' captivity. He left a wife and several children. A journal which he kept to within six days of his death, was recovered by his friends and published in 1748, from which these facts are taken.

* It is singular, that in the elaborate histories of Connecticut no mention is found of this important mission of their statesmen.

Having secured their prisoner, as above stated, the enemy returned and attacked the fort for an hour and a half, but did little damage. They killed all the cattle about the place, cutting a portion of the flesh from the bones the better to transport it. With their prisoner they marched along the river side. At about three miles from the fort a canoe was seen coming down with two men in it. How knew the men and made all the noise he could to alarm them, but the Indians also saw them, and shot at them some twenty or thirty guns, by which they killed one, David Rugg, but the other, Robert Baker, got on shore and escaped. They scalped Rugg, and carried off his scalp in great triumph. On it they painted a face, "with the likeness of eyes and mouth," with red paint, and when they got to Lake George they hoisted a pole some eight feet long, with the scalp on the top of it. At Crown Point they were met by a multitude of Indians. Here Mr. How saw an Indian he was acquainted with, who took him by the hand and was very glad to see him. This Indian then went and brought in another, named *Amrusus*, who was the husband of Eunice Williams, who had lived among the Indians forty-two years, having been carried away from Deerfield in 1704. Amrusus was glad to see Mr. How, and made inquiry about his wife's relations. Many attempts were made to recover Eunice, from time to time, from her captivity to 1713, when she was to all intents an Indian, living among the French Mohawks at Cagnawaga. She had then recently married, and would not converse with those sent to redeem her.

Nov. 16. A large body of three hundred French and two hundred Indians came upon the Dutch settlement at Saratoga, murdering the inhabitants without any opposition. The enemy were commanded by one M. Marin, accompanied by a mischievous and active priest named Francis Piquet. They ravaged a large extent of country, burning all the houses, several saw-mills with much sawed lumber, and a block-house which belonged to John Henry Lydius. Also all the cattle. Thirty persons were killed and scalped, and about sixty taken prisoners. All this was effected without so much as a wound to any of the French. A large number of negroes * were among the captives. In the course of the winter the captives were sent to the prison in Quebec, where many of them died of sickness. The news of this attack reached Albany three days after it happened, and Deerfield nine days after, namely, on the 25th.† A letter of this date was at once dispatched to Boston, to the effect that "two Indians who were taken at Lydius's fort got away from the army near Crown Point, and reported that an army of six hundred men set out from that place in order to fall upon Deerfield, but by reason of a snow were diverted and went to Saratoga. They have burnt Lydius's block-house, and taken his son; Cockensenet was killed there; three hundred of the army went back with the prisoners, and three hundred struck off to come upon our frontiers."

Among the prisoners was Jonathan Hagadorn, taken near Fort Ann, while on a scout. He died on the 3d of January following, a prisoner at Quebec, after a long and painful sickness; as also did Capt. John Fort, March 21, taken at the same time and place.

The Assembly of New York offers a reward for Indian scalps — ten pounds for those of male Indians over sixteen years of age, and twenty pounds for prisoners brought in alive.

---

* Said to have been about sixty, by a prisoner in Canada who saw them brought to Montreal. Some time afterwards their owners sent to redeem them, but they would not go back to slavery, preferring to live with the Indians, where doubtless they had much greater freedom than with their Dutch and English masters.

† The French account may be seen in the *New York Col. Docs.*, X, 38 and 76.

Bounty for Scalps.

"For the years 1745, 1746, and 1747, the premium for Indian scalps and captives was one thousand pounds, old tenor per head to volunteers, and four hundred pounds to impressed men, their wages and subsistence money to be deducted."* At the same time old tenor was to sterling money as one to eleven. Hence it took eleven pounds of the former to purchase what was actually worth but one pound in specie.

Some time in the year 1745, as James McQuade and Robert Burns of Bedford, New Hampshire, were returning from Penacook to their homes, whither they had been to procure corn for their families, they were fired upon by some Indians who appeared to be lying in wait for the opportunity. McQuade was shot down and killed, but they missed their aim at Burns, who ran, tacking at short intervals, and thus escaped unhurt.†

One Bunten was shot by the Indians in what is now the town of Chester, N. H., " near where Head's tavern is in Hooksett. He was from Pelham, and was on his way to Penacook."‡

---

* *Douglass*, I, 565.

† The date of this affair may have been derived from tradition, which is generally very unreliable, especially when not accompanied by any month or day of month on which it happened. There is a history of Bedford, but the author adds nothing more authentic.

‡ *Colls. N. H. Hist. Soc.*, VII, 363. The historian of Old Chester does not throw any light on this murder, not even giving the name of the man killed.

CHAPTER VI.

DIARY OF DEPREDATIONS (continued).

A French Item — A distressing Scene at Gorhamtown — Escape of Prisoners — Captives taken at Number Four — John Spofford — Harvey's Escape — Surprise at Hopkinton — Remarkable Events in the Narrative of Mary Woodwell — Upper Ashuelot Surprised — Death of Holton — Death of Putnam, and Fight at Number Four — Attack on Contoocook — An Indian punished at Ashuelot — Indians fail at Fall Town — John Buck — Attack on Lower Ashuelot — Huntington — Two Men attacked near Fort Massachusetts — Surprise at Colerain, and Death of Matthew Clark — Persons killed near Albany — Others at Saratoga — Houses burnt at Kinderhook — Men killed near Schenectady — Seven killed and taken at Norman's Creek — Great Depredation at Broad Bay — Surprise and Fight at St. George's Fort — Fight at Number Four — Affair at Sheepscott — Retaliation recommended — Forces raised — Surprise at Long Creek — A Surprise prevented at Fort Massachusetts — Hugh Morrison — Joseph Swett killed — Gallant Defense of Number Four — Seven Persons killed at Sheepscott.

THE Chevalier de Niverville, officer, and Sieur Groschesne Raimbault, cadet, left Montreal on March 16th, with some Abenaquis Indians, on their way towards Boston, and returned with some scalps and prisoners, one of whom Raimbault took with his own hand. Sieur Duplessis, Jr., an officer, started at the same time with six Algonkins and Nepissings in the same direction, and joined the preceding party, with whom he returned, bringing in a prisoner who was captured at the same time.

It is not very clear on what point of the frontier this company performed their exploit. Perhaps it was at Number Four, on the 19th of the following April. A French leader, probably the same Raimbault, afterwards fell into the hands of the English, as we shall see.

M

April 19, 1746. At a new township called Gorham Town, in Maine, was perpetrated a tragedy which was thus reported at the time: "Boston, April 28. Last Tuesday morning came in here an express from Falmouth, who informs, that on the 19th instant, about ten o'clock, Mr. Briant of Gorham Town, about ten miles from thence, with three others, went to work in a field three-quarters of a mile from the fort, when the said Briant was shot to death by the Indians; two of the others were taken, and the other made his escape to the fort and informed that he saw about twenty Indians, who went from the field to said Briant's house, and killed and scalped four of his children, three of whom were knocked in the head by an axe, the other had its brains beat out against the hearth. This was discovered in the afternoon by some persons from the fort. His wife was missing, and it is supposed is taken prisoner. One of the persons taken was seen to be stript naked by the Indians." The other persons taken were Jacob Read and Edward Cloutman. These were brought prisoners to Quebec on the 14th of May following. Mrs. Briant was brought in afterwards, who, on the 20th of November, 1746, was married to Leonard Lydle, another captive, by the Rev. John Norton,* also a captive, taken at Number Four, as will elsewhere be seen. Mrs. Sarah Lydle (Briant) died a prisoner on the 7th of May of the next year (1747). Jacob Read was also dead, having died on the 20th of October preceding.† Edward Cloutman and Robert Dunbar broke prison and escaped three days after. Dunbar was taken not long before as he was scouting "on the

---

* Mr. Norton does not mention this circumstance in his Narrative, which is quite remarkable.

† John, son of Jacob Reed, a prisoner at the same time, died eleven days after his father, but had been longer in captivity, having been taken near Annapolis, May 9, 1745, while on duty as a soldier.

Carrying-Place," and his loss was greatly lamented, as he had performed the most important services as a ranger, ever since the war commenced. He was a New York man probably, and the Carrying Place was that between the Hudson and Wood Creek, doubtless. Cloutman does not appear to have reached his home, for Anne, probably his wife, petitioned for relief the next year, as "her husband was in captivity, and she was left with three children, and very poor."

April 19. "The enemy came to the uppermost and most frontier place on Connecticut river, called Number Four, where they took three men as they were going to the mill, about half a mile from the garrison, namely, Capt. John Spafford,* Isaac Parker and Stephen Fainsworth." They were with a team of four oxen. The oxen the Indians killed, and after cutting out their tongues left them. They arrived, with their prisoners, at Quebec the 3d of the following month. All three of them returned home after a short captivity, but whether redeemed or exchanged is not known.

The leader in this depredation was Ensign de Niverville. He took his prisoners first to Montreal, where, May 14th, they underwent an examination. From Spafford and Parker they learned that two regiments were to be sent from Boston to Ile Royale, where over seven hundred men had died; that twenty-two hundred regulars had arrived at New York from London, at the close of winter, and had set out for Louisbourg; that

---

* A Capt. John *Spofford* is conspicuous in the Spofford Genealogy in the *New England Hist. and Gen. Register*, VIII, 340. He settled at Charlestown, N. H. He may be the captive, but as nothing is said about it in the Genealogy, and the discrepancies in the same, render it doubtful, an uncertainty hangs over him. John, the captive, had a wife, and while at Quebec wrote a letter to Mr. John Stoddard, which letter Mr. Stoddard communicated to Governor Shirley, and on October 1, 1746, it was read in the House of Representatives.

two thousand pairs of snow-shoes had been made and laid in at Boston, and what Indian moccasins were necessary.

April 22. A man named Moses Harvey is shot at as he is passing between Northfield and Deerfield, and narrowly escapes, the ball passing through the rim of his hat. He returned the fire, but whether with any effect is not known.

April 22. The fort or garrison at New Hopkinton is surprised, and six days after an account of it was published in Boston to this purport: "We hear that the Indians have lately surprised a garrison house in New Hopkinton, and made eight men prisoners, whom they found asleep in their beds, the door being left open, or upon the latch, by a man who had just gone out a hunting." The names of the captives were Samuel Burbank, his sons Caleb and Jonathan, David Woodwell, his wife and sons Benjamin and Thomas, and daughter Mary. Jonathan Burbank, after his redemption, became an officer and was killed by the Indians, they mistaking him for Maj. Robert Rogers, against whom they had sworn vengeance. Mary Woodwell, after a detention of six months among the French at Montreal, returned to Albany, thence to Hopkinton, her native place. She had been twice married, joined the Canterbury Shakers, and died in October, 1829, in the one hundredth year of her age, having been born May 11, 1730. Her first husband was Jesse Corbett. He was drowned in attempting to swim across Almsbury river, in Hopkinton, since called Warner's river, in 1759. She had two sons by him. She afterwards married Jeremiah Fowler, by whom she had five children. These facts were gathered from her when in her ninety-third year. She stated that there were but six Indians in the party that surprised the garrison. Her mother, also named Mary, died in captivity, December 18, 1747, at Quebec. "She lay

1746.]   *Attack on Upper Ashuelot.*   93

in a burning fever about a fortnight." Samuel Burbank was an old man, and died in captivity at Quebec, May 19th, 1748.

April 23. A furious attack is made by a body of about one hundred Indians upon the garrison of Upper Ashuelot, since Keene, in New Hampshire. The report of the attack made at the time is thus given: "There were about sixty of the enemy, who were discovered in their approach, by the garrison, early in the morning; whereupon the men went out to meet them, and fought, which gave most of the inhabitants time to get into the garrison, so that there were only an old man and a woman killed, and one man missing, supposed to be taken captive. One of our men, being abroad, was surprised by the Indians, and submitted by laying down his gun; but the Indian who pursued, and had, as it were, taken him, coming up to him with his hatchet lifted up to kill him, thereupon, being resolute, struck the Indian with his fist such a blow on the temple as laid him on the ground, which gave him opportunity to recover his gun and make his escape, which he did, to the garrison. The name of this man was Ephraim Dorman, and another says he encountered two Indians, from one of which he tore off his blanket and carried it with him to the fort, leaving him entirely naked."

The enemy had been watching the place, intending, that as soon as the men went out in the morning, to rush in; but the affair with Dorman timely alarmed the rest. It appears that those who sallied out to fight the enemy met with rough usage, one man, Nathan Blake, was captured and carried to Canada, but was redeemed in the winter of 1747. Another, named Allen, was redeemed at the same time. The enemy came on very boldly, shot down one John Bullard, who soon died, and stabbed one Daniel McKenny's wife in the back with a long knife, who also soon died. They burnt six houses and one barn, and killed twenty-three cattle. In the ruins of one of the burnt houses were found the remains of several Indians which had been killed, and placed there by their comrades for concealment, as was supposed. Mrs. McKenny had gone out to milk her cow, at a barn near by, and was returning to the fort, when a naked Indian, probably the one Dorman had stripped, started from the bushes, stabbed her and escaped. She being old and corpulent, walked, but slowly, and continued her progress, notwithstanding her wound was mortal, till nearly at the gate of the fort, when blood gushed from her mouth, and she fell and expired.

April 26. Some of the Indians who did the mischief on the 23d, at Upper Ashuelot, as was supposed, waylaid the road between Lunenburg and Northfield, where they killed and scalped Joshua Holton of the latter town. He was on his return from Boston with a large sum of money for the payment of the soldiers, and parties who had billeted them, among whom was Mr. Benjamin Doolittle. They soon after petitioned the General Court for the amount due them, in which petition they said that the last winter they had billeted the soldiers under Major Edward Hartwell; that the major delivered the money to Joshua Holton to pay them, who was killed by the common enemy as just stated, and the money taken from him. The petition went through the usual stages, and on June 10th following forty-six pounds seven pence half-penny was ordered to be paid the petitioners.

May 2. The enemy came again to Number Four, and in the night hid themselves in a barn some fifty or sixty rods from the fort. As Seth Putnam a soldier belonging to the fort, went out in the morning, he was shot down and killed. Upon which Major Josiah Willard, with two men, ran near the Indians

1746.]   *Attack on Contoocook.*   95

undiscovered, and fired upon them, which caused them to make a hasty flight, with two of their number mortally wounded. They were in the act of scalping the soldier when fired upon. The party of enemy consisted of eight Indians, and was probably the same company, under a chief named Thesaotin of the Sault St. Louis, sent out from Montreal about the 20th of April.*

May 4. At Contoocook, since Boscawen, N. H., a party of Indians fire upon five white men and a negro named Cæsar, kill one of the white men, named Elisha † Cook, and the negro, who was the slave of the Rev. Phinehas Stevens, the minister of the place. They took Thomas Jones prisoner, whom they delivered at Quebec twenty days after. He died in captivity in the following August. He belonged to Sherburne, but was a soldier at Contoocook when taken. At the time of this attack Capt. John Goff of Harrytown, with some thirty-six men, was on a scout from the lower towns in the direction of Contoocook, but was delayed, owing to a failure of a supply of bread, at Pennycook, and there received the news of the murders.

May 4. A party of the enemy secreted themselves about the fort at Upper Ashuelot, and in the night attempted to surprise it by causing those inside to open the gate under the impression that some friend had come to gain admittance; but the Indian who undertook to counterfeit a friend found a sad reception, for the sentinel on duty took the precaution to shoot through the gate before opening it, thus shooting the Indian through the abdomen also. He immediately retreated for Canada, but died before reaching Crown Point.

The same day, at Contoocook, a Mr. Thomas Cook and his

---

* See *N. Y. Col. Documents*, X, 32. which is an error, and Judge Potter did
† Capt. Goff gave his name Thomas,   not correct it.

son, and a negro named Cæsar, are killed in that part of the place called Clay Hill, and Elisha Jones is taken and carried to Canada, where he died in captivity * the 16th of the following August.†

May 6. ‡ At Fall-town, since Bernardston, a party of Indians had concealed themselves near by, intending about midday, when the men were at their labors in the field, to rush in and take the garrison. But a soldier a little space from the fort discovered them, and alarmed those inside, though he could not recover it. There were but three men then in it, yet by the assistance of the women in loading the guns, they successfully defended themselves, though the enemy came on with more than their accustomed audacity. Finding they could not succeed they drew off, the amount of their mischief being the wounding of John Buck (or Burk, as Taylor has the name) slightly, and killing ten cattle. The chief leader of the Indians had his arm broken, and one or two others were wounded. Burk (or Burke, as the name is since written) became a man of considerable distinction, served through the war till the fall of Canada, having attained the rank of major; was in the battle of Lake George, in 1755, and hardly escaped from the Indians at the massacre of Fort William Henry, in 1757.

May 6. At Lower Ashuelot, since Swanzey, Dea. Timothy Brown and Robert Moffet are fired upon as they were leaving the garrison. They returned the fire, breaking the arm of the Indian leader, but both are made prisoners and taken to Canada,

---

* Price, *History of Boscawen*, 37, and Farmer and Moore's *Gazetteer*, p. 83.

† According to *How*, p. 18, who gives his Christian name as Thomas, and says he belonged to Holliston.

‡ The date of this affair is given as happening on the 9th, by Doolittle, and on the 6th, by Taylor. Gen. Hoyt does not give the date. In the *Hampshire Record Book* it is said to have occurred on the 9th of May. See *New Eng. Hist. and Gen. Reg.*, IX, 163.

arriving at Quebec June 22d. They were both exchanged or ransomed soon after.

May 7. One Christian Tedder or Tether is taken at Schenectady. He died at Quebec, after a year and eight days' captivity, namely, May 15, 1747. The same day died, in the morning, a young man of much promise, Mr. Hezekiah Huntington, son of Col. Hezekiah Huntington of Norwich in Connecticut. He was captured in a vessel at sea, on the 28th of June, 1746; hence he had been near a year in captivity. "A hopeful youth of a liberal education;" and another says "he was well beloved and much lamented by all sober, religious persons."

May 9. At Fort Massachusetts, in what is now the town of Adams, as Sergeant John Hawks and John Mihils, or Miles, were riding on a horse, they were fired upon by two skulking Indians, and both wounded. Mihils made his escape to the fort, and Hawks fell from the horse, and, as the Indians ran to scalp him, he recovered and presented his gun, which so damped their ardor that one jumped down a bank, and the other got behind a tree and called for quarter; but Hawks was too confused to understand what he meant, so stood hallooing to those in the fort to come to his assistance; meantime both Indians fled, one having his gun discharged; the other had dropped his, and did not dare to venture from his screen to recover it.

May 10. Some of the party of Indians that had fared so hard at Falltown, waylaid the road at Colerain, about ten miles northwest from Deerfield. Here, as Mr. Matthew Clark, with his wife and daughter and three soldiers, were going from the garrison to Clark's house, they were fired upon. Mr. Clark was killed and scalped, and his wife and daughter were wounded. One of the soldiers fought off the Indians with much bravery, and succeeded in getting the mother and daughter into the fort, having killed one of the Indians. The wounded females recovered. According to Taylor the party of Indians consisted of but five.

May 10. Six persons are killed in sight of the city of Albany, just across the river, two of whom were negroes. Pursuit was immediately made, but before men could cross the river and pursue on the other side, the enemy got into the woods and escaped.

May 13. As three men belonging to the garrison of *Saraghtoga* were fishing near that fort, they were surprised by Indians, who killed a son of William Norwood, took another, a German, who used to live with Col. John Schuyler, while the third effected his escape to the fort. Another person narrowly escaped being taken in his own garden, within a fourth of a mile of the city of Albany. So daring have the enemy become that they are daily seen about the settlements, and yet none of them are either killed or taken.

About the same time two negroes were taken at Stone Arabia, since Palatine, on the Mohawk river, a German settlement, commenced in 1709.

A day or two later they fall upon Kinderhook, burn the houses and barns of Tunis Van Sluyck and Peter Vosburgh, and kill their cattle. The people escaped to the garrison.

About the same time Simon Groot and two of his brothers are butchered three miles from the village of Schenectady. The enemy burnt their buildings, killed their cattle, and destroyed their other effects. They were discovered, while doing this mischief, by the settlers on the opposite side of the river, who knew some of the Indians, particularly Tom Wilemau, who had lately removed from the Mohawk country to Albany.

May. At Norman's creek,* about eight miles to the westward of Albany, as fourteen men, all armed, went with a wagon to bring corn from a deserted farm to a house where several families had removed for safety, they were met by a party of Indians, who killed and took all the party but two, who made their escape to Albany. One of these was wounded in the shoulder.

May 21. At Broad Bay, near the mouth of the Penobscot river, in Maine, the houses of the inhabitants are burnt, and their cattle killed about Pemaquid. Some people were killed, and others carried off prisoners. Among the latter was Capt. Jonathan Williamson, who, on the 26th of April, 1747, was carried to Quebec. He was exchanged, and returned home by way of Boston, after about a year's captivity.† Sullivan was acquainted with Capt. Williamson, and had the account of the affair in which he was taken, from Williamson himself. He was well treated, and being a man of consequence, and well known to the Indians, was taken alive, for the reason that he would be able to give the French valuable information.

May 22. At St. George's fort, Capt. Bradbury having sent out thirteen men about half a gunshot from the fort, to peel some bark for covering of canoes or whale boats newly got ready for making discoveries of the enemy. No precautions are mentioned as having been taken to prevent a surprise, for no sooner had the men commenced their work than they were saluted with a volley from an unseen foe, killing at once Elia-

---

* Although Norman's *kill* falls into the Hudson about two and a half miles *below* Albany, yet the course of it is such, that at eight miles inland the point would lie *to the westward* of that city. See Spafford's *Gaz. of N. Y.*, p. 361, ed. 1824.

† Compare *Sullivan*, 168, with *How*, in *Indian Captivities*, 138. *Williamson* was misled by *Sullivan*. See the former, II, 252. The editor of the *New York Colonial Documents*, following Williamson, has made the same blunder. See X, 95.

kim Hunt, badly wounding Stephen Buxton, Samuel Peirce, John Davis, and Josiah Harvey. They carried off one man, Timothy Cummings, whom they arrived with at Quebec on the 14th of the next April. The captain of the fort lost no time in pursuing the enemy with most of his men, not giving them time to scalp the man they had killed. He captured one of the Indians, took him to the fort and scalped him. This Indian was found to be Job's son-in-law. There is another account of the affair extant, but the above is probably the most reliable. In this version it is stated that two were carried off captive. Of those who escaped to the garrison, one was an old man, who was overtaken by an Indian with his tomahawk raised to cleave his head, but the old man had presence of mind and activity enough to turn and shoot down his pursuer, scalp him, and gain the fort in safety. Cummings stated, on his arrival in Canada, that the Indians killed the ensign as he stood on the top of the fort, and that five of the Indians were killed. Cummings was sixty years old. He died in captivity on the 14th of April following (1747).

May 24. A large body of the enemy appeared again at Number Four. Capt. Paine, with a company of horse, had recently arrived there, having been sent by the government of Massachusetts. About twenty men went out to the place where Seth Putnam was killed, when an ambush rose, fired upon them, and then attempted to cut off their retreat to the fort. Capt. Phinehas Stevens, seeing this from the fort, sallied out with a few of his men, when a fierce encounter ensued. At length the enemy were put to flight, with the loss of five of their number killed. They also left on the battle ground, thirteen blankets, five coats, a gun, and other things. The English lost Aaron Lion, Peter Perrin, and Joseph Marcy of

Capt. Paine's men; and Samuel Farnsworth, and Elijah Allen, belonging to the fort. Quartermaster Bacon was wounded, and with Ensign Obadiah Sartle was made prisoner. Sartle (or Sartwell, as some write his name) returned not long after.

May 25. At Sheepscott some concealed Indians fire upon and kill one man, and wound another. The wounded man seeing an Indian coming swiftly upon him to dispatch him, courageously turned upon him and cut him down with a hatchet. A moment after another appeared, but the wounded man succeeded in escaping to the fort.

This is probably the same event noticed by Smith as happening two days later. He says, as five persons were returning from meeting they were fired upon by fifteen Indians, by which one was killed and one mortally wounded.

On the 30th of May the governor, in a message to the General Court, strongly urged the attention of the members to the distressed state of the people; among other things he said, "At Fort Dummer they are in extreme distress, also at Number Four, and other places, by reason of the great number of Indians that appear there. Upon the advice I had about a fortnight ago, I sent up three troops of horse, as a most expeditious way for a present relief; but there is great inconvenience in this, owing to a want of forage, and they must soon be discharged. The danger there is of the enemy's being masters of these important places, I must desire you to provide for their immediate protection."

On the 31st of May, Governor Shirley laid before the General Court a letter from the Rev. Mr. Serjeant, missionary to the Housatunnuk Indians, in which he recommended retaliation of a character which the governor did not fully approve of, at the same time remarking that he was far from any disposition to countenance cruelty or unnecessary severity; yet whether the practice of the French in this very case, and the great advantage they have over us, unless we make reprisals upon them in the same way, will not justify us therein, is a matter which deserves our deliberation. What the *particular case* was, is not now very clear. However, on

June 3, Massachusetts voted to raise two hundred and seven men to be added to the four hundred and forty posted on the western frontier. Of these, twenty were to scout from Stockbridge (of which sixteen to be Indians), along the river above Northfield; sixty-one to be posted in the counties of Middlesex, Worcester, and on the Merrimack river; ten at Sheffield; ten at Number One; ten at Number Two; the remaining fifty to be a company under such officer as the governor should appoint, to range the woods with fifty large dogs. Also, twenty men to be sent to the frontiers of the county of York, in addition to the six hundred and three already there, and the sixty men now being raised to range the woods in the same county. Also a surgeon to be allowed for the eastern service, who is to reside at Georgetown, on Arowsick island.

June 5. The governor thought it necessary to issue the following proclamation, so constant were depredations on every hand not protected by the open ocean: "Whereas, on the 25th of April last I issued warrants to the colonels of the several regiments of militia within this province, to give out orders without delay, for impressing their respective quotas of men for the defense of the frontiers. And, whereas, it appears to me that there is a great failure in the execution of the said warrants in divers of the said colonels, by which means the inhabitants of the frontiers are much exposed to the attacks of the enemy."

June 6. Two soldiers are killed at the side of Westcot's Field at Long Creek. There were twenty-five soldiers in the field besides Westcot's own people, and only seven Indians drove them all, scalped the two soldiers, took off their clothes, secured three guns, and made a safe retreat. They did not know the soldiers were there till after they had attacked them. Two of the English stood their ground bravely, though to little purpose. Their names are one Skillin, and Stephen Irish.

In another and more circumstantial account of this affair, it is said to have taken place on the 5th of June; that as three soldiers were set to guard those at work in the field, being placed at the entrance of a thick wood, one of them stood with his back against a tree, while his two companions were carelessly diverting themselves lying upon the ground. The Indians stole up to the tree and attempted by a line to tie the man to the tree, and then secure the others as prisoners also; but when seized the man at the tree alarmed the other two by his outcry, and at the same time broke away from the Indians, who immediately fired upon him, wounding him in the arm. They also fired upon the other two as they were rising from the ground, killing them both. Two of the men at work not far off, caught up their guns, and, meeting the wounded man, with him advanced upon the Indians, fired upon and wounded one of them; upon which they all precipitately fled.

The place of this affair was probably where a small stream falls into Back Cove; perhaps on Stroudwater.

June 10. Captain Eleazar Melvin sent in a petition to the General Court, asking for fifty men to be added to the fifty already in his company.

June 11. Some men who were at work not far from Fort Massachusetts, are fallen upon by a party of Indians, who kill and scalp Elias Nims, and wound Gershon Hawks. They had laid an ambush of part of their number to cut off the retreat to the fort of any who might attempt it; and though the ambush rose to carry their plan into execution, were prevented by a sharp fire from the fort. They took Benjamin Taintor captive, but he returned not long after. He was son of Deacon Simon Taintor of Westborough. Near one hundred of the animals belonging to the English and Dutch are killed by this party of Indians, some of whom lost their lives, but how many is not known. The body of one is found a few days after, buried in the bank of the river; also some long cords were found, judged to have been brought along by which to lead captives.

On the same day Hugh Morrison, of Colerain, reported to the General Court of Massachusetts that he had built a good, defensible block-house at his own charge, and also "a garrison round his house." He requested to be reimbursed, because these works were a public benefit. The court thought so too, and ordered the committee which had been appointed to erect block-houses in the county of Hamshire, to adjust the matter.

June 12. Captain Arthur Savage, "late of Pemaquid," reported that he had expended upon the fort there £1136 9s. 11d. more than the court had granted him. £284 2s. 6d. was voted him on the 25th following, "including £100, part of £300 formerly granted and not received."

June 16. Mr. Joseph Swett* is shot from his horse while riding along the road near Blanchard's, in North Yarmouth. He belonged to Falmouth. Blanchard's was where Captain Andrew Blanchard lived afterward.

June 19. Number Four was for a long time a point of great

---

* In another account Swett's Christian name is given *John*, and his death June 17.

attraction to the enemy, and as it stood in the way of their excursions to the settlements below, they seemed determined to destroy it; hence at this time they came against it in strong force, though their exact number is not known. While the enemy lay in ambush about the fort, Capt. Phinehas Stevens, the commander of the post, and Capt. Josiah Brown, from Sudbury, went out with about fifty men to a meadow; they became aware of the presence of Indians by the uneasiness of their dogs, and rightly judged that they were waylaying a certain causey where they were to pass. Capt. Stevens made his approach accordingly. As the English were cautiously proceeding, one of Capt. Brown's men discovered an Indian and fired upon him, whereupon the ambush arose, and a sharp engagement ensued, and with much obstinacy, till several of the enemy had fallen, and were dragged off by their companions. They then scattered in the neighboring woods, leaving behind them one gun, eight blankets, a scalp, and other things. Capt. Stevens lost none of his men in the fight, but Jedidiah Winchell was mortally wounded, and died about fourteen days after. David Parker, Jonathan Stanhope, and Cornet Heaton were wounded also, but recovered. Stanhope belonged to Sudbury. His wound was in the elbow, which disabled him from labor, and government allowed him a pension of four pounds per annum. About thirteen years afterwards he had a further allowance of one pound per annum in addition.*

---

* "They received the loss of no men, but four or five wounded. They sent forty of the men to carry the wounded men to the fort, and the rest maintained the fight and stood them manfully. After the fight was over they found where they drew off several dead Indians into a swamp. They sent down a troop of men to guard Mr. Doolittle and Dr. Williams to cut off the arm of one of their men [Stanhope ?] that was sore wounded." *Deacon Noah Wright's Journal*, in *N. E. Hist. and Gen. Reg.*, II, 208. Mr. Doolittle is the same as is mentioned *ante*, p. 10.

From another source it appears that Capt. Stevens was proceeding from his fort in search of horses belonging to his men, when the Indians were discovered, to the number of one hundred and fifty, as was supposed. The English had the advantage of the first fire. Finding they were getting the worst of it, the Indians fled into a swamp, and the English did not think it prudent to pursue them; and they did not explore the battle ground until the next day, when they found traces of Indians killed to the number of ten or twelve. The blankets, swords, hatchets, and other things found there, were sold for £40, "a large booty from such a beggarly crew."

June 22. Seven persons are killed at Sheepscott; namely, three men, two women, and two children, and a girl is taken captive, as they were at work in a field within a few rods of the garrison.

CHAPTER VII.

DIARY OF DEPREDATIONS (continued).

Return of Pepperrell and Warren from Louisbourg — Ceremonies thereupon — Attack on Bridgman's Fort — People killed at Rochester — Fight at Hinsdale — Capt. Rouse's Failure — Capt. Drake's Expedition — David Morrison lost — Losses at Number Four — The Six Nations — Depredation at Winchester — At Contoocook — At North Yarmouth — At Northfield — At Concord, N. H. — At Black Point — At Shattuck's Fort — At Paquage — Siege and Capture of Fort Massachusetts — French Account of the same — Mohawks at Crown Point — Constant Bliss killed — Depredation at Deerfield — New Casco — Pemaquid — Schodac — Saratoga — Saco — Swivel Guns ordered for Garrisons — A Scalp brought to Boston — Subject of Exchange of Prisoners agitated — Capt. Gorham's Expedition — A French Armada on the Coast — Its Disasters.

BUT amidst the continual alarms from attacks of the enemy upon the frontiers, it was announced in Boston that the admiral and general were coming up the harbor. They appear to have been expected about this time from Louisbourg, and nothing was omitted on the part of the inhabitants to do them honor. They came in a fifty-gun ship, the Chester, Captain Richard Spry, with a blue flag at the mizzen topmast, which denoted that the Admiral of the Blue was on board.

The General Court was in session, and undertook to take suitable action to receive the conquerors, but the excitement seems to have caused a hasty adjournment, leaving their proceedings quite incomplete, and Mr. Secretary Cotton probably forgot to write up his journal after the excitement was over. However, we find that Mr. Speaker Hutchinson was appointed

to welcome the commanders, who seem, somehow, to have gotten into the council chamber of the court-house before the court was ready for them, when the following ceremonies occurred: The Speaker said,

"*Admiral* WARREN and *Sir* WILLIAM PEPPERRELL:

"The House of Representatives of this Province have a high sense of the service you have done for his Majesty's Subjects in general, and for the People of *New England* in particular: And it is with the greatest Pleasure they embrace this happy Opportunity of acknowledging it.

"In their Name and by their Order I Congratulate you on your safe Arrival in the Province, and most heartily bid you welcom.

"To which ADMIRAL WARREN repli'd;

1746.] Surprise near Fort Dummer.

"Mr. Speaker,

"*I am obliged to this honourable House for the great Respect they have shown me: They may depend upon my Zeal and Service while I live for the Colonies in general, and this Province in particular.*

"Sir WILLIAM PEPPERRELL also said as follows,
"Mr. Speaker,

"*I am heartily obliged to the honourable House for the Respect they have shown me; and I hope I shall be always ready to risque my Life and Fortune for the Good of my dear native Country.*"

June 24. About twenty Indians make an attack on Bridgman's Fort,* about two miles below Fort Dummer, and since in the town of Vernon, Vermont. They killed William Robbins and James Barker of Springfield, wounded Michael Gilson and Patrick Ray, and took Daniel How and John Beaman, of Northfield, captive, who not long after returned, and the wounded men recovered. Before they secured Beaman he shot one of the Indians, killing him outright. How was son of Daniel How, and nephew of Nehemiah How, who died in captivity, as already noticed under October 11, 1745. It appears that the men killed, wounded, and taken, were at work in a meadow at some distance from the fort, when they were surprised by the enemy. Belknap gives the names of the men quite different from Doolittle, whose account is followed. Belknap says How killed the Indian, that James *Baker* was killed, and that *John* Beaman was taken. And Nehemiah How records in his journal, that on the 7th of July (1746) John

---

* A little below Bridgman's Fort, at a place called Cold Spring. *Wright's Journal.*

Beman, of Northfield, was brought to Quebec, and that How arrived there on the 10th of February following.*

"On the 18th of July Lieut. Falaise brings into Montreal an Englishman named John Bimant, taken on the 1st instant at Northfils, fourteen miles above Dierfils, by a party of Indians belonging to the Sault" [St. Louis].†

At his examination Beaman did not fail to represent the preparations of the English to take Canada on a scale which caused the French very great alarm. He told them the English army designed against Fort St. Frederick consisted of thirteen thousand men and fifteen hundred Mohawk Indians. This probably did not exceed the will if it did the power of the people. He told them the English were determined to persevere till Canada was taken, and that the King of England had promised to support the colonists till they had effected it.

June 27. A party of Indians came to Rochester, in New Hampshire, on the westerly side of the northern branch of Pascataqua river, about twenty-two miles above Portsmouth, where, discovering five men at work in a field, having their guns within reach, the Indians cunningly induced the English to discharge all their guns at once, by firing one of their own. Having thus in effect rendered the English harmless, they rushed upon them before they could reload their pieces. They retreated to a small deserted house, securing the door after them. The Indians mounted the roof, broke through it, and

---

* Feb. 15th [174⁶⁄₇]. My nephew, Daniel How, and six more, were brought down from Montreal to Quebec, viz: John Sunderland, John Smith, Richard Smith, William Scott, Philip Scofil, and Benjamin Tainter. How's *Narrative*, 21. Philip Scaffield died on the 7th of April following. *Ibid.*

† French account in *N. Y. Col. Docs.*, X, 51; but the dates do not correspond, allowing even for the difference of style. If the French date is right, the people were killed and taken on June 20, which is, indeed, according to Taylor.

with their guns and tomahawks killed Joseph Heard, Joseph Richards,* John Wentworth, and Gershom Downs. John Richards they wounded and took prisoner. They then crossed the river, where, upon another road, they found some men in a field, but all of these escaped. They secured one prisoner, a boy named Jonathan Door, whom they caught sitting upon a fence. In little less than a month the Indians arrived at Quebec with Richards and the boy. The former was kindly used by his captors, and his wounds cured, and after some eighteen months he was sent to Boston under a flag of truce. The boy Door remained among the Indians some fourteen years, but returned after the conquest of Canada, having fully acquired the habits and language of the Indians. At Montreal Richards underwent a close examination, from whom much information was elicited as to the great preparations being made by the English to subdue Canada, more than corroborating the large statements of Beaman. He returned home not long after, and lived to an advanced age, dying in Rochester in 1793.

July 3. A small party of Indians formed themselves into an ambush at Col. Hinsdale's mill, in Hinsdale, N. H., about thirty-eight miles above Northampton. The inhabitants for some miles around were obliged to club together and perform guard duty whenever they wanted their corn ground. At this time Colonel Willard went with a guard of about twenty men to the mill, and, mistrusting an ambush, warily proceeded to discover it, in which he proved himself more alert than the Indians, for he discovered and routed the ambush, obliging

---

* August 1. Lieut. Chatelain, of Three Rivers, arrived [at Montreal] with the Englishman named John Richard, who was taken prisoner by a party of Abanakis twenty-three days ago, near Rochester. *N. Y. Col. Documents*, X, 54.

them to fly, leaving their packs behind them. The plunder thus secured the captors sold for £40, old tenor.

The better to deceive the enemy, probably, the English commenced grinding in the mill before falling upon them, and although the Indians fired upon Willard's party, with great resolution the major ordered his men "to fire and fall on," which they promptly did, and thus causing them to fly in dismay. Of the major's party only one man was wounded, whose name was Moses Wright, two of his fingers being shot off.

July 10. Captain Rouse having been dispatched to the island St. John (since Prince Edward's), to take off the French inhabitants, a party of his men, going on shore, are fallen upon by a large body of Indians, who kill and take twenty-eight of them;* meantime the inhabitants escape into the woods, and thus the object of the expedition is defeated. Rouse had with him several small vessels, which were magnified, in the French accounts, into frigates of twenty-four guns and a transport of seven hundred tons and twenty men. The English landed at Port Lajoie, now Port Joy, near the mouth of York river. The number of Indians who surprised the English was two hundred. They were Micmacs, and under the leadership of M. Croisille de Montesson. "They killed or made prisoners of all of them except a few who escaped by swimming" to their vessels. The English had on shore, "in a park, a quantity of oxen and other cattle," which they had procured for provisions. These the Indians killed for their own use.† But few of the names of Rouse's men are found, and these

---

* *American Magazine,* and *Douglass.* Neither Hutchinson nor Holmes mention this unfortunate affair. The latter is unaccountably deficient and barren of facts in this year; and, indeed, in the greater part of the period of this war.

† *Paris Documents in Col. History of New York,* X, 57.

were among the prisoners, namely, William Daily, of New York, who died at Quebec December 26th, following; Richard Bennet, died 27th February, 1747. He belonged to *the Jersies*. Samuel Vaughan, died April 18th, 1747. He belonged to Plymouth, in New England. William Prindle died July 4th, 1748. William Norwood, who died July 11th, 1748. A soldier of Louisbourg, named Davis, who died Nov. 10th, 1746.

The following entry in How's journal probably relates to this sad affair: "August 15th, 1746, seven captives, who, with eight more taken at St. John's Island, were brought to prison [at Quebec]. They told us that several were killed after quarters were given, among whom was James Owen, late of Brookfield, in New England." *

The same narrator says Robert Downing was brought to prison (at Quebec) September 12th; that he was one of those taken at St. John's; that he was with the Indians two months, and suffered great abuses from them.

To secure the Six Nations of Indians on the side of the English was thought to be of immense importance. Accordingly Governor Clinton, of New York, had by messengers arranged for deputations of them to come to Albany on the 20th of July. He thereupon notified the governors of all the colonies to send delegates to the conference. An expedition against Canada had been resolved upon, therefore the cooperation of the Indians of those nations was thought indispensable; so much so by the commander-in-chief, Gov. Shirley, that, in his request to the General Court to appoint commissioners, he said he had reason to fear the expedition would fail if their aid was not secured. The result was commissioners were appointed,

* How's *Narrative*, p. 18.

although some difficulty was experienced in finding gentlemen to accept the office.

The Indians' services, or rather cooperation, was to be secured by presents. For this end the Massachusetts commissioners were to take with them seven hundred ounces of silver, or an equivalent in gold, which they were to lay out in articles which they should judge suitable for the purpose of presents.

July 28. Captain Nathaniel Drake, of Hampton, New Hampshire, with his troop of mounted men, proceeded to scout in and about the woods of Nottingham, where some Indians had been lately seen, but, after ten days' diligent search, none of the enemy were discovered.

David Morrison, of Colerain, a young lad, seeing a hawk light on a tree a little distance from his father's fort, went out to shoot it. As he was intent on his object, about a dozen Indians sprang from their hiding places, seized and carried him away captive. Nothing was ever heard of him after.

August 2. At the eastward, "the Indians came upon Mr. Proctor's folks, and we hear that they killed one."*

August 3. Number Four is again visited by a large body of the enemy. The dogs belonging to the garrison gave notice of their vicinity. Early in the morning a few men went out, and near a nursery were fired upon by some Indians in ambush, by which Ebenezer Phillips is killed. Some time after, as a company of men from the fort went to bring in the body of Phillips, the ambuscade rose and fired, as it was said, an hundred guns at them. The English returned the fire, retreating to the fort.

---

* Smith's *Journal*. Mr. Willis makes no note of this in his edition of *Smith and Deane*, but informs us that Samuel Proctor was a son of John, who was executed at Salem for witchcraft; that he settled in Portland in 1718.

The Indians besieged it till the next day, the men not being sufficiently strong to make a successful sally. Meantime the enemy killed all the cattle, burnt all the buildings, and drew off at leisure.

August 6. About thirty Indians came to Winchester, N. H., waylaid the road, and, as six of the white people were passing, fired upon them, killing and scalping Joseph Rawson, and slightly wounding Amasa Wright.

This depredation is thus circumstantially narrated by Deacon Wright: "At Winchester, across the way, over against Benainon(?) meeting-house, lay an ambush, as is supposed of about twenty Indians; and several of our men had business to pass by, not knowing of the ambush, while the Indians fired on them and shot two of them. One of them, named Roger [Rawson] killed, the other, named Amasa Wright, being one leg shot through, [and] part of his neck; recovered himself, got up and made his escape with the rest of the men. The Indians fired thick after them, but they all got off alive only said Roger [Rawson].

"About the same time a small number of Indians ambushed the road at the Lower Ashuelot, and a number of our men were passing along that way. Just as they came near the Indians they turned out of the path, and the Indians seeing them, supposed they were discovered, and that the English were surrounding them, rose up and fled through thick and thin; and then our men saw them flying, gave them chase, but the Indians outran them and escaped; and there was no *spile dunne on nary side.*"

Joseph Rawson was son of John Rawson, of Uxbridge, grandson of the Rev. Grindal Rawson, the well known preacher to the Indians, and great-grandson to the old secretary,

Edward Rawson, Esq.* Joseph's father received the wages due his son, the following March, from the treasurer of the colony.

The same day the attack was made upon Winchester, two men were made prisoners at Contocook and carried off.

August 9. Philip Greely is killed at North Yarmouth; some thirty Indians were seen secreted in a gully waiting an opportunity to surprise Wear's garrison, but it was saved by the barking of the dogs.

August 11. At Northfield, as Benjamin Wright, a young man, was riding in the woods to bring the cows home, he was shot and mortally wounded. He kept on his horse, which brought him into the town, but he died the following night, about one o'clock. The ball passed through him, coming out of the opposite shoulder from the side where it entered.

The same day five soldiers fell into an ambush on the road between Concord and Hopkinton, and are all killed. There were about one hundred Indians it was said. The killed were Jonathan Bradley of Exeter; Samuel Bradley and Obadiah Peters, of Concord; John Bean, of Brentwood; John Lufkin, of Kingston; Alexander Roberts,† of Brentwood, and William Stickney, of Concord, were made prisoners. Four Indians were killed, and two mortally wounded.

August 13. Two Frenchmen and an Indian fire on Mr. Allen Dover, as he is passing "through the bog, from Black Point, but miss him. He fired twice on his assailants, and thought he killed one of them."

August 15. A number of Indians approached to the neighborhood of Shattuck's fort,‡ and fired upon four men, but

---

* See *Colls. N. H. Hist. Soc.*, III, 74.   ‡ Miscalled, on a map of the time,
† *N. E. Hist. and Gen. Reg.*, III, 303.   *Shannak's* fort.

1746.] *Siege of Fort Massachusetts.* 117

fortunately missed them. A few days before they hung up a white flag in sight of the fort, intending it probably as a decoy.

August 17. At Winchester, John Simmons, being at some distance from the fort, was shot at by several Indians, who missed him. He turned and fired upon them, *dropping one*. On visiting the spot afterwards, the English found blood upon the ground, and one blanket. They therefore concluded the owner of the blanket was killed.*

August 17. Mr. Ezekiel Wallingford is killed near his garrison, at a place called Paquage, Pequaig, Pequioug, etc., which is in the present town of Athol. He discovered the enemy and ran for the fort, but was shot down before reaching it. His scalp was taken and borne off in triumph.

About the same time a messenger was dispatched to Boston from Number Four, who informed the governor of the *ill state* of that place. The governor, apprehending it of great importance, and not to be quitted but upon absolute necessity, thereupon ordered a troop of horse to Number Four, "to carry as great a quantity of provisions as they conveniently can;" that no part of the forces be withdrawn, except the former troops; and that upon their return, together with the company of fifty men with dogs, be directed to guard off as many of the women and children as may conveniently leave the place."

August 20. Fort Massachusetts, on the Hoosac river, near the north-west corner of the province, was invested yesterday by a body of French and Indians, headed by Gen. Rigaud de Vaudreuil. His army consisted of about seven or eight hundred men, while the fort contained only twenty-two men, three women, and five children.† Of the men, but eight were in

* *Deaçon Wright's Journal.* but accounts differ as to the number, as
† This is according to Dr. Douglass, will be seen.

health and able to do full duty. And then they were nearly destitute of ammunition, having but some three or four pounds of powder, and about as much in weight of lead. The garrison was in command of Sergeant John Hawks. When Vaudreuil had kept up the siege about twenty-four hours he sent in a flag to demand the surrender of the fort. Hawks consulted with his men, who, in view of their desperate situation, thought it their most prudent course to surrender on the best terms they could get. In these Vaudreuil was very liberal. All in the fort were to be well used, and exchanged as soon as it could be brought about. None of the captives were to be delivered to the Indians; and that the sick, and such as were not able to travel, should be carried. Yet it was said that half of the captives were the next day delivered to the Indians, who the next night "killed one of the sick men rather than carry him," and there was "one man killed in the fight," which was the extent of their loss up to the time of their commencing their march for Canada.

It was more than a month before all of this forlorn company arrived at Quebec; then twenty-three at one time entered the prison there.* They reported to their fellow prisoners already there, that two were killed when the fort was taken, namely, Thomas Knowlton and Josiah Read. The names of the twenty-three, as recorded on their arrival at Quebec, are these: The Rev. John Norton, the chaplain; John Hawks, John

* This was the number reported, and including women and children, probably.

1746.] *Captives of Fort Massachusetts.* 119

Smead,* wife† and six children, John Perry and wife,‡ Moses Scott, wife§ and two children, Samuel Goodman,‖ Jonathan Bridgman,¶ Nathan Eames,** Joseph Scott, Amos Pratt,†† Benjamin Sinconds [Simonds], Samuel Lovet,‡‡ David Warren, and Phineas Furbush.§§ On the 1st October, Jacob Shepard,‖‖ of Westborough, taken at Hoosuck, arrived, and on the 5th of October, Nathaniel Hitchcock,¶¶ John Aldrich, and Stephen Scott were brought in.

The captives, even those with the Indians, acknowledged that they were generally kindly treated, "according to their manner," that is, according to the manner of the Indians.

After the enemy had taken and plundered the fort, they burnt it, thus taking revenge for their severe loss of men, instead of murdering their prisoners; for it appears to have been currently reported, and fully credited, that Vaudreuil and his Indian allies lost forty-five of their numbers during the siege, which, considering the weakness of the garrison, is rather incredible.

The chaplain found an opportunity, before leaving the fort,

---

* According to *How*, p. 21, he died April 8th, 1747; but according to *Norton*, p. 3, John Smead, Jr., died April 8th, 1747. Both doubtless refer to the same person. As it will be seen, John the elder was redeemed, but killed at home. See 19th October, 1747.

† She died on the 28th of March following. Her youngest child was born the second night after she was taken. *How*. Her they named *Captivity*. She died at the age of about nine months, at Quebec.

‡ She died December 23d, following, and the youngest child February 10th.

§ She died December 11th, following.

‖ He died on the 23d March, following. He belonged to South Hadley.

¶ Belonged to Sunderland, died in captivity, July 21st, 1747.

** He was of Marlborough. Died Nov. 17th, following.

†† He died on 12th of April, following.

‡‡ He was son of Major Lovet, of Mendon, and died January 23, following.

§§ He died in captivity, July 16th, 1747; belonged to Westborough.

‖‖ He died May 30th, 1747. "A pious young man."

¶¶ He died in prison, at Quebec, May 22d, following (1747).

to write a letter, which he dated August 20th, 1746, and placed upon the well-crotch, of the following purport:

"These are to inform you that yesterday, about nine of the clock, we were besieged by, as they say, seven hundred French and Indians. They have wounded two men, and killed one Knowlton. The General De Vaudreuil desired capitulations, and we were so distressed that we complied with his terms. We are the French's prisoners, and have it under the general's hand, that every man, woman and child shall be exchanged for French prisoners."*

In the course of the following year the most of the captives found their way back to New England. Some by way of France, and some by the West Indies, and some through the wilderness. Imprisonment was so irksome to many of them that they were ready to accept of any change. A number of them arrived at Newport, in Rhode Island, about the 1st of May, 1747, from the West Indies. From them it appears that when Fort Massachusetts was invested there were only twenty-two men in it, including the commander, Sergeant Hawks, and the chaplain before mentioned; that of these one-half was sick of dysentery. Consequently they were dispirited, and too feeble to defend themselves. That the force of Vaudreuil consisted of five hundred French and three hundred Indians; yet by noon of the second day the English had lost but one man,† and two wounded. At this point a parley was entered into. The enemy displayed their means for capturing the fort, as axes, hoes, spades, a quantity of facines ready cut,

---

* Mr. Norton speaks of the terms of capitulation in his *Redeemed Captive*, and of this letter, but he does not give the letter, for the reason, no doubt, that he kept no copy of it. See APPENDIX, E.

† Thomas Knowlton, shot in the watch tower before mentioned. His place of residence is not mentioned, but he was son of Joseph Knowlton, who some time after received the wages due his son when killed.

and a number of grenades; that if they now surrendered they should all be exchanged the first opportunity; which, as they had ammunition to last them "but a few minutes," if the attack was continued, the terms were accepted. They encamped the following night near the ruins of the fort.

These captives give a more favorable account of their treatment than that at first reported. By these it does not appear that the sick man who died the first night after the surrender, was killed, but died of his malady. All the rest arrived in seven days at Crown Point, and in better health than when they surrendered.

The French account of the sacking of Fort Massachusetts sheds some new light on that important event, big with so much suffering and anguish, not only to the immediate victims, but to their numerous relations and friends, who, though they escaped the horrors of Indian captivity, suffered a long mental agony from the harrowing thoughts of what was daily occurring to those friends in the hands of barbarians.

The expedition started from Montreal on the 3d of August, under the conduct of "Monsieur de Rigaud de Vaudreuil, town major of Three Rivers." Under him were "two captains,* one lieutenant, three ensigns, two chaplains, one surgeon, ten cadets of the regulars, eighteen militia officers, three volunteers, and about four hundred colonists and three hundred Indians. They attacked a fort on the Kakekoute† river, near Brockfil, containing a garrison of twenty-two men, with three women and five children. After a fight of twenty-six hours, and the loss of one killed and several wounded in the fort, the garrison surrendered. M. de Rigaud was wounded by a shot in the

---

* The name of one of them was De Sabrevois. *N. Y. Col. Docs.*, X. 65. That of the other does not appear.

† The fort was on a branch of the Hoosuc river, which is doubtless the river meant.

right arm, and three of his Indians killed; four Frenchmen and eleven Indians were wounded. The party set fire to all the houses and grain within a space of fifteen leagues, with barns, mills, churches, tanneries, etc." This is substantially according to the English account.

From an *improved version* of the French narrative, compiled later, it is said: "The fort was attacked on the morning of the 30th of August. [Thus agreeing with the English as to time, allowing for the difference of the manner of dating.] They had been on their march ten days. Three women and five children were found in it. The loss on the part of the English was not ascertained, as they had buried all their dead save one. The French loss was one man killed and twelve wounded. Sieur Rigaud was among the latter. The fort was burnt on the same day, and the prisoners having stated that a reinforcement was to arrive from Dierfil, Sieur Rigaud detached sixty Iroquois and Abenakis on the route they were to come. These Indians having met this reinforcement, which consisted of only nineteen men, defeated it, and brought in four prisoners only, all the remainder having been killed.

"After this expedition Sieur de Rigaud ordered the pillage, and all the settlements were burnt and sacked, and the harvest laid waste within a circle of twelve to fifteen leagues. Only fifty-six prisoners were, however, made in this foray, almost all the settlers having had time to take refuge in Boston, Deirfil, and Orange." [Albany.]

Thus was the French government treated to an account of the Fort Massachusetts affair, with scarcely any likeness to the true original. It was made intentionally false, and displays a wonderful want of knowledge in everything which actually took place, as well as in geography.

After detailing the Sieur Marin's expedition of the 16th of November, 1745 — in the same strain of exaggeration — the writer remarks, that since that foray, "twenty-seven detachments of Indians had been formed, with a certain number of Canadians always at their head, to make incursions on the enemy's flanks, and not one of them had returned without killing or capturing some persons. The number of prisoners was, at the date of the departure of the ships from Quebec, about two hundred and eighty." But the most important expedition of them all was that against Fort Massachusetts, just detailed.*

When an account of the capture of Fort Massachusetts reached Boston, the General Court being in session, Governor Shirley, in a message to the House of Representatives, dated, Province House, September 3d, 1746, communicates the following remarks, just and applicable in this connection:

"You may make a judgment of the unspeakable benefit it would be to this province to have the French dislodged from Crown Point, by the calamitous state of the western frontiers, and especially in the late tragedy at Massachusetts Fort, now burnt down by the enemy, and all the garrison, as well as the women and children, either put to the sword or carried into captivity; the terror of which has reached so far as Northampton, where the enemy have plundered divers houses, and destroyed a considerable number of cattle, all of which you will be informed of by a letter I received last night from Major Williams, which will likewise be laid before you.

"It may be remembered by some of you, that in the former wars, when the Indians were more numerous, and our inhabitants in those parts few and weak, that the Indians never made

---

* See *N. Y. Col. Documents*, X, 76, 77.

such frequent incursions upon them, and very rarely in such great bodies as they have done in this war, which must be principally attributed to the advantage they have of issuing out of a fort so near our borders, where they are furnished with necessary provisions and ammunition, and to which place they retreat with their prisoners and booty."

Of course, when the governor's message was delivered, nothing was known respecting the fate of the garrison, only that all had been carried away captives, and the fort burnt. The great anxiety that prevailed concerning the fate of those captives, is difficult now to be realized; scalping, maiming, starvation, and horrid deaths by torture, harrowed the sleepless nights of numerous friends in various parts of the province, and increased a desire to be rid of such troublesome neighbors; and this desire soon ripened to a determination of an intensity equal, at length, to the sacrifice required.

Near the end of this month (August) it was reported that three Mohawks had killed the officer of the French garrison at Crown Point, and another person, as they were walking in the garden attached to the fort. These they scalped and brought their scalps to *Schenegtade*, intending to present them to the governor.* Sixteen other Indians of the same tribe went towards Montreal with a design to seize some of the French, with a view to bring them to Albany, but what success they met with is not reported.

August 22. As about ten men were going from Deerfield to Colerain, two or three Indians having secreted themselves near the road, fired upon and shot down Constant Bliss, a

---

* It is to this affair that the French officer refers, no doubt, in his record at Montreal: "All the expeditions of our enemies have, up to this time (3 August, 1746), amounted to some Mohegans (*Loups*) scalping a soldier belonging to the garrison at Fort St. Frederick, who had gone out unarmed. *N. Y. Col. Docs.*, X, 35.

soldier from Colchester, in Connecticut, his companions flying from the place as fast as they were able. The Indians found a quantity of rum those men had left, and, after scalping the dead man, got drunk, and in their bewilderment wandered to the vicinity of the garrisons at Colerain, and there slept till the next morning (as they confessed afterwards), where, had they been discovered, they might have easily been dispatched.

August 25. About forty* of the army which had reduced the fort at Hoosuc, stealthily approached Deerfield, about thirty miles easterly of the former, "not being satisfied with the spoil," made at that place. They came first upon a hill at the south-west corner of the South Meadow, where were ten or twelve men and children at work, in a situation in which they might all with ease have been made prisoners—their design being to take prisoners. But this object was frustrated, and the affair ended much more tragically than perhaps it otherwise would. It eventuated thus: Mr. Eleazar Hawks was out that morning fowling, and was at the foot of the hill when the Indians were coming down into the meadow. Seeing him they supposed they were discovered, and thereupon shot and scalped him. This alarmed the people in the meadow, being distant but a few rods from Mr. Hawks when he fell; it also prompted the Indians to act quickly, which they did, killing Simeon Amsden, a lad, whom they scalped and beheaded. Mr. Samuel

---

* Taylor says there were *fifty*, and Doolittle sets them at *thirty*. But the French account is as follows: "Sixty Abenakis belonging to this force, went, after the fight [at Hoosuc] to lie in wait for twenty Englishmen who were to come to the said fort, according to the report of the prisoners; but, not meeting with them, went further, and some returned with seven scalps, one Englishman, and one negro."

"Seventeen Mississagues left De Vaudreüil's party during the siege, went six leagues below Orange, struck a blow and brought back four scalps." *Ib.* See *about the middle of August*, page 127, *post.*

Allen, John Sadler, and Adonijah Gillet, of Colchester, ran a few rods, and then made a stand under the bank of the river, meeting their savage pursuers with bravery, but were soon overpowered by numbers. Allen and Gillet were soon dispatched, but Sadler succeeded in running across the river, and thus made his escape "amidst a shower of bullets." Meantime some pursued Oliver Amsden, stabbed and killed him, after having his hands cut to pieces in trying to defend himself against the enemies' knives. At the same time, three children of the name of Allen (all living in 1793) being pursued, one of them, named Eunice, was struck down by a blow of a tomahawk, "which was sunk into her head," but whom the enemy in their haste omitted to scalp. She afterwards recovered. Caleb Allen, another of the children, made his escape, and the third, Samuel, was taken prisoner, the only captive obtained on this memorable and sad day to Deerfield.

The guns and commotion in the meadow at once raised the town. "Capt. Hopkins, commander of the standing guard," and Capt. Clesson, with a body of the inhabitants, with as much speed as possible, pursued on after the murdering party, but could not overtake them. Two dead Indians were afterwards found near where Allen and Gillet were killed, supposed to have been killed by them before they fell.

It was said, at the time, that but for the delay of the guard in the town, the enemy might have been cut off before they could have gotten out of the meadow. The men had been so heedless in firing guns at all times, that when guns of alarm were fired, they were not heeded.

The enemy reached Crown Point August 31st, about noon, with their six scalps displayed in a triumphant manner, including that of Constant Bliss, killed August 22d.

August 26. At New Casco, Mr. Richard Stubs is taken and carried to Canada, where he arrived in October following. A soldier was killed when he was taken.

The same day John McFarland and his son are severely wounded near Pemaquid fort, and his fine plantation which he had there, entirely laid waste, his cattle all killed, and his buildings burnt.

About the middle of August six men are killed at Scooduck, or Schodac, eight miles below Albany. Another is missing, supposed to be taken captive. Perhaps at the same time, or, it may be, some days earlier, two men are wounded at the same place, "one in the arm, who is like to do well, the other in the neck, which 'tis tho't will prove mortal."

The Indians lately* killed four men and took four others prisoners, at Saratoga. Capt. Schuyler, in command of the militia posted there, went out to their assistance, but came near being cut off, and with difficulty retreated to the fort. Had the enemy effected this, it was thought they would have taken the fort.

To which affair in our narrative the following refers, is not very clear: "A party of Abenaquis, headed by Ensign Monsigin, who had been detached from Sieur Rigaud's (De Vaudreuil) party after his attack on Fort Massachusetts, proceeded towards Fort Sarasteau [Saratoga]. They met seventeen soldiers belonging to the garrison, took four of them and scalped four others. The remainder threw themselves precipitately into the fort, pursued by our people, who killed some of them."†

The following cannot well be reconciled with any known

---

* This account was published in New York, September 15, hence the actual date is uncertain.

† *N. Y. Col. Docs.*, X, 68.

events: "M. de Rigaud has also informed us that several Abenakies, belonging to his detachment, had set out after his expedition, to make an attack towards Dearfille [Deerfield] and Corsac [Hoosuc?] and have taken fifty-six scalps.*

Sept. 6. At Saco one man, Joseph Gordon, is killed, and his brother, Pike Gordon, is taken captive and carried through the wilderness to Canada, after a month's travel. He reported, on his arriving there, that his brother was killed when he was taken. Just two months after his arrival, namely, on December 6th, he died in prison, of a prevailing sickness which carried off a great number of the poor, unfortunate captives. He was sick but eleven days, and all the time delirious.†

The accounts from the western frontiers were still full of terror and alarm, insomuch that Governor Shirley recommended the sending of a number of swivel guns to be used in all the public forts, and some to be loaned to other exposed garrisons.

About the same time an Indian, in the English interest, brought to Boston the scalp of another Indian, probably taken from one killed at Deerfield on the 25th of August. The governor recommended that it might be advisable to grant him some gratuity, but whether any action followed is not known.

Strong appeals from captives in Canada frequently found their way to their friends, and through them to the governor, who would gladly have sent flags of truce for their exchange, if he could have done so without putting at hazard the general welfare of far greater numbers. It was of vast importance to follow up the blow which he had dealt the French at Louis-

---

* *N. Y. Col. Docs.*, X, 68. Probably a great exaggeration.

† There is a fully detailed account in Folsom's *Saco and Biddeford*, 243-6.

bourg last year, by a formidable attack upon Canada, already in preparation; therefore he could not send a flag to the enemy without at the same time conveying intelligence of his preparations. In this judgment all concurred, and the matter was laid aside for the present.

About the end of September, Captain Gorham, who commanded the rangers at Nova Scotia, which consisted of Cape Cod Indians chiefly, with a party of his men went down Annapolis river, and, discovering a number of inhabitants at work in their fields, landed; secreting his Indians, he went alone among the enemy, feigning to be a Canadian officer, and, upon a signal, his Indians sprang from their hiding places and surrounded the whole party. The captain's object being to gain intelligence, he carried off only a few of the most intelligent.

The greatest alarm had prevailed all along the coast of New England, as news was daily brought to Boston that a numerous fleet of French ships of war were seen in the neighboring seas. It proved to be a powerful armada under the Duke d'Anville, quite numerous enough to take possession of New England, and to bring all North America under the yoke of France. That such would have been the fate of the country, had it not been for the opposition of the elements, seemed quite probable. But, like the great Spanish armada of 1588, it could not fight against tempests and pestilence, which came to the aid of New England in 1746, as they did to Old England above one hundred and fifty years before. The cases are quite parallel, though New England had no fleet of a hundred ships, with Drakes, Howards, Hawkins, and Frobishers to resist the French in their approach. Yet a vigorous defense was determined upon, and Governor Shirley had called on the inhabitants of the country to come to the defense of Boston, and in a few days above six thousand men were paraded on Boston Common. But the enemy did not appear, and news soon came that by tempests and sickness the fleet was rendered harmless; whereupon, on the 7th of November, the governor was requested to appoint a day of thanksgiving.

CHAPTER VIII.

DIARY OF DEPREDATIONS (continued).

Saratoga — Sheepscott — Great Sickness among the Indians — Depredation at Concord — Dogs in the Service — Ordered to be disposed of — Discussion respecting Retaliation — Reward for Prisoners and Scalps — Success of some Mohawks — Governor Shirley's Notice of it — General Noble's Disaster and Death — Indian Stratagem to burn Shattuck's Fort — Captain Melvin's March up the Connecticut — Number Four attacked and bravely defended — Commodore Knowles notices Captain Stevens, the defender — The Place named for him — Another Expedition by Mohawks — Narrative of it — French Account — Saratoga attacked again — Depredation at Kinderhook — At Scarborough — At Saccarap — Northfield — Winchester — Ashuelots — Saco — Falmouth — Damariscotta — Canajoharie — Wells — Topsham — Suncook — Pemaquid — Rochester — Some Mohawks bring in Scalps — Attack on Rochester — Saratoga — Lieutenant Chew's Disaster — Hendrik's Expedition — Depredation at Fall Town — Colerain — Burnet's Field — Wiscasset — Epsom — Nottingham — Ashuelot — Northampton — Pemaquid — Fight at George's Fort — David Brainard — Capture of Rainbow — Sergeant Hawks's Mission — John Smead — Depredation at Bridgman's Fort — At Number Four.

HOW the frontier of New York was left so much exposed, has already been explained. On October 12, at Saratoga, sixteen men are killed and taken, about a mile from the fort. They belonged to Langdon and Hart's companies. The men attacked behaved with great cowardice, except one Lieut. Johnston and the ensign of Hart's company. The latter, having killed two Indians, returned to Albany with the gun of one of them.*

* The date of this item is from another source, from which it is learned that the party attacked was guarding some wagons; that the number of the Indians was thought to be one hundred and fifty; that seven men were killed, six of whom were scalped, and seven were missing. Among the prisoners was Philip Scofield, a soldier from Pennsylvania; he died at Quebec the 8th of April, 1747.

About the same time Governor Shirley ordered Brig.-Gen. Dwight to march to the western frontiers with five hundred men, and there to employ them to the best advantage for the defense of the inhabitants.

October 20. At Sheepscott, Robert Adams and John McNeer are taken and carried to Canada. At the same time and place James Anderson is killed. Mr. Adams arrived at the prison in Quebec on the 19th of November following.

November. A great sickness prevailed among the St. John's Indians, carrying off great numbers of them. Thus it was also among those of Cape Sable.

The yellow fever carried off near an hundred of the Mohegan Indians this year also.

The Cape Sable Indians were terribly reduced by a contagion communicated from the French fleet. Admiral La Jonquire's men were carried off by ship fever. The clothing of his men who had thus died was given to those Indians, from which the disease was communicated to them.

November 10. At Concord, N. H., a Mr. Estabrook is shot and killed by some lurking Indians who had waylaid the road near where the men were killed on the 11th of August last.

November 12. The fifty men formerly ordered to range the western frontiers with dogs, not having been provided with subsistence for a continuance of the dogs in the service beyond the present time, John Stoddard, Esq., is directed to order the dogs to be disposed of, and there is no mention that they had been of any service whatever.

Dogs seem to have always been used in the wars with the Indians. The Spaniards employed them in South America, and in King Philip's war they acted their part in that desperate struggle. In the war with the Western Indians, in 1764, among the precautions to be observed by the troops in going against them, was the following: "Every light-horse man ought to be provided with a blood-hound, which would be useful to find out the enemy's ambushes, and to follow their tracks; they would seize the naked savages, or at least give time to the horsemen to come up with them, and they would add to the safety of the camps at night.*

In that cruel and unjustifiable Florida war of near seven years' duration, General Z. Taylor was authorized to import blood-hounds from Cuba, with Spaniards to direct them. Many were thus obtained, and actually employed in the service.†

Early in the winter of 1746-7, an earnest discussion came up in the General Court of Massachusetts respecting a course of retaliation which many had urged should at once be pursued against the enemy, and at his own doors. Precipitate action on the part of the lower house immediately followed, and bounties for prisoners and scalps were authorized; but when this vote was sent to the Council that body nonconcurred, and appointed a conference upon the subject, at which some modification of the vote in the house took place, and the following preamble or explanatory declaration preceded the retaliatory action of the house in these words:

"His Majesty's subjects the inhabitants of the inland frontiers of this province, having both in former and later wars been grievously distressed by parties of French and Indians from Canada, surprising and murdering men, women and children, and taking of their scalps, as a trophy and evidence of barbarity; and it having repeatedly been represented to the governor of

---

* See Bouquet's *Expedition*, p. 50, edition, London, 1766, 4to.

† See *Book of the Indians*, IV, 149, etc., 7th edition, 1841.

Canada, that if this unchristain and unmanly way of making war was encouraged or suffered to be continued, it should be avenged and retaliated on the inhabitants of the French governments; and he the said governor, notwithstanding said representations and warnings, persisting to employ and send out the vassals and dependants of the King his master, French and Indians, who since the commencement of the present war have captivated, destroyed, scalped, mangled and barbarously used great numbers of the good people of this and his Majesty's other governments.

"Therefore, for the future safety and protection of the frontiers of this Province, and more effectually to deter the French, and Indians under their direction and influence, from carrying on the war in a way and manner abhorred by christian and civilized nations, and justifiable from the principles of self preservation only; Resolved, that the following bounty be granted and allowed to be paid to such Indians as shall go out by order or direction of this government, to Canada or the borders of Canada, in quest of the enemy, viz, for every male prisoner above twelve years of age, £40. For every scalp of any male above twelve years of age, that shall be brought as evidence of his death, £38. For every female prisoner, and each male prisoner, under twelve years of age, £20. For every scalp of such female or male, under twelve years of age, £19."

It was also voted that any Indian setting out on an expedition for prisoners and scalps, be allowed five pounds; that it was advised some Englishmen should go with the Indians; such were to receive the same bounty. John Stoddard, Esq., was to have the directing of all such parties, and pay their bounties.

In the mean time news was received from the westward by

express, which arrived in Boston on the 3d of December, to the effect that the Mohawk Indians had made a successful incursion into Canada. One party struck a blow at Caderougui-Lake, killed eight persons and brought away six scalps, and took seven or eight Frenchmen prisoners, all of which prisoners and scalps they brought to Albany. Another party, under the chief Hendrik, went to Montreal, and after a conference with the governor of Canada, went to Isle La Mott, in Lake Champlain, where they fell upon some Frenchmen getting out ship timber, killed and scalped one, and took another prisoner. The report of the guns alarmed some men in a house not far off, who, on coming out to discover the cause, were also fired upon with buck-shot. The Mohawks then immediately took to their canoes, and with their prisoners and scalps proceeded to Albany.

In his message to the General Court on the 30th of this month, Governor Shirley alludes to such retaliations in these words: "Since the last sitting of the Court I have received advice that two parties of Indians of the Six Nations have been engaged in acts of hostilities against the French of Canada, within their own settlements, in which they have killed five persons and taken nine prisoners: the first open breach of those nations with the French in this war will, I doubt not, be attended with considerable advantage to us if we rightly improve them by encouraging the Indians."

January 31. From untoward circumstances, the expedition against Canada the last year could not be prosecuted. In order to improve some of the men raised for that service, Governor Shirley set on foot a winter campaign to drive the French and Indians out of Nova Scotia. About seven hundred men were employed in this service, under Col. Arthur Noble. But the

French were beforehand of them; for M. De Ramesay had already garrisoned Minas, the objective point, with a superior force. In his march to that place Noble was surprised in his camp by a superior body of French and Indians, himself and four of his principal officers, and seventy men, are killed, and the rest made prisoners.* But few of the names of those engaged in this disastrous expedition have been met with. Among them is that of William Nason, of Casco Bay. He was taken, carried to Quebec, and died in prison there, June 20th, 1747.

March 30. About forty Indians came to Shattuck's fort, between Northfield and Col. Hinsdale's, with a design to burn it. Having prepared faggots of spruce and pitch pine wood with the ends dipped in brimstone, with fire in a kettle covered with a blanket, they crept silently up to the fort in the night, and succeeded in setting it on fire, which burnt down that part of it which stood on the south side of the brook. Immediately after the wind changed and blew from the opposite point of the compass, and the soldiers and people within, getting into the other part, by the help of the brook and wind, stayed the progress of the flames. The Indians were amazed to see their prospects thus blasted, and soon after retreated. The soldiers fired upon them, breaking the leg of one of the assailants. Captain Daniel Shattuck was the owner of the fort. He removed to Northfield, from Worcester, about 1723, and to Hinsdale about 1736, where he died in 1760, aged sixty-seven. His fort was about one hundred rods east of Connecti-

---

* A minute detail of this affair by the French officers engaged in it is given in *N. Y. Col. Docs*, X, 91, 92. A more favorable account to the English will be found very clearly detailed in a very able work entitled *Memoirs of the Last War* (London, 1757), pp. 85-89. The English called the French commander *Ramsay*.

cut river, one mile south of Fort Hinsdale, and one mile southeast of Fort How, on the west side of the river, and three miles south of Fort Dunner.

March 31. Capt. Eleazer Melvin being at Northfield with some of his company, on hearing of the attack on Shattuck's fort, marched at once in pursuit of the enemy. But they had crossed the river, and at Great Meadow were discovered on the opposite side and fired upon, by which one was killed. Melvin then went to Shattuck's fort, which was deserted, and burnt the rest of it, to prevent the enemy from having the gratification of doing it, if they should return.

At the urgent and frequent solicitations of Gov. Shirley, the General Court passed the following order for the better security and defense of the frontiers.

April 1, 1747. "Ordered that there be pay and subsistence allowed for a garrison of twenty men to be posted at Northfield, and twenty at each of several block-houses to be built four miles distant one from the other, and to extend on a line from Northfield to Townshend; said men to be constantly employed in scouting from one block-house to another; and that there be allowed two swivel guns to each block-house; and that there be pay and subsistence allowed for a garrison of twenty men in the block-house at Fall Town;* twenty at a new block-house to be built between Fall Town and Colerain; twenty at Colerain; twenty at the block-house commonly called Fort Shirley;† twenty at Fort Pelham;‡ twenty at a new block-house to be built west of said Fort Pelham; and thirty at a block-house to be built near where Fort Massachusetts stood; and that two swivel guns be allowed to each block-house, except the two block-houses west of Fort Pelham, which are to be

---

* Since Bernardston.   † Heath.   ‡ Rowe.

S

allowed one swivel and one four-pounder each; and scouts constantly maintained from one block-house to another, and also west from Fort Massachusetts; and that a number not exceeding ten of the inhabitants of Colerain, and ten of those at Green River, above Deerfield, be kept in pay of the Province.

"And it is further ordered, that pay and subsistence be allowed to thirty men at the block-house on George's river, near the fort there; and also pay and subsistence to three hundred and seventy men for the defense of the eastern frontier from Berwick to Damarascotty; and that His Excellency be desired to cause one hundred and fifty of said three hundred and seventy to be employed for the defense of the frontier from Berwick to Pesumpscot river, and two hundred and twenty from said Pesumpscot river to Damarascotty; and that of said three hundred and seventy there be one hundred and fifty of such of the inhabitants as are so exposed to the enemy as to be unable to support themselves by their labor, the pay and subsistence of the aforesaid forces, both for the eastern and western frontiers, to continue till the first of July. Said forces to be inclusive of those already on the frontiers."

April 3. A company of Mohawks were sent out from the Mohawk Castle towards Crown Point by Col. Johnson, in pursuance of orders from Gov. Clinton. The following is Johnson's report of the doings of the party which was led by Lieut. Walter Butler, Junior.* "They went to Crown Point, where they lay two days upon a hill, from whence they had a good view of the fort. They discovered nothing except two large canoes full of men, that they saw go from the fort towards Albany; and, by the shouting the men made as they left the fort, it was concluded they were going to scalp. The third day the

* *Documents, Colonial History of New York*, VI, 343, 344.

1747.] *Mohawks surprise the French.* 139

party came down from the hill and divided into two parties, one of which consisted of thirteen men came upon the track of several persons going towards the garrison; they pursued them till they got within half a mile of the fort, when they discovered a party of the garrison resting on a fallen tree, and were employed in beating and dressing touchwood, which they had found in the woods where they had been upon the patrol. Our thirteen Indians took the opportunity of approaching under a bank. By the advantage of the bank they got very near the French without being discovered, and found that the enemy consisted of twenty-seven soldiers and three Indians. Our Indians fired upon them and killed three; whereupon the enemy flew to their arms and returned the fire briskly, but without any execution. Our Indians having loaded again, gave them a second volley, killed one more and wounded three; upon which the enemy retreated, but one of their officers brought them back to their ground again, and then they fought smartly, and the chief of our Indians was wounded through the breast and one arm, and another slightly on the knee. Upon this, it is said, our Indians, enraged, fought more like devils than men. One of our Indians run up (on observing one of the French Indians presenting his piece) within ten yards of him, and discharged his piece loaded with swan shot, into his breast, upon which he fell down dead; the other two French Indians, on this, run for it. This discouraged the French so much that they all likewise fled towards the fort, except two officers and a sergeant, who continued fighting bravely till they all three fell. Part of our Indians, in the meantime, pursued those that fled till they came within musket-shot of the fort, and say they saw nine wounded men carried into the garrison by the others. They then returned to the place of action, but observing a party from the garrison coming after them, they had only time to take six scalps. The enemy pursued them closely two days, till they came to the lake from whence a river issues that runs towards the Mohawk Castle. One of the French officers, the Indians say, was a young man dressed in blue, with a broad gold lace, who fought with undaunted courage till he was grievously wounded, and then called out for quarters in the Indian language; but, perceiving his wounds were mortal, they dispatched him. This is considered the gallantest action performed by the Indians since the commencement of the present war." The party returned to their head-quarters on the 24th of the same month.

This expedition is thus noticed in the French accounts: "We learn (May 7th) by a courier just arrived from Montreal, that in the last days of April a party of Mohawks and English had fallen on twenty-one French scouts near Fort St. Frederic, and killed and scalped five of them. Sieur Laplante, an officer, had been very badly treated on that occasion, having received seven gunshot wounds. This unfortunate occurrence was the result of too much confidence on the part of the French, who have been surprised." *

The Sieur Laplante was doubtless the officer in blue with gold lace trimmings, just mentioned in Johnson's report.

April 7. Number Four had been abandoned some time previous to this, and was taken possession of by Capt. Phinehas Stevens and about thirty men, who were employed in ranging the wilderness to intercept parties of the enemy. They had had possession but a short time before *an army* of French and Indians under Mons. Debeline appeared before it. Meantime Stevens had strengthened the fort and took every precaution to

---

* *Colonial Documents* before cited, X, 96.

1747.] *French repulsed at Number Four.* 141

prevent surprise. Debeline and his men attacked the place with much confidence, shooting fire arrows, running up carriages by long poles, loaded with faggots, to set fire to the log fort; but Stevens "had dug trenches from under the fort, about a yard outwards, in several places, at so near a distance to each other, as by throwing water we might put out the fire." This and other precautions had the desired effect, though the enemy continued their attack with fire arrows for near two days. Then Debeline sent in a flag for a parley. Stevens consented, and hostages were given and taken. The surrender of the fort was demanded, with the usual promise of good quarter and a safe conduct to Montreal. Stevens answered promptly that he would never give up the fort. Then the enemy proposed to buy some corn of him, but Stevens said he would not sell them a kernel, but he would give them five bushels apiece for every hostage they would send in, to be retained till they should return a like number of captives.

Finding they could gain nothing by diplomacy, they resumed their fire arrow operations; but pretty soon became convinced that they had men to deal with that were not to be frightened; so, to make a safe exhibition of their courage, they commenced formidable preparation to storm the fort, which they probably had no intention to put in practice, for on the night of the third day of the siege they decamped, and were seen no more for this time. All the damage the garrison sustained was the wounding of two of Stevens's men slightly, namely, Joseph Ely and John Brown.*

The news of the gallant and successful defense of Number Four, caused much rejoicing all over the country. At the same time Commodore Knowles, afterwards Sir Charles

---

* The French account will be found in *N. Y. Col. Docs.*, X, 97.

Knowles, arrived with a small squadron in Boston harbor. He had been governor of Louisbourg since its capture. On hearing of Stevens's success, the commodore was so well pleased that he afterwards sent him a silver hilted sword. It was in compliment to the commodore that Number Four was named Charlestown.

The enemy appeared in large force at Saratoga the same day. As Capt. Trent, with Lieut. Proctor's party, went out along the river to the ruins of Capt. Schuyler's house, in order to cross the river, they were ambushed by sixty French and Indians, who killed eight of them on the spot, and wounded several others. Trent and Proctor rallied their men, and bravely fought the enemy near an hour. In the meantime Capt. Livingston dispatched Capt. Bradt with a company, who came up on the opposite side of the river, and soon after the enemy drew off, leaving some plunder and one wounded Frenchman behind them.*

April 10. The same party of the enemy next appeared at Kinderhook, where they surprised a party of eleven men at work, killed two of them, and made the other nine captives. They then burnt the house and barn of Mr. John Van Alstine, and escaped unmolested.†

April 13. A young man named Nathaniel Dresser is killed at Scarborough, within two hundred yards of a garrison,‡ and the day following,

April 14, the enemy appeared suddenly at Saccarappe, six miles from Portland, captured and carried off William Knight

---

* This was one of M. de Rigaud's expeditions, sent out by him from Fort St. Frederic under the immediate command of M. de St. Luc, at the head of two hundred Frenchmen and Indians. See *New York Colonial Documents*, X, pp. 112, 115.

† See *Ibidem*, 116.

‡ See more full particulars in *Colls. Maine Hist. Soc.*, III, 170, 171.

and his two sons. Within the same week they killed a Mr. Eliot and his two sons, and carried a Mr. Marsh or Murch into captivity.

April 15. At Northfield, a little after sunset, Nathaniel Dickinson and Asahel Burt are killed and scalped as they were bringing cows out of the woods. They then made their way to Winchester and the two Ashuelots, and burnt all the three places, which had been deserted by the inhabitants, the government not being able to protect them. They complained mournfully that the soldiers had been withdrawn, leaving them with no means of taking away their effects.

On the same 15th of April two men are killed near a garrison at Saco, and a third is made prisoner. The three men had been weighing hay in a barn, and when they left their work were fired upon. This mischief was done in sight of a shipyard where some carpenters were at work.

April 21. A party of the enemy to the number of fifty, as some reported, came within the bounds of Falmouth, killed a Mr. Foster, and made captives of his family consisting of his wife and six children.

April 25. The Indians appear again at Saco; some fifty or sixty of them attacked the block-house there, and endeavored to burn the mills. They kept up the attack all day, and were prevented effecting their object by the few brave men stationed there, and had two of their number killed.

April 27. Eleven Indians appeared at Damariscotta, killed two women and scalped one of them. The husband of another of them, Capt. John Larman, is made prisoner, carried to Canada, and delivered at Quebec on the 14th of May following. One account says the women killed were wife and daughter of Capt. Larman. Smith appears not to have heard of the attack until the 8th of May, and then not to have had the names of the sufferers. His entry in his journal is: "May 8. We hear the Indians yesterday, at Damariscotta, took a man and killed his wife and daughter-in-law."

At Canajoharie a party of ten French Indians captured a man. Two others heard the man halloo for help, and ran to his assistance, and fired upon his captors, killing one and wounding another; at which the rest fled, leaving their dead companion behind them.

May 2. Five Indians have this week killed two women about Falmouth.

May 4. A man is chased into the center of the town of Wells, and the day following one Hinkley is killed at New Meadows Neck. He had a brother killed at another time.

May 9. At Topsham a canoe, in which were three men and one woman, is shot into by Indians in ambush, by which two of the men are killed and the other sorely wounded, but the woman escaped unhurt.

May 21. As two men were returning with their grist from a mill, between *Amauskeeg* and Suncook, they were fired upon by a party of Indians, supposed to be about sixteen, and one of them was killed on the spot; the other escaped remarkably, as three bullets went through the brim of his hat, and ten through several parts of his coat, while only two of them grazed the skin of his arm and side. The man killed was named Starkee, whom the enemy scalped.

May 22. Fourteen men and a lad, belonging to two fishing vessels at Pemaquid, went up to the Falls to take some alewives for bait, and coming near the Falls in a whale-boat and canoe, belonging to the fishing schooners, six of the men went on shore, and while dipping for alewives were shot upon, but none were killed. All retreated except Capt. John Cox, who stood his ground and was killed. The other five on approaching, as was supposed, a more advantageous ground, faced the enemy, but were soon overpowered, and four of them killed. The other seven of the company had got about half way from the boat when they were attacked and immediately scattered, and were pursued by the enemy, who killed two of them; the remaining four men and the boy recovered the whale-boat to escape, but were shot upon and two more killed outright, and Mr. Abner Lowell sorely wounded, and Capt. Joseph Cox severely, whom they put on shore on the other side of the river, being followed by four of the enemy in the canoe, who soon overtook Capt. Cox and killed him, cutting open his skull with their hatchets. Mr. Lowell and the boy not being able to manage the boat, watched their opportunity and fled on shore. The lad, being fatigued, ran into some bushes and effectually hid himself. Although the Indians made much search for him they did not find him. Mr. Lowell and the boy finally escaped to a sloop, Capt. Saunders, who brought them off. Three of the men were supposed to have been taken prisoners, viz: Reuben Dyer, Benjamin Cox, son of Joseph before mentioned, and Benjamin Mayhew. Those found killed and scalped were Captains John and Joseph Cox, Lieut. Hawes, Nathaniel Bull, George Clark, Jacob Pett, George Caldwell, John Smith, and Ezekiel Webb. Those not accounted for were Edward Bull, and Josiah Weston or Wesson.*

* The names are obtained from several sources; and although some of them differ, and no one account contains all the fifteen, the above list is believed to be correct. Smith has a *Vincent*, but I find fifteen without that name. All agree that there were fourteen men and a boy or lad. The party which committed this savage action consisted of fourteen Pannaouamske Abenaquis. French accounts in *N. Y. Col. Docs.*, X, 107. See also *Boston Gazette and Weekly Journal*, June 2d, 1747.

John and Joseph Cox belonged to Falmouth, Smith and Weston to Purpooduck; Dyer, Mayhew, and Benjamin Cox to Falmouth.

May 23. At Rochester, New Hampshire, Samuel Drown is shot in the hip, in which he carried the ball till his death, which happened in 1795, at the age of ninety years.

May 25. Some of the forces destined for the expedition against Canada, had been ordered to rebuild Fort Massachusetts at Hoosuck. The enemy's scouts appear to have watched the undertaking, for they partially surprised a party of one hundred and two men which had been sent thence to Albany on the 19th of May, to guard stores for Fort Hoosuck. The guard was under the command of Major William Williams of Stockbridge, Capt. Elijah Williams, Lieut. Groves, and Ensign Ingersole. On the 24th they were sent out from the fort to meet this convoy; another detachment, which met them twelve miles below, aided Major Williams's party in passing Hoosuck river, and then returned to the fort. On the morning of the 25th, Major Williams had out five scouts, one of which was under Ensign Konkapot. He also sent squads of men forward to clear the way for the wagons. These having performed that service, came "stringing along (contrary to order)," and were fired upon by an ambush, by which a Stockbridge Indian was killed, and two others of the party wounded. And though our men "pushed the enemy like lions, those serpents got off the Indian's scalp, about as big as three fingers." All the rest reached the fort, except Zebulon Allen of Deerfield, who was captured, as was supposed. Three of Williams's men were wounded, but not dangerously. The enemy were met near a swamp, and a considerable skirmish followed; and seeing the English were likely to have the advantage, they retreated into the swamps, but the discharge of a cannon at the fort caused them to make a precipitate retreat, leaving behind them twenty blankets, one coat with frosted buttons, three of a meaner sort, ten pair of woolen stockings, one pair of leather, sixteen guncases, six *muttump* lines, four pairs of Indian shoes, looking-glass, four shirts, twelve knives, five hatchets, eight petunks, etc., etc. The Indians reported that they lost ten of their men.

June 1. About this date the Indian chief Kintigo returns to the lower Mohawk Castle, whence he went against the French with six men. They brought in seven prisoners and three scalps taken at St. Pierres, a little above Montreal.

June 4. It was reported that a man had been killed at Rochester, N. H., in the course of the week previous, but his name is not ascertained. Encouraged by this success it would seem, for on

June 7, a party of the enemy came to the same town, and as they were stealing upon a party of men at work in a field, they were discovered by three boys, on whom they fired, but did not hit any one. John Place, one of the three, fired and wounded an Indian; another of the boys, Paul Jennens, aimed his gun at the Indians, but did not fire, though it had the effect to check them, and in the meantime the men at work came to their relief and put the enemy to flight.

June 15. News came to Boston that the fort at Saraghtoga had been attacked by two thousand French and Indians, who had killed sixty of the garrison, and the attack was still in progress. The place was relieved soon after by the arrival of Col. Schuyler.

June 20. Lieut. Chew, with one hundred and two men, went on an expedition towards Canada, was attacked and had fifteen of his men killed, and forty-seven wounded. The lieutenant and the rest of his command were made prisoners and sent to Crown Point.

June 26. The well known Indian chief Hendrik returned from a march into the enemy's country. He had some thirty Indians and ten white men under him. They were surprised on an Island in the St. Lawrence above Montreal, by the enemy's Indians, in which four of the white men and nine of the Indians are killed by the first fire. The names of the whites were Cornelius Van Slyck, Johannis Pottman, —— Le Roy, and —— Gott. Hendrik and the rest succeeded in escaping.

June 30. Matthew Loring died in prison at Quebec. He was captured at sea, May 29th of the previous year, but under what circumstances is not known, nor is it known to what place he belonged.

July 15. About thirty or forty Indians came to Fall Town (since Bernardstown), shot and mortally wounded Eliakim Sheldon as he was hoeing corn in the field, and, although he escaped to the fort, he died the following night.

July 21. "One day last week a young man was shot through the body in two places by Indians as he was traveling between Northfield and Falltown, wounding him in so terrible a manner that 'tis thought he is dead before this time." The man killed was probably John Mills of Colerain, who, according to Taylor in the *Redeemed Captive*, "was passing from what was called the South fort to his own house."

At the same time it was reported that a woman and six children were carried off from Burnet's Field, on the Mohawk river, the only out settlement undisturbed hitherto in that region.

July 28. At Penacook a party of the enemy were discovered by their shooting at some cattle, and are pursued by fifty men. They made a hasty retreat, leaving their packs, blankets, and other things behind them.

July 31. At Mount Swag* [Wiscasset] Ebenezer Hilton, Joseph Hilton, and John Boynton, are killed by Indians, who took William Hilton prisoner.†

August 19. A man is fired upon at Brunswick and wounded.

August 20. A large ship arrives in Boston harbor with two hundred and seventy-one persons which had been prisoners in Canada; thirty were left there sick, seventy had died, and one hundred remained.

August 21. At Epsom, N. H., a Mr. Charles McCoy, having seen some signs of an enemy in his neighborhood, concluded to repair to the nearest garrison, which was at Nottingham. He and his wife went out to catch their horses, and, becoming separated, Mrs. McCoy was seized by the Indians, who carried her to Canada and sold her to the French. At the end of the war she was liberated and returned home. She and her husband lived to a great age, he being a hundred and five years old at his death.‡

The same day a party proceeded to Nottingham, ambushed and killed Robert Beard, John Folsom, and Elizabeth Simpson, a little to the south of the plain since called the Square. The woman, though reported killed, it is believed recovered from her wounds.

About this time (the exact date has not been ascertained) a party of the enemy appeared at one of the Ashuelots (which,

---

* Sullivan writes *Montsweag*, one of the places occupied by the Wewenocks, in 1749, who sent six deputies to the treaty of Falmouth. See *post*. Dr. Morse has *Montsiogue* in his *Gazetteer* of 1795, and says it is "a river or bay in Lincoln county, Maine, which communicates with the rivers Sheepscut and Kennebeck."

† See *N. Y. Doc. Hist.*, X, 121.

‡ The reader will find some additional details in Judge Potter's *History of Manchester*, pp. 230-3.

is not stated), killed three cattle, and would doubtless have done greater mischief, but for their having been discovered by some of the inhabitants, who fired upon them. The Indians returned the fire, but none were killed or wounded.

August 26. At Northampton (in the part since Southampton) Elijah Clark was killed and scalped as he was threshing grain in his barn. "He was the last of between fifty and sixty deaths by the Indians, as stated on the records of the town."

August 27. At Marblehead, since Windham, Maine, one William Bolton is captured, and a lad of Mr. Mayberry wounded.

BENJAMIN COLMAN, D. D.

August 29. The Rev. Dr. Benjamin Colman dies in Boston, at the age of seventy-three. He served long as a Commissioner of the Indian Corporation of London, and was one of the ablest ministers in New England. He was once a prisoner to the French, having been taken at sea, after "fighting bravely," according to his biographer.

Sept. 2. Some sixty of the enemy hovered about Pemaquid, and finally attacked it, but were beaten off. They surprised two men at some distance from the fort, shot them down and scalped them. These were soon after found by men from the fort. One was not quite dead, and was able to make them understand that he was scalped by a Frenchman, and that not far off were two dead Indians who were killed from the fort. On going to the spot no Indians were found, but a great amount of blood.

At the same time came the account of a fight at St. George's fort. Lieut. T. Kilpatrick went out with twenty-five men to scout and procure wood. While upon this duty a large number of Indians attacked him. Capt. Bradbury of the fort, hearing the firing, sent out another party which were soon engaged with the enemy, and the fight continued about two hours. The enemy finally withdrew, carrying off their dead and wounded. Of our men four were killed, namely, John Kilpatrick, Nathan Bradley, John Vose, and Benjamin Harvey — the two former they scalped — and there were three wounded. The loss of the enemy was considerable, as was evident from the amount of blood discovered. Three scalps were taken from the enemy.

The party of Indians who did the mischief consisted of about sixty Abenakies, twenty of whom returned to Quebec October 3d, N. S. They reported that the English had been too hard for them; that the two chiefs had lost two of their children, one was the son of Sagonaurabb, and a third the son of Louis Meseadoue.*

October 1. Peter Boovee, or Bevoee, is captured near Fort Massachusetts. He was a soldier belonging to that fort, and was out hunting. He returned after peace.

October 3. A small exchange of captives was effected at Isle de Basque, thirty-five leagues below Quebec, by an agent of Massachusetts, who left Boston August 1st, and delivered there sixty-three French prisoners, and received in return sixteen of the English. He made this journey in two months and three days.

October 9. David Brainerd, a noted missionary to the Indians, dies, at Northampton, aged twenty-nine. His life has been published and republished, on both sides of the Atlantic,

* *New York Colonial Documents*, X, 127, 130.

drawn up from his journals principally, by the eminent divine, Jonathan Edwards.*

October 16. Major Willard, Capt. Alexander, and others, were coming from Ashuelot to Northfield; in Winchester they met some cattle running as though pursued. Capt. Alexander, being forward, saw a Frenchman in the path, coming towards him. When he saw our men he jumped behind a tree. Capt. Alexander fired and wounded him in the breast, whereupon he made up to the captain and saluted him *handsomely*, then fainted and fell. Supposing the main body of the enemy at hand, and that the Frenchman was mortally wounded, he was left behind. Presently his Indian companions came to him. They took him up and carried him some distance; but, like the other party, they, supposing the English close upon them, left the wounded Frenchman and retreated. A few days after, having revived, he made his way into Northfield, surrendered himself to the English, and was confided to the care of the Rev. Benjamin Doolittle, who acted the part of surgeon, and his wounds were soon healed;† after which Capt. Alexander conveyed him to Boston, where he was kindly treated, and in February following he accompanied Sergeant Hawks with a flag of truce to Canada, to be exchanged, and was quite serviceable to him in his mission. His name appears to have been Pierre Raimbault,‡ which the English generally understood to be *Rainbow*, though they sometimes wrote it *Rainboe*. On Sergeant Hawks's return, on

---

* His life is given in Dr. Allen's *Amer. Biog. Dictionary*, and is one of the many in that work drawn out at an unreasonable and disproportionate length.

† Mr. Doolittle does not mention these facts in his *Memoirs*. See *N. Y. Col. Docs.*, X, 147, 153.

‡ Or Sieur Simblin, according to the French report of the affair. Perhaps he passed himself off with the English under the assumed name above given. See *Ibidem*; also *Ibidem*, X, 32. Rainbow made quite a sensation in Boston, being much noticed by the ladies.

the 4th of May of this year, the governor of Canada sent Raimbault, with five other Frenchmen, and two or three Indians, as a guard to accompany him, which they did, to within a few miles of Number Four. Sergeant Hawks brought along with him two that had been some time in captivity, namely, Samuel Allen, taken at Deerfield, August 25th, 1746, and Nathan Blake, who was taken at Upper Ashuelot, April 23d, the same year (1746).

October 19. As Mr. John Smead was traveling from Northfield to Sunderland he was killed by an ambush and scalped. The fortune of this poor man was of the most melancholy kind; having been one of those who were taken prisoners at Fort Massachusetts, with his wife and six little children, and carried to Canada, as already related, and was but recently returned out of captivity. His son Daniel died in prison at Quebec, after a long and distressing sickness of several months, May 13th, 1747.

October 22. About forty of the enemy came to Bridgman's Fort, near Fort Dummer, took Jonathan Sartle, or Sawtelle, as he was going from Col. Hinsdale's Fort into the woods, then burnt Capt. Bridgman's Fort, house and barn.

Nov. 14.* As twelve men were drawing off from Number Four, a considerable party of the enemy waylaid them as they passed down the river, within half a mile of the garrison, shot upon them, killed and scalped Nathaniel Gould and Thomas Goodale; Oliver Avery was wounded, and John Henderson was taken captive. The rest escaped by flight.

The French account of this affair is as follows: The party consisted of forty Indians from the Lake of the Two Mountains, and were led by the Chevalier de Longueuil, Jr. They

---

* Taylor dates this massacre October 24th, but I follow Doolittle.

called Number Four Fort Oequarine; they attacked nine men who were going out of that fort, killed two of them and took one prisoner, whose name was John Anderson, an Irishman, twenty years of age, by whom they learned that the captain of the fort was named Elias Williams. Longueuil returned with his prisoners to Montreal not long after.* His report of the news he obtained on this expedition was a singular medley, and could have afforded little satisfaction to the governor. Some of it is thus detailed: "That the fleets of Admiral Townsend [he means Admiral Anson and Vice-Admiral Warren] were appointed this year for the Canada expedition, but that the battle they fought has prevented their coming. That in the propositions of peace the king [of France] had demanded the restitution of Louisbourg, and that King George had answered, it was not at his disposal; it was a conquest of the people of Boston."†

It does not appear that Anson was destined for North America at the time mentioned, but was stationed in the Channel to intercept the shattered fleet of D'Anville on its return to France. "The battle" mentioned was that of Anson's fleet with that of De Jonquiere's off Brest. De Jonquiere was fitted out to reinforce the Duke D'Anville, but, with all his fleet, was overpowered and taken. The English had five hundred and twenty men killed and wounded. Their ships were double the number of the French, and Anson was seconded by Boscawen, Brett, and Saumarez.

---

* How the Frenchmen got the name of the fort it is not easy to see. Whether the prisoner's name was Anderson or Henderson is a little uncertain. By *Elias Williams* they can hardly mean *Josiah* *Willard*, who was in command of the fort not long before, and perhaps when this attack was made. See *N. Y. Col. Docs.*, X, 147.

† *Ibidem.*

CHAPTER IX.

DIARY OF DEPREDATIONS (continued).

Men killed at Number Four — At Fort Dummer — Poquoig — Sheepscot — Suncook — Rochester — Brunswick — North Yarmouth — Southampton — Berwick — Fort Massachusetts — Hollis's Attempt to civilize Indians at Stockbridge — Captain Melvin's Surprise — Ambush near Kinderhook — Men killed between Hinsdale's and Fort Dummer — Captain Hobbs' Expedition and Surprise — News of Peace — Capture of John Fitch and Family — Depredations at Upper Ashuelot — Falmouth — Butchery near Fort Dummer — Other Details — Surprise near Schenectady — The Six Nations at Albany — Depredation at Northfield — Fight at Fort Massachusetts — Flag of Truce from Canada — Depredation at Sheepscut — Captives returned — Treaty of Aix la Chapelle — Depredations on the Frontiers continue — Captains Prebble and Coffin attacked at Annapolis Royal — A Deputation of French and Indians in New York City — Peace proclaimed in Boston — Sartell killed at Number Four — Eastern Indians at Boston — Treaty made with them at Falmouth — An Indian Trick — Efforts to recover Captives from Canada — Incidents.

THE snow being very deep, on March 15th, the enemy were not supposed to be about; some eight men went out from Number Four to procure wood. When about sixty rods from the fort, ten Indians, or, as some judged, twenty, sprang up, and by a volley killed Charles Stevens, wounded one Andrews,* and took Eleazer Priest captive. They then retreated at their leisure, our men having no snow-shoes to enable them to pursue, while the enemy were well supplied with them. It is said the French had been apprised of this fact, which was the occasion of their undertaking an enterprise under the very walls of the fort.

* Andreas. *Doolittle.* Androus. *Taylor.*

March 29. About fifteen Indians waylaid the scout path between Fort Dummer and Colerain. Lieut. Serjeant went out in this path with four other men, to obtain timber for oars and paddles. At about one mile from Fort Dummer they were fired upon. Moses Cooper was mortally wounded the first fire, yet escaped to the fort, but died the next night. Lieut. Serjeant, his son, and Joshua Wells, engaged the enemy, fighting as they retreated. Wells was killed. Serjeant encouraged his son, saying they should have help from the fort, charged many times, shouted as often as the enemy did, and called to them to come out and fight like men; but after a retreat of half a mile the lieutenant was killed and his son taken prisoner. It is said they received no help from the fort because some of the men were sick of the measles, and the others had no snowshoes!

There is a circumstantial account of the murder of a man at Groton, and the killing of the murderer, said to have happened in that town some time during this war; but as the relation is unaccompanied by any date, it may have occurred much earlier, or even later than the period assigned to it. The following are the facts as recorded, probably long after:

An Indian had been seen, for several days, lurking about the town, upon some ill design, as was supposed. One Jacob Ames, who lived on the intervale, on the west side of the Nashaway, on land now, or since, owned by John Boynton, Esq., went into his pasture to catch his horse. Discovering the Indian, who, it would seem, had lain in wait for him, he ran for his house with all speed. The Indian gained upon him, leveled his gun and shot him dead as he was entering the inclosure surrounding the house. Ames's son and a daughter were in the house. The son, seeing his father fall, sprang forward to close the gate, but was prevented by the dead body of his father. The Indian now came up, and as he was attempting to pass the gate, young Ames fired upon him. The ball struck the latch of the gate and was thus cut into two parts, one of which struck the Indian, slightly wounding him; not, however, sufficiently to prevent his attempting an entrance into the house; but young Ames pressed the door against him, yet the Indian thrust one foot in, and was there held while Ames's sister passed him his father's gun, which was in the house. Thus both parties were fully occupied for the moment — the Indian in attempting to force the door, and Ames in holding it against him. In another second Ames brought down the but of the gun upon the Indian's foot, which made him make a hasty withdrawal of it. The latter now commenced reloading his gun for a new campaign; but Ames had the advantage, for his was already loaded, which he discharged through a loophole or crevice, and killed the Indian. The report of the guns soon brought two men to the scene of disaster, Ezra and Benjamin Farnsworth, who were at a mill about a mile off; they found the elder Ames and the Indian weltering in their blood not many paces distant. This depredation is thought to be the only one which happened in Groton during this war.*

April 16. As Jason Babcock was at work in his field, at "Poquoig,† about seven miles from Nichewag," he was surprised and carried off prisoner, but returned by way of the St. Lawrence and the Atlantic, arriving in Boston the 6th of October following.

April 24. From the eastern country came the following dis-

---

* For the facts in this narrative I am indebted to Butler, *Hist. Groton*, 110-11.

† Afterwards Athol. But in what direction *Nitchewog* lay from Poquoig, is not easily determined. The name is not found on the maps consulted.

tressing news, in a letter dated, Georgetown, the 29th of April; namely, that on Sunday, the 24th, James Kincaid was killed. He had been in captivity nearly two years, having returned in a French flag last summer. At Avery's garrison at Sheepscut, were killed one Carr and one Ball, and Avery was led away captive. It appears that from the uneasiness of the dogs in the garrison there were thought to be Indians in the vicinity, and the above-named men, with two others, went out, and but two of them returned. Two days after five Indians were seen going up a creek in Georgetown, as unconcernedly as if it had been a time of peace, and there was no one to molest them. On the following day,

April 27, within gunshot of the fort, the enemy took Job Philbrook and Samuel McForney and carried them off. The same day one of the garrison at St. George's, named Presbury Woolen, was captured and carried to Canada, but he returned in October following. He belonged to Sandwich.

April 30. While at work on the western bank of the Merrimack river, opposite the mouth of the Suncook, Mr. Robert Buntin, in company with James Carr and his son, a lad of ten years, were surprised by a party of Indians. Carr, in endeavoring to make his escape, was shot down and killed. Buntin and his son were taken and carried to Canada, and there sold to a Frenchman in Montreal. With other prisoners they were sent to Boston by way of Louisbourg, where they arrived October 6th following, after the comparatively short captivity of five months. The name of the son of Robert Buntin was Andrew. He went a soldier in the war of the Revolution, in which service, at White Plains, he died.

Besides the above mischief at Suncook, the enemy killed the

cattle of two teams, consisting of nine oxen, six of which they cut up and carried off, with the tongues only of the other three.

May 1. At Rochester, about ten miles northwesterly of Dover, in New Hampshire, a Mr. Jonathan Hodgdon and his wife went out to find and milk their cows, and, taking different paths, some Indians sprang from a thicket and seized Mrs. Hodgdon, and would probably have carried her off alive, but she screamed to her husband, and would not cease until they gagged her, nor then could they stop her entirely, whereupon they cut open her head with their hatchets, killing her immediately. Mr. Hodgdon heard her cries, and was near enough to see the fatal blows dealt, but, as he was powerless, and could do nothing to save her, he fled to the garrison, closely pursued by the murderers of his wife. She was a young woman much beloved for amiable and virtuous qualities, by whose death two young children were left motherless.

Mr. Hodgdon married a second wife, and had, in all, twenty-one children, and lived to the great age of ninety years, dying in 1815.

May 3. Several persons are killed at Brunswick, among whom was a Captain Burnet, or Burnel, and no further record is found of this depredation. Not far from the same time a man is killed at North Yarmouth, named Ebenezer Eaton, and another, Benjamin Lake, captivated; and "all the houses to the eastward of Weirs" were burnt down. The number of the enemy was computed at an hundred, as they were able to waylay "all the road to New Casco."

May 8. About twelve Indians laying in ambush near a house in Southampton, shot and killed Noah Pixley. A William Pixley was an early settler in Westfield, from whom Noah was probably descended.

Affair near Fort Massachusetts. [1748.

May 10. At Berwick, on the east side of Salmon Falls river, a town about seven miles northwest from York, in the district of Maine, a young woman named Morell, going out a short distance from a house, is seized by Indians, who, after barbarously murdering her with their hatchets, tore off her scalp and escaped.

May 21. About thirty Indians came and formed an ambush near Fort Massachusetts, hoping to take some of the men of the fort prisoners, as they might come out to pass towards Deerfield. It so happened that Serjeant Elisha Chapin, with a number of men, went out from Deerfield towards the fort. As they marched cautiously along they discovered one of the enemy standing and earnestly watching the fort. The sergeant thinking they might be some of the friendly Stockbridges, called to them. Supposing they were discovered, the enemy jumped from their hiding places and ran. Upon this Chapin and one or two of his men fired upon them, killing one of them, the rest making their escape, leaving on the place a gun, several blankets, and many other things. With these trophies, and the scalp of the Indian, Chapin and his party pursued their march to the fort.*

May 23. Amidst all the trying scenes of the war efforts were not relaxed by benevolent Christians to civilize such of the Indians as they could have access to. Especially had efforts been made among the Stockbridge tribe. Owing to hostilities it was not thought advisable to set up a school at Stockbridge, although Mr. Isaac Hollis of High Wycomb in Bucks had made a donation for the support of twelve boys "of heathen parents" to be educated in "letters and husbandry." It was therefore concluded to engage the boys and to send them into

* See APPENDIX F.

the settled part of the country, and thus carry out the benevolent purpose of Mr. Hollis. Accordingly, Mr. Sergeant, the missionary at Stockbridge, engaged Captain Martin Kellogg of Newington, in Connecticut, to take and support the twelve boys, and thus carry into effect the object which had been for some time in contemplation. The boys having been selected, set out for Newington at the date above given. After they had spent a year under the direction of Captain Kellogg, they accompanied him to their former home, and a favorable report was given of their progress in education and civilization. Captain Kellogg was selected as their tutor and governor, as he had a knowledge of the Indian language, having been twice captivated and carried a prisoner to Canada in his youth.

May 25. Captain Eleazer Melvin was surprised and had a severe fight with the Indians at a point on West river. With eighteen men he marched into the Indian country, from Fort Dummer, upon a scouting expedition, on the 13th of May. After marching, by the captain's estimation, about ninety miles, he arrived at the shore of Lake Champlain, having till then (May 25th) discovered no Indians. He now discovered a large canoe in which were six Indians, but beyond the reach of his guns. Soon after another was seen with twelve in it. By running to a point of land, about half a mile nearer Crown Point fort, they got within some fifty or sixty rods of the boat or canoe; thinking he might have no better opportunity to annoy the enemy, he ordered his men to fire into their canoe, which they did, firing six times each in about three or four minutes. At the first shot all in the canoe lay down close, but when three rounds had been poured into them, "they made a most terrible outcry," cut down their sails, and about six of them commenced paddling to get out of the reach of their assailants. At the fourth volley from Melvin's men, three of the enemy made a shot at them, by which one man had his hand grazed by one of their balls. By this time the alarm had reached Crown Point, of which notice was given by firing three of the cannon of the fort. The assailants now thought it time to make good their retreat; and fearing the enemy might intercept them in their return march, they waded swamps and flowed land, and scaled mountains in various directions. At length they reached West river, thirty-five miles from Fort Dummer, on the last day of May. Now feeling that they had got safely thus far, they probably were a little too secure, and were not sufficiently cautious, and allowed themselves to be surprised, and, in a feeble fight that ensued, Melvin lost six of his men killed outright, namely, Joseph Petty, John Howard, John Dod, Daniel Man, Isaac Taylor, and Samuel Severance.

It appears that as soon as Melvin was attacked his men scattered, a few of them faced about and made some shots on their pursuers, but no considerable stand was made by any of them, and all except the six above named came into Fort Dummer at different times; and at the time it was remarked, that "it was a surprising stroke, and struck a great damp into the spirits of our men who had thoughts of going into their [the Indian] country; when they found how far the Indians would pursue them to get an advantage upon them." But the same writer had remarked before, that there was a probability that the Indians that surprised Melvin were the same that had been discovered and routed by Sergeant Chapin on the 21st of May. How this may have been it would be useless to conjecture.

Whether any charge of remissness of duty was brought against Captain Melvin, no mention is found. Perhaps his explanation, and his former services under Captain Lovewell sufficiently shielded him from suspicion of cowardice or want of capacity in such commands.

As twenty men were on their march to Kinderhook they fell into an Ambush of French and Indians, who killed five of them and took two prisoners. Another party of English, consisting of fifteen, soon after came up with the enemy, killed their leader, a Frenchman, and two Indians on the spot; recovered the two prisoners, and put the enemy to flight, who left their accoutrements behind them.

June 16. A large body of the enemy having waylaid the road between Col. Hinsdale's Fort and Fort Dummer, fired upon a company of thirteen men as they were passing from the former to the latter fort, where, by one volley, were shot down and killed, Joseph Richardson, Nathan French and John Frost. Three only escaped; the rest were taken prisoners. It afterwards appeared that one of the prisoners was mortally wounded, as the bones of a man were found where the enemy encamped the first night after their murderous exploit, and W. Bickford was missing. The names of the men thus captured were Henry Stevens, Benjamin Osgood, William Blanchard, Matthew Wyman, Joel Johnson, Moses Perkins, and William Bickford.

June 26. An expedition under Captain Humphrey Hobbs went out from Number Four. It consisted of forty men. Their march seems to have been early known to the enemy, whose spies were probably secreted near the fort when Captain Hobbs commenced his march, for when he arrived at a point about twelve miles northwest of that fort he found he was pursued by one hundred and fifty of the enemy. It being the middle of the day, he had halted his men to allow them to take some refreshment, when the approach of the enemy was announced by a gun from the sentinel stationed in the rear.

Whereupon, almost momentarily, the enemy came on with their accustomed shouts and yells; and yet, notwithstanding the great disparity in numbers, Captain Hobbs and his men stood their ground, giving them "a warm reception," and, in the manner of battles of those times, continued the fight for four hours, during which Hobbs lost three men in killed, namely, Samuel Gun, Ebenezer Mitchell, and Eli Scott, and three more very badly wounded, whose names were Samuel Graves, shot in the head, by which some of his brains came out; Daniel McKeney, who had his thigh broken; and Nathan Walker, who had an arm broken, the ball lodging between the bones, and Ralph Rice slightly. Up to this time the enemy unflinchingly continued the fight; but now, fortunately, Capt. Hobbs got a shot at their leader, the Indian chief who had encouraged his men, and it was supposed killed, or so badly wounded him that they all left the ground and drew off, and Capt. Hobbs was able to carry off his dead and wounded men. He buried the killed about half a mile from the scene of the fight, "as well as he could in the dark," and the next day continued his march to Fort Dummer with his wounded, and the following day he proceeded to Northfield.

Considering all the circumstances, there had hardly been a more desperate action between the English and Indians since that at Pequawket in 1725, when the "brave Lovewell with fifty men from Dunstable," encountered Paugus in the wilderness of the Aucosisco. And yet it is scarcely mentioned in any considerable work of history, and is yet to be sung by some native poet in the perhaps very distant future. But it is sure to be immortalized in song, no doubt worthy of the occasion. One local writer has indeed said in prose, that "it was a very manly fight;" and another, that "our men fought with such boldness and fortitude, as that had they been Romans, they would have received a *laurel*, and their names would have been handed down with honor to posterity."

What loss the enemy sustained in this severe conflict was never known; but as they were near three to one of the English, they must have, in all probability, suffered at least in as great a proportion as their opponents. They also retired from the field without giving even a single shout, which they never do when successful. It was also observed, that when about a week after the battle they met some of the English captives, they looked downcast, "like dogs that had lost their ears."

July 2. News reached New England that preliminary articles of peace had been agreed upon between the contending powers in Europe.

July 5. A large party of about eighty Indians, and a few Frenchmen, surprised the garrison at Lunenburg, took prisoners Mr. John Fitch and his family, consisting of his wife and five children, and carried them through the wilderness to Canada, where they remained till the news of peace between England and France was received there; after which, with other captives, Mr. Fitch returned home by way of New York. Like hundreds of others he returned a beggar to his desolate home, with several small children dependent upon him. As he left under his own hand a circumstantial account of his capture, the reader may desire a more detailed narrative of the affair. It therefore follows:

Mr. Fitch was a carpenter by trade, and, having a young and growing family, he determined to make a farm in the wilderness, and accordingly purchased, in the year 1739, one hundred and twenty acres of land about seven miles and a half above Lunenburg meeting-house, and about three miles and a half beyond any inhabitants, on the road to Northfield. He there built a house, and from the produce of what land he had from time to time cleared, supported his family, "and some to spare, whereby he entertained and refreshed travelers." On the breaking out of the war, knowing his very exposed situation, the people of Lunenburg urged upon him the importance of having a garrison at his place. The result was, with their assistance one was soon erected, and soldiers stationed in it by the government. From that time forth it was a place of resort and refreshment for town scouts, as well as for the larger government scouts. This year four soldiers were allowed for his garrison, and it was also ordered that the scouts from Lunenburg and Townsend should visit the place once every week. From which circumstance the authorities probably imagined that if the enemy came to attack the garrison they would come at the same time the scouts were there to entertain them! But, if this was their calculation, "they reckoned without their host." And, to add to the desperate situation of this pioneer family, half of the regular soldiers belonging to the garrison (namely, *two*) were too sick to be upon duty, and this was the time the enemy came for entertainment. They did not even wait for a scout which was to arrive as a reinforcement the same day, but appeared before the garrison in the forenoon. Mr. Fitch and his two defenders, Blodget and Jennings, were outside of the garrison when the enemy made their appearance, and as the disparity of the forces was too great to warrant a prolonged action, after having half of his small force shot down, with the remaining half (namely, *one* man) Mr. Fitch retreated within his garrison. Nothing daunted, the enemy came on with their usual bravery, and vigorously continued the attack, while those within defended themselves until Mr. Fitch's last man was killed by a shot which came through one of the port-holes of the garrison.

Thus reduced, and no hope of succor, Mr. Fitch, with his wife and five children, became captives to the Indians. After plundering the place, taking whatever they could carry away, they set fire to and burnt the rest, with the garrison and other buildings. Then, says the owner, "we entered into a melancholy captivity, with one small child on the mother's breast," and two others, to prevent their starving, she was compelled to nourish in the same manner while on their journey through the wilderness. This distressing hardship, with other privations, broke her constitution, and, although she survived her captivity, she died before the end of her journey homeward.

About the 23d of September, conducted by five French officers, Mr. Fitch and his family, with many others, arrived in Boston, his wife having died at Providence, on the passage from New York hither. With his five children, one of whom was sick, Mr. Fitch was entirely dependent on charity; all his stock of cattle, hogs, and other animals, destroyed, and his tools and household utensils burnt up. In December, 1749, he petitioned the government of the colony for help, and on the following April (1750) the treasurer was directed to answer his order for eight pounds! "in consideration for his sufferings!"

The names of Mr. Fitch's five children were Catharine, John, Paul, Susannah, and Jacob. His wife's name was Susannah.

The part of Lunenburg since Ashby, includes the farm and residence of John Fitch.

July 8. A party of Indians came to Upper Ashuelot and killed eleven head of cattle, which is all the damage they did, so far as known.

The night of the same day, a man of the name of Whitney died at Falmouth of the wounds he had received from the Indians.

July 14. The road between Fort Hinsdale and Fort Dummer is again waylaid by a large number of Indians, reported to have been a hundred, and as Sergeant Thomas Taylor, with a company of seventeen men, was on his march from Hinsdale's Fort to Fort Dummer, the Indians fired upon them and then rushed upon them with their tomahawks and war clubs. The sergeant ordered his men to fight, but the odds was too great, and the English were quickly overpowered, and all were killed or taken except four who escaped by flight. The killed were Joseph Rose, Asael Graves, —— Billings and —— Chandler; nine were taken prisoners, namely, Sergeant Thomas Taylor, Thomas Crisson, John Henry, —— Lawrence, —— Walker, Daniel How, Jr.,* —— Edghill, Daniel Farmer,† and Ephraim Powers. Of the four that escaped, one was badly wounded. Two of the captured men being severely wounded also, were carried about a mile and then killed. The Indians which performed this bloody work were said to have been a part of those who had the four-hour fight with Capt. Hobbs.

The following is the report of this disaster published about fourteen days after it happened: "From the westward we have intelligence that Captain Stevens, having been lately out with a number of men, found four of the seventeen men that were fallen upon by the enemy between Hinsdell's Fort and Fort Dummer, dead; nine more are supposed to be in captivity. He also found one of the ten who were missing some

---

* He had been in captivity about two years before. See 24 June, 1746.

† The circumstance here recorded seems not to have been known to the genealogist of the Farmer family, Mr. John Farmer.

time before. He followed the enemy, but could not come up with them. He also buried Capt. Hobbs's three men which the enemy had not found."

July 18. About three miles from Schenectady, Daniel Tol, Dirk Van Vorst and a negro went to a place called Poependal to catch their horses; but not finding the horses as they expected, they went into the adjacent woods to a place called the Claypit. They discovered Indians and attempted to escape from them, but were pursued by them, and both Tol and Van Vorst were shot down, but the negro escaped. Van Vorst, though wounded, was not killed, but taken prisoner. The firing was heard at Maalwyck, about two miles distant, and the people there, knowing that Tol and Van Vorst had gone for their horses, suspected the occasion of the firing. This was about ten o'clock in the morning, and a messenger was at once dispatched to the town, where the alarm was sounded about twelve. Some of the inhabitants, with a company of the new levies posted there under Lieutenant Darling of Connecticut, in all seventy men, marched out towards Poependal, cautiously searching for the enemy, as far as the lands of Simon Groot, but made no discovery of the enemy. At this point the negro before mentioned came to the party and told them where the body of his master was. The negro was furnished with a horse, and they (about forty in number) were piloted to the spot where his master lay dead; and near Poependal, at Abraham De Graaff's house. They immediately entered the woods with the negro, where they at once discovered the enemy in great numbers, upon whom they discharged a volley with a shout. The enemy shouted in return, accompanying it with a volley also. This was the commencement of a most desperate fight. All but two or three of the English stood to it manfully, although

W

they were hemmed in on every side by the great numbers of the enemy, and fought over a space of about two acres; yet the battle ground was left in possession of the settlers. In this hand to hand encounter twelve of the inhabitants of Schenectady were killed outright, five taken prisoners, and seven of Lieutenant Darling's men, including himself, were killed, and six of them missing, supposed to be taken prisoners.

The news of this battle reached Albany in the evening of the same day, and by midnight Lieutenant Chew, with one hundred English and about two hundred friendly Indians were on the march for the scene of action, but to no other purpose than as showing their willingness to meet an emergency of this kind.

The names of the people killed, so far as ascertained, were Daniel Tol, Frans Vander Bogart, Jr., Jacob Glen, Jr., Daniel Van Antwerpen, J. P. V. Antwerpen, Cornelius Vielen, Jr., Adrian Van Slyk, Peter Vroman, Klaas A. De Graaf, Adam Conde, John A. Bradt, John Marienes.

There were missing Isaac Truax, Ryer Wemp, Johan Seyer Vroman, Albert John Vedder, and Frank Conner, all belonging to *Schenectade*. Of the soldiers seven were killed and six missing.

July 22. An immense concourse of Indians of the Six Nations assembled at Albany, at the invitation of the governor of New York. His object being to keep them to the English interest. Several governors of the other colonies were present. It lasted four days, during which time the Indians were feasted, and presents were made to them at a cost of above two thousand pounds; upon which it is reported that they were well pleased, and promised to take up the hatchet against all enemies of the English. There were fourteen hundred and fifty of them.

July 23. At Northfield a few Indians, the number not known, but said to be six, waylaid the *Town Street*, and as Aaron Belden was passing along before sunrise, they killed and scalped him, and fled into the woods before the people were aware of what had occurred.

August 2. A party of some fifty French and Indians went into the immediate vicinity of Fort Massachusetts and placed themselves in ambush. By the furious barking of the dogs in the fort, the officers concluded there were Indians not far off. Capt. Ephraim Williams was in command, and in the afternoon, while he was consulting with his men upon some method by which he could surprise the ambush, several soldiers ran out of the fort without orders, following a direction indicated by the dogs. A part of the ambush jumped up and fired upon the men. Upon this Captain Williams sallied out with a strong party to rescue those already engaged; and, not knowing where the ambush was, found he had passed it, or a part of it, and was in imminent danger of being cut off in a retreat; but he and his men courageously fought retreating, and gained the fort with the loss of one man only killed and two wounded. The man killed was named Abbot. The wounded were Lieut. Hawley, shot through the leg, and Ezekiel Wells, who had his thigh broken. The enemy was thought to have sustained considerable damage, as they were seen to drag away several dead bodies. Captain Williams's men made a stand before retreating, and fired several times apiece without any shelter.

August 4. It had been some time known in Canada that preliminaries of peace had been agreed upon in Europe, but the news had not reached Boston in any authentic shape until this date, and then it came from three French Indians who came to Albany from Canada to announce it. Yet depredations continued.

August 16. The governor of Canada having dispatched from Quebec, on July 27th, a flag of truce ship for Boston, it arrived here after a passage of twenty days. When the ship sailed there were about one hundred and seventy-five captives. One or two died on the voyage.* In all there had died in captivity and on shipboard, one hundred and seventy-three; all, or nearly all New England people. While in captivity, in the hands of the French, they were allowed each one pound and a half of bread, half a pound of beef, one gill of peas, "with spruce beer," per day.

August 23. The enemy appeared again on Sheepscot river, where they killed two men and captured another; but their names are not mentioned.

October 6. The schooner Brittania, Aylmer Graville master, from Louisbourg, came into the harbor of Boston, with a great number of persons who had been in captivity among the French and Indians in Canada. Many of them had been captured at sea, and belonged to various sea-ports in England.

October 7. The treaty of Aix la Chapelle was signed by the envoys, but the fact was not formally proclaimed at Boston until about six months after, so slow was the communication between distant places at that period. Hence war parties from Canada hovered upon the borders of New England as though no treaty had been made. Although the treaty of Aix is a noted epoch, it proved to be nothing but a kind of armistice, a

* Douglass mentions some of the facts detailed in this paragraph, but under the wrong year. His dates are often erroneously given, yet his work is valuable.

"hasty and ill-digested affair, determining none of the points in dispute.*

October 20. Captain Jedediah Prebble and Captain Coffin,† with thirty men, embarked at Annapolis Royal for St. John's river. The next day Captain Gorham embarked with thirty more. Captain Gorham on board the Anson‡ with the same number, sailed on the 24th. On the 28th Captain Gorham, with "ten men and paddles," went to the east of the harbor, and Captain Prebble and Captain Davis of the Warren, with five oarsmen, went to the westward of the harbor to make discoveries, and on going on shore were fired upon by the Indians, who killed William Croxford, one of Captain Prebble's men; they also killed two of Captain Gorham's men and wounded three others, Captain Prebble at the same time having a very narrow escape. Seeing an Indian in the edge of a wood taking aim at him with his rifle, at about eighty yards distance, the captain stepped behind a small tree which at the same moment received the ball from the Indian's gun. Captain Prebble immediately fired upon the Indian "with a brace of balls," as also did Captain Davis; but whether with execution, they could not tell, as all the party retreated to their boats and returned to the place of their departure, with two Indians prisoners. By what manner the prisoners were taken is not stated, although it is mentioned that one was a son of a chief, but the chief was able to make his escape.

February 17. Nineteen Indians and Frenchmen arrived at New York from Canada. Their object seems not to have

---

* Wynne, *Brit. Emp. in America*, II, 5.

† The genealogist of Newbury does not seem to have known anything about this Coffin, consequently his Christian name is unknown. I have supplied that of *Preble* conjecturally.

‡ Doubtless so named for the Commodore.

been generally known. Perhaps it was in consequence of the news of an armistice. They continued there until the 9th of April following, causing much speculation respecting the objects of their visit.

May 10. A proclamation of peace is made with great demonstrations of joy at Boston. The regiment of the town was ordered out, and paraded in King street; and being drawn up before the Town Hall, the proclamation was read from the balcony, and received with great and unfeigned delight by the people. But, like the ocean long lashed by the tempest, its fury does not entirely abate with the going down of the wind.

June 20. The frontier towns were again thrown into excitement and alarm. The repeated news of peace in Europe had inspired many with confidence that the war was at an end, and hence they repaired in many instances to their abandoned farms and dwellings. Under this hope of security a band of savages made their appearance at Number Four, just after the soldiers which had been stationed in the fort there had left, having been ordered elsewhere. This morning (June 20*) Ensign Obadiah Sartell went into the field to harrow corn, taking Enos Stevens with him to ride the horse. The Indians were concealed in the bushes which skirted the field, and from which they fired upon and killed Sartell, also the horse on which the boy was. The Indians then, ten or twelve in number, quite naked, rushed upon and scalped Sartell, took the boy and carried him to Canada, but the authorities there discountenanced the depredation and had the boy sent back immediately.

---

* Mrs. Johnson, in her *Captivity*, gives the particulars of this affair, but was mistaken in saying it was in May. Her well written account is quite erroneous in its dates generally. The third edition of it was edited by a scholar (the late Rev. Abner Kneeland, as he informed me), from such materials as the Johnson family had preserved. A reprint is in Farmer and Moore's *Hist. Collections*, I, 177-239.

Close of the War.

The Indians at the eastward had been quite as troublesome as those on the western border; and although they generally knew of the armistice before the English were apprised of it, they did not entirely cease their depredations for some time after they had received the news. And although they had exceedingly annoyed and distressed the English settlers on all their borders, and were almost always successful in their forays against them, yet in the past five years of war they had, through casualties of battles, infectious diseases, and rum, become amazingly reduced, so that the better part of them, especially in the eastern country, were quite as ready as their English neighbors to make terms of peace. The murders and other mischiefs perpetrated during several months past was the work of straggling parties which had not acknowledged accountability to any body, but operated through a thirst for plunder and revenge.

Early this year the chiefs of the eastern tribes met in council, and agreed to make overtures to the government of New England for a settlement of difficulties. This they made known to the authorities by a messenger dispatched for the purpose.

Other preliminary arrangements are not found upon record before the 3d of June. Then Gov. Shirley wrote to Gov. Benning Wentworth, and probably to the other New England governors, that there were then nine Indians in Boston, six from the Penobscot and three from the Norridgewalk tribes; that they stated they had been sent here by their own, the St. François and St. John's river tribes to assure the authorities of their desire for peace, and to request that a time and place of meeting might be fixed for holding a treaty; that he had, in accordance with their request, appointed the 27th of September ensuing for a meeting at Falmouth, and desired that New Hampshire would be represented on the occasion, and that as suitable presents would be expected by the Indians, he had given orders for such on the part of Massachusetts.

On the 17th of June seven other Indians arrived at Boston from the eastern coast, in the province sloop, commanded by Capt. Thomas Saunders, but in what capacity is not ascertained.

Agreeably to the promise of Gov. Shirley, commissioners on the part of Massachusetts and New Hampshire met the Indians at Falmouth on the 14th of October. From the former province were Thomas Hutchinson, John Choate, Israel Williams, and James Otis (the father of the famous James Otis, who was also there), Esqrs. From the latter, Theodore Atkinson, and John Downing, Esqrs.

The Norridgewaks were represented by six chiefs, viz, Toxus, Eneas, Magawambee, Harrey, Soosephinia, Naktoonos, Nesaqumbuit, and Pereez.

The Penobscots by five chiefs, viz, Eger Emmet, Maganumba, Nictumbouit, Esparagoosaret, and Neemon.

The Weweenocks and Arresuguntoocooks by six chiefs, viz, Sawwaramet, Aussaado, Waaununga, Sauquish, Wareedeon, and Wawawnunka.

The usual articles were drawn up and subscribed October 16th, 1749. These were mainly confirmatory of Gov. Dummer's treaty of 1727. And on the 27th of the same month Lieut.-Gov. Phips issued a proclamation in conformity therewith, at Boston.

Peace was now fully established, and the people felt relieved from the perils to which they had for the last five years been subjected.

At the late treaty, and before it was fully opened, an incident occurred which for some little time seemed to portend a disagreeable rupture to further proceedings. It may be well to premise that Indians delight in innocent mischief. It appears to have been a sine qua non in the preliminaries to this treaty, that the Indians should bring forward and deliver up the English captives among them. The following circumstance in relation to this matter is detailed by Gov. Hutchinson, then one of the commissioners there present. It therefore follows in his own words: "Notice had been given that they must bring in such English captives as were among them, and particularly a boy whose name was Macfarlane, and who was taken in the beginning of the war. They apologized for not bringing Macfarlane, and feigned some excuse, promising he should be sent when they returned home. The commissioners showed great resentment, and insisted upon the delivery of the captive previously to their entering upon the treaty. Some time was spent in altercation. At length an old sachem rose up, and took one of the likeliest and best dressed young Indians by the hand, and presented him to Mr. Hutchinson, the chairman of the commissioners, as the captive Macfarlane. This increased the resentment, and it was thought too serious an affair to be [thus] jested with. The young man then discovered himself, and (having spoken nothing before but Indian), in the English language thanked the commissioners for their kind care in procuring his redemption. He had so much the appearance of an Indian, not only in his dress, but in his behavior, and also his complexion, that nobody had any suspicion to the contrary. He had made himself perfectly acquainted with their language, and proved serviceable as an interpreter at the French house so long as he lived."

The boy Macfarlane is probably the same Waltar *McFarland* who, in 1752, was one of the witnesses to the treaty of that year, made at St. George's. Whether he were a son, or

X

belonged to the family of Mr. John McFarland, of whom mention has been made under Aug. 26, 1746, is as yet uncertain.

After the close of hostilities there was much to be done. Many of the English, Dutch, friendly Indians, and negroes were still in captivity, or whose fate was unknown to their friends. Consequently it was the desire as well as the duty of the government to use efforts to recover such as were yet living and held by the Indians. Accordingly commissioners or agents were sent to Canada early in 1750 to endeavor to bring from that country all that could be obtained. They found some of the captives indisposed to return, having become attached to the manner of life of their Indian masters, and some of them thoroughly imbued with the Roman Catholic religion; others refused to return to their native land, alleging as a reason that they would be obliged to labor a long time to raise the money paid for their ransom; that now they had their liberty and could do as they listed.

In the month of June, 1750, Gov. Clinton, of New York, sent Lieut. B. Stoddert to Montreal, where he met the French authorities, from whom he received twenty-four prisoners. He learned the whereabouts of many others, and with Captain Anthony Van Schaick went into the Indian country to obtain them, but without much success. The names of those which returned with Lieut. Stoddert were as follows: Capt. Anthony Van Schaick, John Vroman, Peter Vosborough, William Goff, Christopher McGraw, John Philips, Edward Varen, Benjamin Blachford, Peter Clincton, John Thompson, Daniel Eden, Albert Vedder, Adam Mole, Francis Conner, Cornelius Sprong, Elisha Stansbury, Timothy Colbe, Southerland Fort, Timothy Colson, Peter Dogaman, Mattée Gatroup, and three Mohawks.

Efforts were made to induce others, of whom he had information, to return, but could not prevail on them. The following is a list of them: Rachel Quackenbus; Samuel Frement, a negro; Simon Vort, Philip Philipson, Thomas Volmer, Jacob Suitzer, Jacob Volmer, Joshua Nicolson, Henry Piper, Christian Volmer, John* [――], Edward Cheaole, and an old man whose name is not known. He was away on a hunting expedition with the Hurons of Lorette, and it was not known whether he desired to return to New England; if, on coming from hunting, he wished to go to his former friends, he should be at liberty to do so. Rachel Quackenbush † abjured the English religion, and Lieut. Stoddert could not persuade her to return. The negro, Frement, was held on the principle that negroes were slaves in all countries, and that the English had acted upon that principle, and an instance was given wherein they had so acted. Vort, Phillipson, and T. Volmer had made abjuration, and desired to remain with the Iroquois. Vort, or as his name is elsewhere written, Fort, belonged by adoption to a sister of a chief named Agouareche. She refused to give him up at any price, though it does not appear that Stoddert was provided with any means for paying a ransom, as his instructions were only to exchange prisoners. But Capt. Van Schaick offered six hundred *livres* for Fort without succeeding in obtaining him. On the contrary, so determined was his squaw owner to retain him, that she said she would obey the French commandant and deliver him up, but that she and her husband

---

* His surname does not appear in our documents, though they inform us he was an Englishman by birth, and that he was captured near Caskebee [Casca Bay] in 1746.

† Another (whether of the same family is unknown) Marthy *Quaquinbush*, taken at Saratoga, Nov. 17th, 1745, died a prisoner at Quebec, Dec. 7th, 1746. Two men of the same surname, Jacob and Isaac, father and son, died there, both on the same day, May 26th, 1747. They also had been taken at Saratoga, Nov. 17th, 1745.

would follow him, and he should not reach home alive. The authorities therefore thought it best not to urge the matter further. Suitzer was living at the Falls of St. Louis, and did not desire to leave his Indian associates. J. Volmer, Nicolson, and Piper, were at the Lake of the Two Mountains, with the Iroquois and Nipissings. These Indians refused to give them up, because "they loved them very much." Nicolson was disposed to leave them, but was not permitted to do so. C. Volmer was at the Lake of the Two Mountains, and when he returned to Montreal he was to be allowed to go home if he inclined to do so. The captive John [———] lived with the St. Francis Indians, by one of whom he was captured. John refused to be delivered up, and Lieut. Stoddert, who understood the Indian language, visited him and tried to persuade him to go home with him, but without avail; said "he had been instructed in the Catholic, apostolic, and Roman religion, in which he wished to live and die." Edward Cheaole had married a squaw among the Lorette Hurons, and desired to remain with them.

Lieut. Stoddert left Canada on the 28th of June with his twenty-four prisoners. He was to proceed to Fort St. Frederic, having given the Marquis de la Jonquière a receipt for them, purporting that he was to send to the governor of New York, requesting him to forward "all the prisoners, both French and Indians, in his hands, to Mr. Lydieus, and give orders to the officer who shall have charge of them to send me an express on their arrival at that place, to inform me thereof, and to tarry one day, so that they may be exchanged, one against another, at the foot of the Great Carrying Place of Lake St. Sacrament, whither I will repair in order to conclude the reciprocal exchange of the French and English prisoners."*

* *Colonial History of New York*, vol. X, 209-15.

APPENDIX A.

(Page 29.)

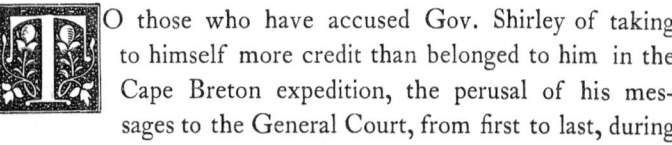O those who have accused Gov. Shirley of taking to himself more credit than belonged to him in the Cape Breton expedition, the perusal of his messages to the General Court, from first to last, during it, is earnestly commended. Space cannot be allowed here for all of them, but the following are fair specimens of the whole. They are elegant compositions, and will compare favorably with the best parliamentary speeches of the time; and as to their accuracy in statements of facts, there can be no space for a question.

On April 3d, 1745, Gov. Shirley made the following communication to the "Gentlemen of the Council and House of Representatives: In pursuance of the resolution of this Court for forming an expedition against the French settlements on Cape Breton, passed the 25th of January last, which is agreeable to His Majesty's pleasure signified to me upon the present rupture with France, 'That I should take all opportunities, as depended upon me, to distress and annoy the French in their settlements, trade and commerce.' I have raised three thousand volunteers, under proper officers to be employed in His Majesty's service upon that expedition, two thousand eight hundred of which by the 24th day of last month, and the remainder within two days after were embarked, and sailed for Canso, where they were to be joined with three hundred and fifty troops more, raised by the government of New Hampshire for the same service, upon my application to Gov. Wentworth, and to proceed from thence by the first favorable opportunity to Chappeaurouge Bay, to which place I expect they will be followed some time this week by five hundred troops more from Connecticut, raised likewise for the same service by that government, upon my application to them. And after the most diligent and exact inquiry into the state of the enemy's forces and fortifications upon that island, from persons intimately acquainted with both, I have endeavored to form such a plan of operations to be executed immediately upon the landing of our troops there, as may, I hope, with the blessing of Divine Providence upon His Majesty's arms, render our attempts against the enemy under their present circumstances, successful, provided our naval forces shall prove sufficient to hinder them from being reinforced in the meantime with recruits and supplies from France. For preventing which, as well as to cut off all intelligence from the enemy, and intercept any provision vessels which might arrive to them from other parts, I sent away, near three weeks ago, three ships of twenty guns each, two snows of sixteen guns, and an armed brigantine of near the same force (which, together with some other vessels of war, are employed by this government in the service of the present expedition) well manned and equipped, with orders to cruise before the harbor of Louisbourg till the arrival of our land forces at Cape Breton, after which those vessels will be immediately joined by Captain Rouse in a snow of twenty-four guns, and the Connecticut colony sloop, in order to block up the enemy's harbor more closely. And that I might procure as strong an armament by sea as well as land, as may be upon this occasion, I not only applied to the neighboring

governments of New England, New York, the Jersies and
Pennsylvania to furnish their respective quotas of sea as well
as land forces for this enterprise in the common cause, but to
the commanders of His Majesty's ships of war stationed in
these parts for their assistance also, as far as His Majesty's
service in their several stations would admit; and particularly
apprised Commodore Warren by an express sent to Antigua,
of the whole scheme of the expedition, representing to him the
advantages we have over the enemy at present; and that for
securing the success against them, 'it was necessary that we
should have a sufficient naval force before the harbor of Louisbourg by the middle of March at farthest (if possible), not only
to intercept the enemy's provision vessels, but Monsieur Du
Vivier, who was expected by that time with recruits and supplies for the enemy's garrison, and perhaps some troops designed
against Annapolis Royal, under convoy of a fifty-four and sixty
gun ship; the intercepting of which would be a killing blow to
the town and garrison of Louisbourg; but that it would be
impossible for us to muster up here a sufficient naval force for
that purpose without the assistance of two fifty or forty gun
ships;' and therefore pressing him in the strongest terms, 'if
he could possibly spare two such from the squadron under his
command, to dispatch them away instantly upon the receipt of
my express; and that if he could not spare two such ships, he
would assist us with one, which might, perhaps, be sufficient,
as I was in hopes from advice I received from England, that
one, if not two, of His Majesty's ships of war might be expected to arrive here with stores for New Hampshire and Annapolis Royal by the middle of March, though I could make
no absolute dependence upon that.' And as His Majesty's ship
the Bien Amiè prize, Captain Grayton commander, then and

still in this harbor, and which I understood was sent here, partly to load with masts of such dimensions as could not be got ready before the latter end of June, 'I desired that we might have the assistance of that ship for the expedition, or Mr. Warren's orders to His Majesty's ships stationed at Virginia, for that purpose;' and requesting that what ships he sent us might proceed directly to Canso; for which purpose I sent him two skillful pilots, and apprising him that I should send His Majesty an account of the expedition by a Bristol vessel the day following. In answer to this letter I received another from Mr. Warren, dated February 24th, by return of the express boat, which arrived at Boston the 19th of last March, wherein he informed me, that 'he should be very glad to be employed in this expedition, but that the unhappy loss of the Weymouth,* in which ship he should have come here some time in March, pursuant to his orders to attend on New England, had prevented him; that he had sent my letters and scheme by a vessel of war express to the Admiralty, by the return of which to Antigua he should, no doubt, receive full instructions for his future proceedings; and that in the mean time he should, in a very few days, dispatch the Launceston to attend on New England, and the Mermaid to New York, pursuant to his directions from the Rt. Hon. the Lords Commissioners of the Admiralty.' And by the same express boat Capt. Gayton received orders from Com. Knowles, which have prevented him from assisting us with his ship in the expedition. Since this (five days ago) I have received two other letters from Mr. Warren, dated the

---

* She was a sixty gun ship, Captain Warwick Calmady, cast away at the Leeward Islands in 1744, having been run aground through the ignorance of the pilot, as appeared by the evidence at a court-martial, for which he was sentenced to two years' imprisonment in the Marshalsea. The crew were saved. *Ed.*

9th and 15th of last month; the first at Antigua, and the latter from on board the Superbe, informing me 'that on the 8th of last month His Majesty's sloop Hind arrived at Antigua, and brought him orders to proceed with the Superbe, Launceston, and Mermaid, without loss of time, to Boston; on his passage to which place he was at the writing of his last letter, in the latitude of 22°; and that he hoped soon to arrive at Nantasket road, and concert such measures with me as may conduce most to the protection of the colonies and trade, and the carrying on of His Majesty's service in general.' Upon the receipt of which I dispatched a letter by a schooner sent express to meet him, apprising him of the departure and state of our land and sea forces, and recommending to him to send one of his ships at least forthwith before Louisbourg, to join our cruisers there, without coming first to Nantasket, which I apprehend to be of great consequence to His Majesty's service. And I am now in hourly expectation of hearing further of Mr. Warren, and the ships under his command, and hope they may come in time to secure success to the present expedition, which, according to the ordinary course of human events, may be looked on as most probable, if these ships shall arrive seasonably before Louisbourg.

"Gentlemen: As I am persuaded it must be a satisfaction to you to be informed of these several steps hitherto taken for conducting this important enterprise, with the success of them, I have been induced to be the more particular in my account of the success of my endeavors for procuring a sufficient naval force for the service of it. And I may assure you that no vigilance or attention has or shall be wanting in me to make the other necessary dispositions for the support of it with all possible dispatch, and to make the event of it answer the great ends proposed by it for His Majesty's service, and the general interests of his British dominions, as well as the particular interests of New England, and the other British colonies on this continent, and to provide a safe retreat for our forces on any extraordinary emergency that may require it. In the meantime it must afford you the highest satisfaction to observe the particular regard which His Majesty's ministers have shown for the protection of these colonies by their beforementioned orders to Commodore Warren, and the warm assurances I received from His Majesty's governors in the colonies of New York, the Jersies, and Pennsylvania, of their most hearty endeavors to engage the colonies under their respective governments in the support of the common cause upon this occasion, have given me great encouragement to proceed in the expedition, towards securing the success whereof I immediately received from Gov. Clinton, upon my request to him for that purpose, a considerable train of artillery, without which we could not have had the same prospect of reducing the island as we now have.

W. Shirley

APPENDIX B.

(Page 69.)

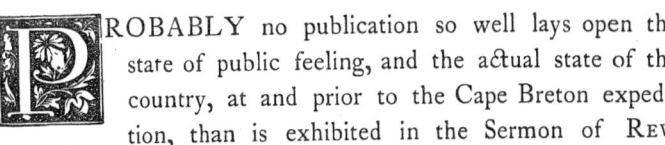ROBABLY no publication so well lays open the state of public feeling, and the actual state of the country, at and prior to the Cape Breton expedition, than is exhibited in the Sermon of REV. THOMAS PRINCE, preached in the Old South Meetinghouse in Boston, on a Thanksgiving, appointed for that occasion, just one month and one day after the surrender of Louisbourg. That performance is thus entitled: "*Extraordinary Events the Doings of* GOD, *and marvellous in Pious Eyes.— Illustrated* in a SERMON on the GENERAL THANKSGIVING, Thursday, *July* 18, 1745. Occasioned by taking the City of *Louisbourg* on the Isle of *Cape Breton*, by *New England* Soldiers, assisted by a *British* Squadron. Psal. xcviii. O sing unto the Lord a new Song, [etc.] BOSTON: *Printed* for D. HENCHMAN in *Cornhill.* 1745."

The Dedication follows entire:* "To His Excellency WILLIAM SHIRLEY, ESQ; Captain General and Governour in Chief in and over His MAJESTY's Province of the *Massachusetts Bay* in *New England*, and Vice Admiral of the same: Your *Excellency* being, under the Divine Conduct, the principal *Former and Promoter* of the prosperous *Expedition* to *Cape Breton;* of such vast Importance to the Trade, Wealth, and Power of Great Britain, as well as Safety of Her American Colonies; and so much to the Glory wherewith GOD has crowned His

---

* Capitalized and italicised according to the original.

188   *Taking of Louisbourg.*   [APPENDIX.

MAJESTY's happy Reign: The following SERMON is, in Gratitude and Justice, with all Submission, DEDICATED by your EXCELLENCY's *Most obliged, Obedient Humble Servant,*

"THOMAS PRINCE."

After a philosophical introduction, in which the author hints at the influences of good angels and bad angels on the actions of men, and gives Satan a recognition in the management of affairs, he proceeds : " But we must hasten on to APPLY these things, in pursuance of our first design, to the *great* and extraordinary *occasion* of this happy Solemnity : A surprising course of Providence has led us into a most adventurous enterprise against the French settlements at Cape Breton, and their exceeding strong city of Louisbourg, for warlike power the pride and terror of these northean seas ; and by a wonderous series and happy coincidences of various means, delivered them into our hands. And this in a most signal manner, is the LORD's doings in the present day ; and is truly marvellous in every pious, yea, I may say, in every unprejudiced and considerate eye.

" The island belonged originally to the British empire : * was at first comprised in the general name and grand patent of New England in 1620; but in the following year set off and included in Nova Scotia by a separate patent ; and since, in Nova Scotia comprehended in the royal charter of the Massachusetts province in 1691. It abounds in the best of pit coal known in

---

* Assuming that the English first discovered it, which the French never admitted. "On [the English] prétend que les Cabots reconnurent l'Isle de Terre Neuve . . . . cependant de bons auteurs assuré qu'ils n'avoient débarqué en aucun endroit," *et cet. Charlevoix*, II, ix. *Ed.*

See also Lahontan *Nouveaux Voyages*, II, 7, who says : " Il y a plus d'un siecle et demi que le Canada a été decouverte ; Jean Verasan sut le premier qui le découvrit, mais à son malheur, car les sauvages le mangerent." *Edition la Haye*, 1705, page 7, vol. II. *Editor.*

America; and so near the surface of the earth and coast of the sea, as to be very easily dug and put in vessels. Yea, from 1703, Lahontan had told us* of the French ships loading with and carrying the same to Guadaloupe and Martinico, for the refining of sugars, to their great advantage. And its commodious harbors; with its happy situation in the center of our fishery, at the entrance of the bay and river of Canada, and in the wake of all the trade from Europe to the British colonies on the main land, of [North] America, and both from them and our West India Islands to Europe, rendered the place of such vast importance." †

It will be very difficult for the casual reader of the present day to have even a slight appreciation of the situation in which our fathers saw themselves at the period of this French war. The resources of their immediate country had scarcely begun to be known; coal had not been discovered, and although the abundance of wood rendered it almost useless, yet they doubtless looked forward to a time when coal would be of consequence, as it had long been in England and other parts of Europe. To look upon Nova Scotia as a *central* position to the country in our time would excite a smile. But at that period the country to the westward of Boston was mostly a wilderness.

---

* This reference to Lahontan is not very intelligible. The author probably meant *before* 1703, instead of *from* 1703. *Editor*.

† "I remember while in England, when we came to know the Tory Ministry had by the treaty of Utrecht in 1713, resigned it to the French, all true-hearted Britons who knew the circumstance of the island, most grievously lamented the resignation, as full of teeming mischief to the British trade, wealth, and power, and as one of the most fatal acts of that unhappy ministry." *Prince*. Up to this period much had been written on "The Importance of Cape Breton:" that the French annually employed 1,000 vessels in the fishery, of 200 to 400 tons, and 20,000 men; curing 5,000,000 quintals of fish. In 1730 they carried to Marseilles alone, 2,200,000 quintals. *Amer. Magazine*, II, 216. *Ed.*

New York was of small account, and places further westward amounted to very little, and were almost entirely confined to the mouths of rivers upon the sea coast. The West, the GREAT WEST was practically unknown.

"The French well knowing the vast advantage of their acquisition, have built a walled city on the most convenient port both for trade and fortification; for these thirty years been adding to its natural and artificial strength; and by immense sums and the utmost art and dilligence, made it one of the strongest fortresses in America, if not in Europe; such as was not like to be taken without a very powerful, skillful and resolute army both by sea and land, or being starved to a surrender. In short, it was the Dunkirk of North America, and in some respects of greater importance.

"For, by means of this island and fortification, the French have every year enlarged their fishery, and thereby their trade, wealth and shipping; and by fishing cheaper than we, they have more and more commanded the trade of Spain, Portugal, and Italy; drawn away their gold and silver, and greatly diminished our trade and fishery, a principal source both of the British wealth and naval power.

"So pernicious a settlement was this, that for above these twenty years, it has seemed to me, it were worth the while to engage in a war with France, if it were for nothing else but to recover this most important island to the British empire.*

---

* This was a rather hard philosophy, in view of its source. It is the same as though a man, having sold an article at too low a price, should knock down the purchaser, take the commodity sold and make off with it! As old Thomas Fuller would say, "This might do in sea divinity, but justice is quite another thing." If Queen Anne's ministers made a foolish bargain, it is a sorry argument to base a murderous war upon. It is the argument made use of by small boys about their playthings. It certainly comes with bad grace from our author. *Ed.*

Though a war was dreadful, the necessity and hazard seemed every year to increase; the longer it was deferred, the more powerful and dangerous they grew, and the less our hope of their being ever reduced.

"At length, without our seeking, and in the most critical time, the LORD was pleased to leave them to precipitate a war upon us. An unexpected season opens to make the dangerous trial, if the ALMIGHTY would please to prosper us. And now all the northern colonies, and ours especially, began to feel their destructive power and influence. In a few months' time infesting our coasts, taking our shipping, ruining our fishery and trade, destroying Canso, invading Annapolis, reducing us to straits, and carrying our people into a place almost impregnable. [Louisbourg.] And as it was a source of privateers and men of war distressing to us, it was also a safe resort both of their West and East India fleets, to their great advantage in returning homeward. Of such vast importance was this strong port of our enemies; and this possessed by one of the most enterprising, powerful, and active nations.

"But in the wisdom of GOD, the stronger it grew, the better in the issue for us. The French having built a regular city, and laid out immensely more to render it both strong and commodious, than we should, if the place had been in our power. Yea, it seems most likely, that if they had not possessed it, there would neither have been a battery, nor even a house in the port to this day;* no more than in many fine harbors of

---

* Had the author written this at a much later period, he could not have made a truer prediction. After it fell into the hands of the English in 1758, it was demolished, and has never since been anything but the residence of a few fishermen with some farms of little importance. See Parsons's *Life of Pepperrell*, 332, 333. See also Halliburton's *Hist. Nova Scotia*, II, 214-218. *Ed.*

Nova Scotia; which though so near the fishery, have been neglected by us for so many years, from the peace of Utrecht. But now, in a few weeks' time, the sovereign GOD has pleased to give us the fruits of these thirty years' prodigious art, labor, and expense of our enemies; and this by means of so small a number, less than four thousand land men, unused to war, undisciplined, and that had never seen a siege in their lives.

"Let us therefore look into the wondrous scenes of providence, and see some of the various and surprising steps which led to the happy acquisition: 1. Our enemies, being left of GOD, in opposition to all rules of policy, but in too early confidence of their sufficient growth of power, while engaged with the queen of Hungary, to hurry into a war with us; while their trading ships were mostly abroad, their navy not so well prepared, and ours by the previous war with Spain, equipped and ready to employ its power for our defense and their annoyance; it seems in as happy a juncture as we could wish for; without which we should not have had the advantage or opportunity which they have opened to us.

"2. The people of Cape Breton early and suddenly seizing Canso, invading Annapolis, and M. De Vivier going to France for additional forces by sea and land, to renew the assault in the spring of the year; were improved by GOD as a means of rousing us up with the sense of danger, and of exciting our Governor to implore the KING for some naval help; without which it seems that commodore Warren with his three ships of war had not been ordered from our West India Islands to New England; though then, I suppose, without any special view to this important enterprise.

"3. By the Cape Bretoners taking and carrying so many of our people into their harbor and city, they were obliged to return them to us; whereby we came to be more acquainted with their situation and the proper places of landing and attacking. And at the same time it is in the issue happy they were not fully aware of the prodigious strength of the fortifications, or of the great number of men within and near them, or we never had presumed on such an enterprise. Yea, it is happy that some few, who better knowing the place, gave the more exact accounts and spake discouraging; yet we were so set on sending, they were not regarded.

"4. God was pleased to give last summer a great plenty of provision to our northern colonies, whereby we were this spring prepared to supply so great an armament, and at the same time cut short the crops in Canada and the French West India Islands; whereby it was apprehended that those at Cape Breton were considerably straitened, and that both the Canada French and Indians were hindered the last year from troubling our inland borders.

"5. By our account of the uneasiness of the Switzers there, for want of pay and provision; and the call and wants of their East and West India fleet in the Fall of the year, and their supplies with men and victuals, if not ammunition, it was represented the remaining French were further weakened; and we were the more encouraged. And it was further remarkable, that their store ships from France in the Fall came so late on their coast, and the winter there set in so early and fierce, as to keep them out of their harbor and drive them off to Martineco.

"6. From the sanguine representations made by our returned captives, of the easiness of our taking the place by an early surprisal before any help could come, either from France or Canada, God was pleased to lead our Governor, vigilant and active for our safety and welfare, into the project; and early forming the scheme, in the most timely season, in the midst of Winter, when our intercourse abroad was sealed up, to move and press it on the General Assembly; and after, in convenient time, on our neighboring governments; and with wonderous resolution, circumspection and assiduity to pursue the same.

"7. Though when the affair was first proposed to the General Court, the difficulties seemed so great, and the expense so sinking to this poor people, that they saw no light to venture without a powerful, previous help from England; yet, upon further representations, that the season would likely be lost forever, &c., the affair was unexpectedly reconsidered: And the sovereign GOD so over-ruled the absence of divers worthy representatives, who judged it too vast an undertaking for us, that, it is said, the final resolution for it, on January 25, was just carried by one majority; and even that and other votes had been lost, if the superior greatness of the expense had been then imagined; it soon abundantly exceeded their expectations.

"When the General Court had agreed on this great enterprise, it is surprising to think, with how profound a secrecy so many members in the center of so populous, observing, and inquisitive a town as this, for so many days, kept their consultations, until the various parts of the plan were settled, committees chosen, and all things ripe for enlisting soldiers, hiring vessels, buying materials and provisions: and as surprising to see with what a general silence all these things were done in this city and land; and the army and fleet equipped and ready to sail, while the rest of the world had scarce any intelligence of our preparations.

"9. As soon as ever the design was known among us, it was a marvelous thing, that when this province had lately lost so many hundred men, volunteers in the sad expedition to Carthagena* (not one in ten being left alive to return), their wives left widows and their children orphans, yet to see so many likely men, and I conclude the most of them owners of lands and houses, or heirs of the same, and many religious, in all our towns, readily listing even as private soldiers; with the small wages of twenty-five shillings (new tenor) a month, to leave their gainful farms and trades, as well as parents, wives and children; all as free volunteers, to serve their GOD, their king and country, in this hazardous enterprise. Yes, more to list than the court desired; and that so many men of distinguished figure should cheerfully offer themselves — even four of his majesty's council;† as also the Hon. Deputy Governor of Connecticut colony,‡ and divers others of public esteem and character.

"10. It was wonderful also to see that during those two usually stormy months of February and March, the only season for our preparation, God was pleased to give us such a constant series of moderate and fair weather, as in that time of the year has scarce ever been known among us. So that there was hardly any impediment to our officers going about and enlisting, our soldiers in marching, or our vessels in fitting, or our coasters in bringing us provisions, or our committee of war,§ in their various preparations, until all were ready to sail.

* That pestilential expedition was in 1740, under Admiral Vernon. There were in the expedition, according to good authority, 27,000 men, of whom 15,000 were seamen. The English loss, chiefly by sickness, was about 20,000 men! *Ed.*

† Colonel Pepperrell, Samuel Waldo, Joseph Dwight, and Jeremiah Moulton. *Editor.*

‡ Roger Wolcot, Esq. He was the second in command of the land forces, was a native of Windsor in Connecticut, and attained a high military rank. He died at the advanced age of eighty-eight, May 17th, 1767. His father was Henry W., and his mother was Martha, sister of Gov. William Pitkin. Oliver W., signer of the Declaration of Independence, was his son. *Ed.*

§ Instead of a commissary general, an officer appointed by the governor, a committee of war was chosen by the two houses out of their own members. *Hutchinson*, II, 412. *Ed.*

"11. The extraordinary thought, contrivance, order, management, and quick dispatch, not only of his Excellency, but also of our Council of War, seems wonderful; that gentlemen unused to such affairs, should, in two months time, think of and get ready everything suitable for so great and various an armament by sea and land; so that nothing proper seems to have been omitted. And I have heard some express themselves with wonder to see how things would happen; just as they wanted some kinds of materials or provisions, an unexpected vessel would come in and bring them.

"12. It was also wonderful, that though the small-pox, which has been so fatal and dreadful to us, came into this town [Boston] and harbor, as our troops were coming in, both by land and water, and continued all the time they were quartering and anchoring here, very few of the officers and soldiers having had it, and we were full of anxious apprehensions; yet, it neither hindered them, nor did the dangerous infection spread among them; which, in that critical juncture would, after all, have wholly overthrown the enterprise.

"And now our army of three thousand land soldiers, with all kinds of stores being ready to sail on the 20th of March, in about a hundred vessels, besides five hundred soldiers more sent from Connecticut, and three hundred and fifty from New Hampshire, we had almost every gloomy prospect to make us tremble: for our inland borders were now left bare of a great part of their strength, by listing of so many of their able men volunteers in the expedition. And if the enterprise succeeded, the heavy debt would almost sink us. But if, for our offences, God were carrying forth a great part of the flower of the country to be destroyed, a most dismal scene of ruin seemed to follow! They were to sail five hundred miles to the enemy's island, in a raw and stormy time of the year. And if the feared infection had taken place and should break out among them, especially after their landing, what a general terror would seize them from the hand of God which there was no resisting, and in what a miserable case would they be!* A naval power with stores and disciplined troops were also early expected there from France to conquer Nova Scotia. And after all the labors of our unwearied Governor, to obtain some men of war from our neighboring colonies and West India Islands to come and protect and help us, our hopeful prospects seemed to dwindle away, and we could do no other but that, if two sixty gun ships of our enemies, which were early expected, should arrive before we took the place, they would soon make our fleet and army captives, and then what would become of this country!

"So they must run the most desperate hazards. The hearts of many of the wisest ashore now seemed to fail. Some repented they had voted for it, and others that they had ever promoted it. Some judged it best after all for every man to go home; and the thoughtful among us were in great perplexity. But yet a wonder it was to see, that those who were venturing into the danger, seemed to be fullest of trust in GOD and courage. Many filled their vessels with prayers; and asking ours, they threw themselves into the divine protection, in the name of GOD they set up their banners, and away they sailed. Pray for US, and we will fight for YOU, was the valiant and endearing language wherewith they left us.

---

* In one day, March 5, the small-pox appeared in three different parts of the town. No care was taken to remove the levies to some of the many convenient islands in the bay. Miraculously, by the care of some guardian angel or genius, they escaped the infection. It was lately imported in Capt. Snelling's ship, which was taken into the service of the expedition. *Douglass.* Ed.

"Such were some of the remarkable steps which led to the dangerous enterprise. We come now to the more surprising ones which succeeded therein to the happy accomplishment:—

"1. As it was very encouraging to think how many pious and prayerful persons were embarked in the cause, which we accounted the cause of GOD and his people; it gave further ground of hope, to see such a spirit of Supplication given to many in this town and land on this occasion. For besides the solemn days of public and general prayer appointed by these three governments,* there were particular days observed in several congregations. There were also in divers towns religious societies, some of women as well as others of Men, who met every week, more privately to pray for the preservation and success of their countrymen. And I have been well informed of their extraordinary fervency, faith and wrestlings, as so many Jacobs in this important season. Psalm CVIII, 10-13, was usually among our petitions: As also 'That GOD would preserve, direct and spirit our friends, and surprise and terrify our enemies, and in such a manner as the work and glory might appear to be his alone.'

"2. God then began in a remarkable manner to hear our prayers, in that when so many vessels sailed from hence and from New Hampshire and Connecticut, in such a turbulent time of the year, through a course of five hundred miles on the ocean, they every one arrived at Canso, the place of Concourse, about fifty miles on this side Cape Breton, without the loss of more than one soldier and three seamen, and but fifteen sick;†

---

* They were New Hampshire, Massachusetts and Connecticut, probably. Rhode Island was hardly allowed to be a Christian community, by many in those days, yet they were glad enough of its help in fighting Indians and Frenchmen. *Editor.*

† This was the report of Gen. Pepperrell in a letter to Governor Shirley, as communicated to the General Court,

and time enough to meet together and refresh themselves, and get into order for their descent at Louisbourg.

"3. It was remarkable also, that God was pleased to keep our enemies' shore and harbor environed with ice longer than usual; so that none of their vessels could enter nor go forth for intelligence, till our twenty gun cruisers (which our Governor sent above a fortnight before the rest of the fleet) came thither; and that some of their vessels coming early to them, both before and after the harbor was open, were happily intercepted and taken by ours; whereby our enemies within failed of their supplies, and we were recruited by those without.

"4. That by a most gracious, seasonable and wonderful Direction of GOD, through our Governor's solicitation* the Fall before, the brave and active Commodore Warren, a great friend of these plantations, is ordered by the government in England, to come immediately with three men of war from Antego to Boston; that on his voyage hither, near Cape Sables, on April 12, he met with a fisherman, who informed him of our army's being gone to Canso the week before; that on board the fisherman there was one of the best pilots, who had got out of the way of our committee of war, to avoid being pressed for the service; that though the Commodore wanted fresh provision

April 25. The general said he had reviewed the forces on Canso Hill, and found them in good health; that Capt. Donahew had taken three Indians, from whom he had learned that the French and Indians had intended to make a fresh attack on Annapolis, and that Mons. Duvivier, with two ships of war from France, was expected to join them. *Ed.*

* It will all along be seen that nothing by way of a wise precaution was wanting in Gov. Shirley. As little was left to chance, apparently, as in any similar expeditions, whatever writers have said to the contrary. It is a very cheap kind of wisdom to foresee what would have been the result of an undertaking if a deluge or an earthquake had intervened. If it was providential that neither of these happened, it is equally providential that the internal fires of the earth were quiet during the Louisbourg campaign. *Ed.*

and clothes for his men in so cold a climate and season, he wisely considered the necessitous case of our army, took the pilot, generously tacked about, went after them, overtook them at Canso, to their great joy; and, instead of stopping, passed on to watch the harbor of Louisbourg, that no supply from Canada, Martinico or France might slip into it; without all which a sixty-four gun ship with near six hundred men and full stores had entered, and this great affair had soon been defeated.*

"5. That the Commodore, by the fishermen sent his order for the king's ships that should be found in these parts, forthwith to follow him; that the fisherman timely arriving, our Governor immediately sent the order to a forty gun ship at Piscataqua ready to convoy the mast fleet for England; and though she was got to sea, yet by a boat the order reached her; and sending her fleet into harbor, she bore after the Commodore and quickly joined him. So that our army before they sailed from Canso, had the comfort of four men of war to protect and help them.

"6. That though our fleet and army stayed near three weeks at Canso, within twenty leagues of Louisbourg, and within sight of their island,† yet the people there knew nothing of it till early in the morning of April 30, when they were so surprised to see us, that they had no time to get in the fresh provision and force of the neighboring country to help them. It seems very wonderful, that none of the French or Indians near Canso should happen to see us, and give our enemies intelligence of us. And, when our fleet and army were complete

---

* It is by no means certain that the arrival of this ship would have defeated the capture. It might have retarded it. See *ante*, p. 72. *Ed.*

† The Gut of Canso, separating Nova Scotia from Cape Breton, is "very narrow;" and as it is of very unequal width, geographers do not give us even an average of it. *Ed.* It is six leagues in length. See *Douglass*, I, 346. *Ed.*

and ready, the ice went off at once, and the winds and weather conspired to favor our descent on the island.*

"7. It is also remarkable that the French had made no fortification at the place of our landing, though it is said they designed it, and were preparing for it. And though they had six hundred regular troops, and about fourteen hundred other men in the city, that yet they should make so small an opposition at our going on shore: That GOD so encouraged and helped the few who landed first and engaged them, as to beat them away with the loss of eight of their men slain, several wounded, and ten taken captive, without the loss of one of ours; that thereby he struck terror into our enemies; And though our people were so eager of landing, they were ready to quarrel to get into the boats, and the surf ran high, yet all our army landed safely, without oversetting a boat or losing a man.†

"8. That he moved them to improve the time, and forthwith march up five miles through a thickety, rocky, hilly and boggy country, and enclose the city; that in the following night he led some of our soldiers through strange places to the storehouses near the Grand Battery which was strongly fortified with walls and ditches, and at each end a very thick bombproof tower; that the store-houses, full of combustible matter, being set on fire burnt and flashed in a horrible manner, and in

---

* Pious men saw the immediate hand of Divine Providence in all this. *Hutchinson. Ed.*

† The forces under Admiral Boscawen, Sir Charles Hardy, and Gen. Amherst, found things vastly changed when they were sent to retake the place thirteen years later. The men led by Wolfe, Whitmore, and Lawrence, were not less eager to land, though in the face of fortifications which made terrible havoc among them; besides the drowning of twenty-two men by the staving of boats. *Editor.*

the night increased the enemy's terror; that the wind also bearing a prodigious black smoke upon them, in which expecting our army to enter, they were every soul frighted out of it into the city; and that in the morning, but thirteen of our men observing there was neither flag flying, nor chimney smoking, nor person appearing, but the gates open, ventured in and took possession.*

"9. That yet the enemy aware of their fatal error, soon after came with forces in many *shallowaes*† to recover it; but eight of the thirteen going out of the battery, and meeting with about eight more of our friends, ran to the water side, and so plied the boats with small arms, as damped and hindered them, till seeing more of our forces coming, the boats turned back to the town again. If they had come but one hour sooner, they had regained the battery before we found it deserted. And thus this strong fortress of thirty-two great cannon (thirty of them forty-two pounders), which might alone have maintained itself against all our army, the Lord delivered into our hands, without the loss of a man, or shot of a gun, and before we demanded it; whereby He at once saved us both time, toil, and blood, and surprisingly gave us a great power over the harbor, as well as so many of the largest of the enemy's cannon, with a great number of their own balls and bombs to improve against them.

"10. That our army was preserved from the dangerous infection; and though being open to the air, fogs and dews, upon the melting of the ice, in a raw climate and season of the year, the camp dysentery seized many, yet some of our physi-

---

* This was Col. Vaughan's exploit. It will be found differently reported in APPENDIX D.

† Perhaps flat bottomed boats. The only instance of the occurrence of the word recollected. *Ed.*

cians, in their letters signified, that it looked almost miraculous they should so soon and generally, without means, recover.*

" 11. That they should be inspired with wondrous courage, eagerness, activity, and unfainting strength ; be supported under their extraordinary and constant toils, fatigues, and labors, in carrying stores, drawing cannon over hills and vallies, among rocks and through morasses, up to the middle in mire ; and digging trenches, raising batteries, firing shot and bombs almost incessantly, both day and night, against the city ;† and that God so speedily 'taught their hands to war, and their fingers to fight,' as presently to throw them with great exactness, and do continual execution among our enemies ; dismounting their cannon, beating down their houses, gates, walls, flankers, and greatly distressing them.‡

" 12. That when a new sixty-four gun ship from France, with near six hundred men, and great quantities of arms and stores,

---

* During the siege was constant dry, favorable weather. Next day, June 18, after we had possession of the town, the raining season set in, which, for want of our men being clothed and well lodged, would have broken up the siege. *Douglass. Ed.* These contingencies served a good purpose then and long after.

† Here we may observe, that by the herculean labor of our militia (many of them were used to masting and logging), whose great achievements were most remarkable in quality of pioneers or laborers, they dragged these heavy cannon upon sledges over morasses not practicable by horses or oxen. By good providence they had no occasion to show their conduct and courage in repulsing of soldiers. *Douglass. Ed.*

‡ The transporting the cannon was with almost incredible labor and fatigue, for all the roads over which they were drawn, having here and there small patches of rocky hills, was a deep morass, in which, while the cannon, was upon the wheels, they several times sunk, so as to bury not only the carriages, but the whole body of the cannon likewise. Horses and oxen could not be employed in this service, but the whole was to be done by men themselves, up to the knees in mud ; at the same time the nights, in which the work was done, cold, and for the most part foggy; their tents bad, there being no proper material to be had for tents in New England, at the time the forces were raised. Governor Shirley's *Journal,* page 24. *Ed.*

came so near the mouth of the harbor, and before a fair wind, that two hours more would have given her entrance, she was happily discovered by some of our smaller ships, who led her along to the larger, and soon made her strike, though after near two hours' close engagement, wherein she lost above thirty men, and ours but five.* And though by the fog in the night they lost her, yet in the morning they happily recovered her; to the growing discouragement of the besieged, and our increasing strength and benefit.

"That though to show our dependence on GOD continually, He was pleased to suffer the barbarous Indians twice to surprise and murder some of our people; yet in several land encounters, both with French and Indians, in divers parts of the island, He was pleased to give us the victory.

"That by means of extraordinary quick dispatch of a messenger, our Governor in February sent to the King for naval help. GOD was pleased to send so many men of war, successively, as by the 12th of June, with the 64-gun prize and those who were there before, to amount to eleven, to the sinking fear of the enemy, and the rising joy of our fleet and army; and also to preserve a happy harmony between our various officers.

"That though God was pleased to humble us in defeating our attack in the night, on their strong Island Fort,† yet he

---

* Besides the Superb, the Mermaid, Eltham, Massachusetts Frigate, and Shirley Galley were all in the engagement. Gov. Shirley's *Journal*, page 28. *Ed.*

† This was the most unfortunate part of the whole siege, and was apparently very ill advised. Mr. Prince passes over it altogether too slightly. Dr. Douglass treats it more as it should be treated. He says, "About four hundred men, in whaleboats so thin and light that a few musket balls were sufficient to sink them, rashly attempted the Island Battery, where is bad landing, against thirty guns of twenty-eight pound ball, served by one hundred and eighty men. We lost in this mad frolic, sixty men killed and drowned, and one hundred and sixteen taken prisoners." Ib. 353. *Ed.*

happily guided, and with surprising strength, agility and quickness, helped us to hoist up some of the heaviest cannon and mortars on the Light House Cliff, which overlooked that fort in which they trusted to hinder our entering into their harbor; and then assisted in casting our bombs so exactly, as after the two or three first to throw in every one of the rest, and do such execution as quickly to beat them out of this strong hold they thought impregnable, and frighten the city to a quiet surrender.*

"That God should move them to it in that critical moment, when the navy and army had just agreed on a general, desperate and fierce assault, both by land and water, which was like to be exceeding bloody and of doubtful consequence; for upon the capitulation, when our forces entered the city, and came to view the inward state of its fortifications, they were amazed to see their extraordinary strength and device, and how we had like to have lost the limbs and lives of a multitude, if not have been all destroyed; and that the city should surrender when there was a great body of French and Indians got on the island, and within a day's march to molest us.

"That in all our close and constant assaults and skirmishes, some of our batteries being within pistol-shot of the city, and receiving such a vast number of balls and bombs almost continually by day and by night, we should not have above twenty slain in our batteries, and not above a hundred in all, in so raw a climate and season, and under such fatigues, not loose above a hundred more by sickness. And of so many vessels transporting and cruising, in so many storms in March and April,

---

* June 15th, when the mortar began to play from the Lighthouse battery upon the Island battery, out of nineteen shells, seventeen fell within the fort, and one of them upon the magazine. — Shirley's *Journal*, p. 30. *Ed.*

loose but one,* though this a cruiser of a hundred men, supposed to be overset, is a grievous loss.

"That in the time of the siege, there were many other surprising events in our favor,—such as timely supplies to our army, either by transports or prizes, as we were near to want them ;† that the very balls from our enemy's cannon were of no small service, being as fast almost as they fell catched up and put into ours, and returned with advantage ; that digging a trench to protect our men, and meeting a rock in the way we could not remove it; just as we left it, a bomb from the enemy came down in the most suitable spot, and without any harm, removed it for us.

"That from the army leaving Canso, April 29th, to their landing, April 30th, and during all the siege, there should be such a continual series of fair weather, as was never known in the place before at that time of the year, till their entering into the city, June 17th, and then the clouds to gather blackness and pour down rains for ten days together, which would have spoiled our batteries, filled our trenches, and greatly hindered and disabled us ! It seemed to close the scenes of wonder !

"In the mean while, it is also remarkable, that the North American coasts have been unmolested by both French and

---

*This "one" was the snow Prince of Orange, of sixteen guns, Capt. Smithurst. It is to be regretted that in all the accounts of the Cape Breton expedition which I have consulted, nothing is learned of this serious disaster, but its casual mention.

† "The English, by the situation of their colonies, have had facilities which we do not possess. Boston is only one hundred and sixty to one hundred and eighty leagues distant from Louisbourg ; the passage is usually made in three or four days ; therefore, after landing at Gabarus [Chapeau rouge] Bay, they were within reach of supplies."—*New York Colonial Documents*, x, 4. See, also, Halliburton, *Hist. Nova Scotia*, I, 116.

Spanish West India privateers, till this great affair was ended.* And that by means of Du Vivier's project of taking Annapolis in the Spring or Summer, both our French and Indian enemies have been all this time diverted from our exposed inland borders ; they being drawn to Menis, and to make a trancient show at Annapolis. So he was guided into his mischievous but fruitless project, and to go even to France to promote our safety, and give us an unmolested season for the taking of Louisbourg."

Respecting the combination and continuance of fortunate circumstances which contributed to the capture of Cape Breton, a judicious writer has remarked: " But these circumstances did not lessen the merit of the man who planned, nor of the people who effected the conquest; which exhibited a high spirit of enterprise, and a generous participation in the war of the mother country."†

It was customary at this period, as well as in the earlier periods of the history of New England, to make a providential interposition answerable for whatever fortune befel the country, either good or bad. Hence our amiable author (Prince) has laboriously made it appear, that, in the Louisbourg expedition, more than in all others, the hand of Providence was especially on the side of the English ; that this was a proof that a Papal empire in North America was not to be tolerated by that Providence. That the men who undertook this enterprise against the French, deserved any better success than those who

---

* But they had previously annoyed the English commerce exceedingly; treating the seamen in the most barbarous manner. "Captain Jenkins, master of a Scotch vessel, being rumaged by the Spaniards, they tore part of his ear off, and bid him take it to the English King, and tell him, that they would serve him so, if they had him in their power."— Biggs's *Military History*, page 1.

† Halliburton, *History of Nova Scotia*, I, 120–1.

had before gone on similar attempts under Sir William Phips, Sir Hovenden Walker, and others, is hidden from the scrutiny of the historian.

Had the expedition against Louisbourg been undertaken without orders from Great Britain, as its enemies said, its failure would have been the ruin of the country, as no relief could be expected from the crown. This argument was made use of to prove that it was a visionary undertaking. But it was *not* undertaken without the authority of the British government, as has already been shown. War existed between the two crowns, and the Governors of the respective colonies were ordered to annoy the enemy to the utmost of their ability. Hence the undertaking was in strict compliance with the commands of the government.

APPENDIX C.

Page 72.

THE fortunate interception and capture of the French ship Vigilant, of sixty-four guns, Captain De la Maison Forte, are but incidently mentioned in the published accounts. The capture was of too great importance not to have a very prominent place in the history of this war. It follows here, detailed by Captain Tyng, one who bore a considerable part in the fight, in a letter dated May 23d, 1745, probably on board his ship, the Massachusetts Frigate.

"My last was the 4th of April from Canso; since which I have been at sea, and had no opportunity nor anything material to write about till now.

"I now congratulate you on the good news of our taking a French man of war of sixty-four guns and five hundred men, about three days ago. (She is quite new.)

"The manner of taking her was thus: The Commodore [Warren, in the Superbe of sixty guns], the Eltham [of forty guns, Capt. Durell], and the Launceston [of forty guns, Capt. Calmady*] lay off Louisbourg harbor. Mr. Warren had sent the Mermaid [Capt. Douglas, of forty guns] to cruise further to windward. About one in the afternoon, we saw the Mermaid and the French ship engaged. They were standing right for us, till the Frenchman discovered us to be English. We

---

* The same, doubtless, who lost his ship the year before at the Leeward Islands, as already mentioned. He continued in the service till 1757.

all gave chase, but Rouse, in the Shirley Galley, being ahead, got up with him first, and gave him several broadsides into his stern. Capt. Durell was the next that gave him a broadside. It being very foggy, and night coming on, we steered by the report and flash of the guns. When the brave Commodore got alongside of him, yard arm and yard arm, they fired so briskly, with great guns and small arms, that tore his rigging and sails all to pieces. His intention was to board the Frenchman and mine the Commodore, and to run our men over him, but we could not get up in time; our ship sailing much worse than before we lost our head and bowsprit.

"The Commodore fired one broadside into him after they had struck; he not knowing they had cried for quarters. He shot by him and lost sight of him in the fog. The Eltham and our ship soon after took him in the night for the Commodore, till the Eltham fired, and we upon his bow had an opportunity of firing at him again; the Eltham's guns firing over us, and ours over him, in such manner we were forced to leave off firing. We all lost sight of him in a minute, except the Mermaid, who presently got sight of him again, and sent his boat on board, took the Captain out, and left only four men on board, and thought we had lost her. We lay by the Commodore all night. In the morning it cleared up a little, so that we saw the French ship lie like a wreck, with Capt. Douglas at a little distance from him (who had lost him in the night). We sent all our boats and some men on board, and took the prisoners out, and hope you will have them and about one hundred more in Boston shortly.

"The Frenchman had about thirty-five killed and twenty-six wounded, and on our side not above six; one aboard [me], three in the Mermaid, and two in the Eltham; and most of these by our own guns.*

" EDWARD TYNG."

Upon the capture of this ship (the Vigilant) Doctor Douglass took occasion to make a display of his superior knowledge of naval and other warlike affairs. The following is extracted, not for the value of his opinions, but for some facts then familiarly known, yet not recorded by others. He had the acquaintance of the French commander while that officer was a prisoner at Boston, and learned from him several particulars of much interest. He says of the commander: "M. le Marquis de la Maison Forte was son-in-law to M. Chiconeou, first physician to the French king. This gentleman was too rash in firing; as he met with British men of war, he should have made the best of his way to port, and only have put his men in a posture to prevent boarding, without firing, which stops the ship's way, and have received the fire of our ships silently. Notwithstanding of this misconduct, the Marquis was a man of good sense and observation, he made this good remark; that the French officers of Louisbourg, in bad policy, hindered the English from viewing at all times the strength of their forts; because if the English had been well informed of its strength, the most sanguine, rash, wrong-headed person, if not a natural fool, could not have imagined such a reduction without regular troops, and without artillery." Hence the inference from this historian's assertion is, that Gen. Pepperrell,

* Had the Rev. Mr. Alden seen this letter of Captain Tyng, he would not probably have stated, in his memoir of the captain, that he captured the Vigilant. See *American Epitaphs*, I, 54. Captain Tyng certainly does not make such claim.

Gen. Waldo, Gov. Shirley, and all the officers engaged in the expedition, however experienced in fighting the Indians and French from year to year, and all the prisoners that had been captives at Louisbourg, and had reported upon its fortifications and condition, were "wrong-headed persons if not natural fools!" It is now left for the future reader to judge where the defect of *wrongheadedness* was prominent among the craniums of that day; while it may be conceded that the French commander committed a mistake in attempting to fight the English ships, instead of making all sail for the port without losing any time; but Mons. Maison Forte was fairly surprised, having no knowledge of the large force of ships on the lookout for him. In the *Journal of the Siege of Louisbourg*, is this concise paragraph: "May 21. A letter came to the General from the Commodore, acquainting him he had taken the Vigilant, a French ship of sixty-four guns; besides the Superb, the Mermaid, Eltham, Massachusetts frigate, and Shirley Galley, were all in the engagement, and at the taking of her. Three days after the taking of the Vigilant, Capt. [Richard] Edwards, in the Princess Mary of sixty guns, joined the Commodore; and the next day Capt. [Frederick] Cornwall, in the Hector of forty guns."

APPENDIX D.

Page 81.

 LETTER from William Shirley, Esq., Governor of Massachusetts Bay, to his Grace the Duke of Newcastle, with a journal of the siege of Louisbourg, and other operations of the forces, during the expedition against the French settlements on Cape Breton; drawn up at the desire of the Council and House of Representatives of the Province of Massachusetts Bay; approved and attested by Sir William Pepperell, and the other principal officers who commanded in the said expedition. Published by authority. London: Printed by E. Owen in Warwick Lane, 1746."

Such is the full title of Governor Shirley's authentic narrative of the expedition against Louisbourg. It is an admirably well written document, and would be copied in this appendix had not all, or nearly all its facts been already given in our preceding pages; and it not being our object to go more into this part of the history; a few extracts, however, to show with what admirable clearness the Governor has narrated the facts here follow:

In his "Letter to the Duke of Newcastle," dated October 28th, 1745, he says: "The Council and House of Representatives of the Province, under my government, having taken occasion, in a late address to me, to desire, that upon my arrival here, 'I would give orders, that a full account of the proceedings of the New England forces raised under my commission, for the reduction of Cape Breton, during the late siege of this

place, to the time of its surrender, should be transmitted in the most effectual manner, and as soon as possible to his Majesty.'*
The sum of this account is, that the New England troops having sailed from Canso the 29th of April, till which time they were detained there by the unusual quantity of ice in Chappeau-Rouge-Bay, came to an anchor the next morning, between nine and ten, in the bay, at the distance of about two miles from Flat-Point Cove, where being discovered by the enemy, a party of about one hundred and fifty men were detached from Louisbourg, under the command of Captain Morepang and M. Boularderie, to oppose their landing; that General Pepperell having made a feint to land a party in boats at the Cove, in order to draw the enemy thither, did, by a signal from the vessels, cause those boats suddenly to row back, and join another party of boats under his stern, out of which were landed, at two miles distance from the Cove, about one hundred of our men, before the enemy could come round to oppose them, who, notwithstanding the enemy had the advantage of being covered by their woods, attacked them so briskly, that they killed six of them upon the spot, took as many prisoners (among whom was M. Boularderie), wounded several more, and, after exchanging some shot, put the rest to flight (some of whom were taken prisoners the next day), with the damage sustained on our side, of only two men's being slightly wounded. That two thousand of the troops were landed the same day, and the remainder, being near two thousand more, the day

---

* It was early seen by people of discernment, in New England, that the English naval officers would, or might, through a selfish jealousy, attempt to rob the army of its hard and well earned honors in the expedition. This narrative letter of Governor Shirley was to counteract the effect of any claims which might be made, not warranted by the genuine facts taken on the spot at the time, and amply vouched for by all the chief actors therein.—*Ed.*

following. That on the next day, a detachment of four hundred of our men* marched round to the North-East Harbor, behind the range of hills there, where they burnt all the enemy's houses and stores in that neighborhood, at the distance of about a mile from the Grand Battery, whereby such a terror was struck into them, that the same night they deserted that battery, leaving the artillery, consisting of twenty-eight cannon of forty-two pound shot, and two of eighteen pound, and the ordnance stores belonging to it (except the powder, which they threw into a well), so precipitately that they only spiked up their cannon in a slight manner, without knocking off any of their trunions, or doing other damage to them, and but very little to the carriages. That the next morning, being the third of May, a party of about fifteen or sixteen of our men discovered that the enemy had abandoned the Grand Battery, and drove off a party of them which attempted to reland there that morning, in boats, notwithstanding they stood on the open beach, exposed to the fire of the enemy's cannon from the town, and their musquetry from the boats.† That notwithstanding an incessant fire from the enemy's cannon and mortars in the town, at the distance of five thousand nine hundred and

---

* They marched under cover of night, and were led by Lieutenant-Colonel William Vaughan. The buildings which his party set on fire produced a dense smoke, which the wind carried directly into the Grand Battery. This was the cause of its being abandoned by the enemy. See Belknap's *History New Hampshire* (Farmer's edition), p. 274. The four hundred, or all except thirteen under Vaughan, appear to have retreated after setting fire to the storehouses.

† These "fifteen or sixteen men" were of Vaughan's party, Vaughan himself at the head of them. The enemy were coming to attempt to retake the Grand Battery; "but Vaughan, with his small party, on the naked beach, and in the face of a smart fire from the city and the boats, kept them from landing, till the reinforcement arrived. In every duty of fatigue or sanguine adventure, he was always ready; and the New Hampshire troops, animated by the same enthusiastic ardor, partook of all the labors and dangers of the siege."—*Belknap.*

thirteen feet from it, and from the Island Battery, at the distance of four thousand eight hundred feet, our troops, by the next day cleared three of the cannon in the Grand Battery, which pointed against the town, and returned their fire upon the enemy there, and also from other of the guns, which pointed against the Island Battery, and were by degrees unspiked in a few days.* That our troops, within the compass of twenty-three days from the time of their first landing, erected five facine batteries against the town, consisting of cannon, some forty-two pound shot, and others of twenty-two, and others of nine pound. Mortars of thirteen, eleven, and nine inches diameter, with some cohorns; all which were transported by hand. But notwithstanding these difficulties, and many of the people being barefooted and almost without clothes, by means of this service, in which they had worn them out, and their being taken down with fluxes, so that at one time there were fifteen hundred men incapable of duty, occasioned by their fatigue, they went on cheerfully without being discouraged, or murmuring, and, by the help of sledges, transported the cannon and mortars over these ways, which the French had always thought impassable for such heavy weights, and was indeed

* Some singular incidents, which the general plan of the Governor's narrative did not admit of his going into, are not to be overlooked: a few are here given: "The next morning [after the enemy had been smoked out of the Grand Battery], as Vaughan was returning with thirteen men only, he crept up the hill which overlooked the Battery, and observed, that the chimneys of the barracks were without smoke, and the staff without a flag, with a bottle of brandy, which he had in his pocket (though he never drank ardent spirits), he hired one of his party, a Cape Cod Indian, to crawl in at an embrasure, and open the gate. He then wrote to the General, 'May it please your honor, to be informed, that by the grace of God, and the courage of thirteen men, I entered the Royal Battery, about 9 o'clock, and am waiting for a reinforcement and a flag.' Before either could arrive, one of the men climbed up the staff, with a red coat in his teeth, which he fastened by a nail to the top." Vaughn was a volunteer without command.

APPENDIX.] *Siege and Capture of Louisbourg.* 217

impracticable by any people of less resolution and perseverance, or less experience in removing heavy bodies; and besides this, they had all their provisions and heavy ammunition, which they daily made use of, to bring from the camp over the same way upon their backs.

"To annoy our people in making their approaches, and carrying on their batteries, the enemy erected new works, where they mounted some cannon, from whence, as well as from the cannon of other batteries, and from their mortars, they continually maintained a strong fire, till their cannon was silenced by being dismounted, or having their men beat off by our cannon.

"The most advanced of our five batteries, which was finished on the 17th of May, was within a distance of two hundred and fifty yards from the west gate of the town; so that from this battery several of the enemy were killed by our musquetry, as were some of our men by the enemy's from the walls; and indeed this battery was so near the enemy's works, that our men were obliged to load the cannon there under the fire of their musquetry, which was very sharp on both sides, the enemy generally opening the action every morning with the fire of their small arms upon this battery, for two hours, which was constantly returned with advantage on our side. The execution done from these, and the Grand Battery, was very considerable. The west gate was entirely beat down, the wall adjoining very much battered, and a breach made in it at about ten feet from the bottom of the wall. The Circular Battery of sixteen cannon, twenty-four pounders, near the west gate (and the principal one against ships next to the Grand Battery and Island Battery), was almost entirely ruined, and all the cannon but three, dismounted. Their north-east battery, consisting of two lines of forty-two and thirty-two pounders, in all seventeen

Cc

cannon, another principal battery against ships, was damaged, and the men beat off from their guns. The west flank of the King's Bastion belonging to the citadel, and the battery there of six twenty-four pounders, which pointed to the land side, and greatly annoyed our works, was almost demolished. Two cavaliers of two twenty-four pounders, each raised during the siege, and two other cannon of the same weight of metal, run out at two embrazures, cut through the parapet near the west gate at the same time (all pointing against our batteries), were damaged and silenced. The citadel was very much damaged; several houses in the city entirely demolished, and almost every one more or less hurt; and Maurepas Gate, at the easternmost part of the city, shattered. And as cross fires from the cannon and mortars, and even from our musquetry, ranged through the houses and streets in every part of the city, and through the enemy's parades, whereby many were killed, it drove the inhabitants out of their houses into casemates, and other covered holds, where they were obliged to take refuge for several weeks; and besides this, the fire from the Grand Battery damaged also the barracks of the Island Battery.

"During this time, our parties of scouts so thoroughly ranged the woods, that they seldom returned without bringing in some prisoners,* which very much confined the enemy within their walls, who were constantly worsted in all skirmishes, and repulsed in every sally which they made, and frequently by an inferior number of our men, and with very little loss, upon these occasions, sustained on our side, the chief of which was a party of eighteen of our men straggling contrary to orders,

---

* There were some of our men surprised by the Indians in their straggling in the neighboring woods, and some by going on shore unarmed, as will presently be seen, though the exact date is not learned. *Ed.*

APPENDIX.] *Siège and Capture of Louisbourg.* 219

being surprised and cut off by a large number of Indians, and another of nine, coming on shore out of one of the cruisers to water, without their arms, being likewise surprised and cut off by some Indians.* That on the 26th of May, after some ineffectual preparations for making an attack upon the enemy's Island Battery, which is a strong fort built on a rocky island, at the entrance into the harbor, mounted with thirty cannon of twenty-eight pound shot, and having several swivel guns upon its breast works, and two brass ten inch mortars, and one hundred and eighty men, it was at night attempted by a party of four hundred men in boats ; but from the strength of the place, and the advantage which the enemy had by being under cover, and our men exposed in open boats, the surf running high, our men not being thoroughly acquainted with the best place for landing, and the enemy besides (as is most probable), being apprised of their design, they were repulsed with the loss of having about sixty killed and drowned, and one hundred and sixteen taken prisoners ; yet under these disadvantages, several of them advanced within the enemy's battery, and maintained a fight with them for some time before they surrendered, and killed some of them. That it being judged of the utmost consequence to make ourselves masters of the Island Battery, as it was thought extremely dangerous for his Majesty's ships to have entered the harbor till the enemy could be annoyed in that battery ; and it being after the last attempt thought impracticable to reduce it by boats, it was determined to erect a battery near the Light-House opposite to it, at three thousand four hundred feet distance from it; and the same was, by the 11th of June, notwithstanding the almost insuperable difficulties, which

---

* These two serious disasters are omitted in our author's " Memoirs of the War," published two years later. The particulars should have been given. *Ed.*

attended the drawing of the cannon up a steep bank and rock, raised in such manner, as not to be exposed to more than four of the enemy's cannon, and at the same time to flank a line of above twenty of their guns; and two eighteen pounders were on that day mounted, and began to play, and by the 14th of June, four more cannon of eighteen pound shot were added, and on the 15th, a mortar of thirteen inches diameter was removed thither, out of which nineteen bombs were thrown, seventeen whereof fell within the Island Battery, and one of them upon the magazine; and this, together with the fire from our cannon, to which the enemy was very much exposed, they having but little to shelter them from the shot, which ranged quite through their line of barracks, so terrified them, that many of them left the fort, and ran into the water for refuge. And now the Grand Battery being in our possession, the Island Battery (esteemed by the French the Palladium of Louisbourg), so much annoyed from the Light-House Battery, that they could not entertain hopes of keeping it much longer; the enemy's North-East Battery being damaged, and so much exposed to the fire from our advanced batteries, that they could not stand to their guns; the Circular Battery ruined, and all its guns but three dismounted, whereby the harbor was disarmed of all its principal batteries; the west gate of the city being demolished, and a breach made in the adjoining wall; the west flank of the King's Bastion almost ruined; and most of their other guns, which had been mounted during the time of the siege, being silenced; all the houses and other buildings within the city (some of which were quite demolished) so damaged, that but one among them was left unhurt; the enemy extremely harassed by their long confinement within their casemates, and other covered holds, and their stock of ammunition being almost exhausted, Mr. Duchambon sent out a flag of truce to the camp on the 15th day of June, in the afternoon, desiring time to consider of articles of capitulation, which was accordingly granted them till next morning, when they sent articles in, which were rejected by the General and Commodore, and others proposed by them in their stead, and accepted by the enemy. And hostages being exchanged on the same day for the performance of the articles, on the 17th of June the city was surrendered to Mr. Warren and General Pepperell, and the garrison, consisting of about six hundred and fifty regular troops, and the inhabitants of the city, being about thirteen hundred and sixty effective men, besides women and children, made prisoners by capitulation, with the loss on our side of no more than one hundred and one men killed by the enemy, and all other accidents from the time of their landing to the reduction of the place, and about thirty who died of sickness.*

"I omit mentioning the breaking up of the settlements at St. Peters, and eight other fishing settlements upon this island; and the burning of several houses at St. John's Island within the time of the siege, by companies put on board of some of our cruisers."

On the 12th of September, M. De Beauharnois and M. Hocquart wrote to Count Maurepas: † "You will have been informed, long before this reaches you, of our loss of Louisbourg. The officers of the garrison, and particularly those

---

* M. Duchambon wrote to the Count D'Argenson, August 13th [N. S.] 1745, from Belle Isle Road: "The enemy was greatly superior in number to us, having about thirteen thousand sea and land forces, and I had at the commencement of the siege, including good and bad, but twelve to thirteen hundred men, who have been reduced to eleven hundred."— *N. Y. Col. Docs.*, X, 3. It would be interesting to know how Mr. Duchambon made out his thirteen thousand men for the English. Dr. Douglass's charge of *poltroonary* may not have been very wide of the truth. See *ante*, p. 54. *Ed.*

† See *N. Y. Col. Docs.*, X, p. 3. *Ed.*

who may be deserving of your confidence will have rendered you an account of all the circumstances which have accompanied the blockade, the siege and the surrender of that place. We have not been able to learn any particulars thereof, except from some seamen who made their escape, from time to time, from the different harbors of Isle Royal [Cape Breton], and have arrived at Quebec, the major portion of them in *Biscayennes* (long boats); among the rest one Lacroix Girard, ship master, a native of St. Malo. This individual was in the place during the whole of the siege; his journal of it has appeared to us true, because of its simplicity, and this circumstance induces us to address you a copy of it.* According to what M. Duchambon has communicated to Sieur Marin, in his letter of the 29th of June last, that commandant was obliged to capitulate, on account of want of men and powder." †

These gentlemen give the English great credit for their perseverance and management of the expedition. They do not, like some of the English, attribute all their success to good luck. On the other hand, they attribute it to their diligence, courage, and preparing beforehand to meet all emergencies, although they take into the account the favorableness of the weather during the early part of the campaign, namely, in April, May and June. Capt. Girard, before mentioned, left Louisbourg on the 15th of July [10th, English account]. He reported that the English had at that time begun to remove the artillery out of the Vigilant, and place it upon the ramparts of the fortifications.

* Thus it appears there was a journal kept, within the walls as well as without, of the famous siege; but that kept within does not appear ever to have been published, and this is the only reference to it I have ever met with. *Ed.*

† By what will presently be seen, there was a large quantity of powder found in the city by the captors. *Ed.*

APPENDIX.] *Siege and Capture of Louisbourg.* 223

The following letter, dated Louisbourg, July 4, 1745, is not only valuable for its facts, but for the picture it exhibits of the spirit of those who had participated in the great acquisition. The ensuing is an extract:

"The more I view the works, the more is my admiration, and instead of twenty-five hundred [men] for the attack or siege, if the strength had been known before, ten thousand would not have been thought sufficient. The Island and Grand Batteries are the weakest of their works; for nature has on the back of the Grand Battery provided a shelter for an enemy's bombarding them out, which Providence gave us no occasion for, and the Light-House the same, which did such execution on the Island Battery, that the enemy was glad they could have recourse to the water to avoid the impending destruction of the balls and bombs. Our men, to their great honor, have been perfect Herculeses in their labors and fatigues, and were so hardened to the enemy's fire, that they would run and stop the career of the shot, before they had run their distance. The French say they are devils, for the hotter they fired, the nearer advances they made to their fire, and let what will have been said to their prejudice, four times their number of regular troops would not have undergone the Herculean labors of drawing forty-two pounders over hills and dales, rocks and swamps, three or four miles. God has greatly blessed the whole undertaking; and to describe the strength of Louisbourg city, and the vast labors of the French in casting up works while besieged, is beyond my pen to express; and the additions we are making of forty pieces of cannon out of the Launceston, will make it almost impregnable.* Underneath is an account

---

* The armament was taken out of that ship to prepare her for the reception of the prisoners, who were to be transported to France in her. *Ed.*

of the guns and ammunition found in the several batteries, viz : in the town, one hundred and forty-eight embrazures, eighty-five cannon, five brass mortars, and one iron. In the Island Battery, thirty-four embrazures, thirty cannon, two brass mortars, two small brass mortars in the store. In the Grand Battery, thirty cannon. Found in the town and the Island Battery, one hundred and twelve barrels of gunpowder, and some cartridges."

To avoid foot notes the above paragraphs have been interpolated into Governor Shirley's letter, which is here resumed. This closing part of the letter is separate from the narrative part, and was evidently added to impress on the home government the great and just claims which New England had in the acquisition of Cape Breton.

"By this representation of the services of his Majesty's land forces, I would not be understood to intend to exclude his Majesty's ships from their just share in the reduction of this place. Mr. Warren, upon whom I very much depended from the beginning for assistance and success in this enterprise, did, upon his receiving orders by his Majesty's sloop Hind, the 9th of March, to proceed to Boston, and concert measures with me for the protection of Nova Scotia, and the annoyance of the enemy's settlements, &c., immediately proceeded with his Majesty's ships Superb, Mermaid, and Launceston, under his command, for Boston; but, upon getting intelligence at sea of the departure of the New England land forces for Canso, though he was then within thirty leagues of Boston, without refreshments, or his complement of ordnance stores, and one of his ships not very fit for immediate service, sailed directly for that place, where, having overtaken the forces, and conferred with the General by letter, upon his Majesty's service in the

APPENDIX.] *Siege and Capture of Louisbourg.*   225

expedition; and it being thought advisable by both, that the ships should directly proceed before Louisbourg harbor to cut off all supplies and intelligence from the enemy, immediately proceeded there, and most effectually blocked up the harbor; and by engaging and taking the Vigilant, a French ship of war of sixty-four guns, bound for Louisbourg with some ordnance stores, cut off from the enemy all hopes of any supplies or succors, and gave great spirits to the land forces in carrying on the siege; and afterwards, upon his Majesty's ship Chester's arrival from England, to reinforce him, and receiving advice that the Canterbury and Sunderland were following, determined to enter the harbor as soon as those ships should join him, and attack the town and batteries with his Majesty's ships, whilst the land forces made an assault upon the city by land; which was agreed on, between Mr. Warren and the General, to be made the 16th of June, and the ships were accordingly clearing on the 15th of June, in order to enter the harbor, but were prevented by the enemy's making proposals for a capitulation. And indeed, Mr. Warren offered his assistance for his Majesty's service in every shape.

"It is unnecessary for me to trouble your Grace with a detail of the plans proposed during the siege for a more speedy reduction of the place; as far as I can judge, it was effected most happily in the manner which it was reduced in, as the success of the event was much more secure in this way; and it has cost fewer lives; and the place was gained without the least damage being done to any of his Majesty's ships.

"I hope these services of the New England troops in the field, which seem to have equalled the zeal of the Massachusetts Council and Assembly within their province, for his Majesty's service, upon this occasion, may be graciously accepted by his

Dd

Majesty, as a proof of that perfect duty and firm loyalty which, I am persuaded, all the colonies concerned in the reduction of this place (but especially that of the Massachusetts Bay, for which I can more particularly answer), bear to his Majesty's sacred person, and to his government, and of their ready disposition to promote the general welfare of his dominions; and I humbly beg of your Grace to lay this account before his Majesty, in such manner as your Grace shall think most proper.

"I am, &c.,

W. SHIRLEY."

SUFFERERS IN THE CAPE BRETON EXPEDITION.

THE following list has been prepared from the General Court Journals and other materials. It is not given as complete in any respect, but to aid those who may desire to do something more in the same line. A principal design being to notice such as are not met with in the general accounts of the period :

Allen, Benjamin. In answer to a petition to the General Court of Massachusetts, was allowed "two pounds and fourteen shillings, in full for wages and expenses in sickness," while in the Louisbourg expedition.

Allen, Joseph, was allowed four pounds and ten shillings for his services and sufferings in the expedition, in August, 1746. He had previously petitioned.

Bacon, Ebenezer, was of Woodstock, "being wounded and lost his gun, valued at twelve pounds, O. T.," was allowed three pounds for his gun, and "four pounds for loss of time, sufferings, &c."

Bane, David, was of York; went as a volunteer, and had received no recompense. On the 9th of January, 1747, the General Court voted him ten pounds. The family name was doubtless *Bean,* which was generally pronounced as given in the records, *Bane.* He was probably a son of Joseph Bean, long time a captive among the Indians, and an interpreter between the English and Indians on many important occasions. He was at the treaty of 1749, and 1753, and is frequently mentioned in the affairs of those times. He was afterwards a captain, and employed in building the fort at Penobscot, and in 1759 petitioned for additional wages. "Steeven" Beane, aged twenty, and Thomas Beane, aged twenty-one, were emigrants to America in 1635.

Baron, Timothy. He belonged to Westford, had an allowance granted him for wounds received during the expedition, and on the 13th of November, 1746, another of five pounds.

Bell, John, was an armourer in the expedition. He appears to have been incapacitated by sickness, and to have returned home in consequence, but recovered and went a second time. On the 13th of August, 1746, a petition of his and Edward Bemis was acted upon in the General Court of Massachusetts; said petition setting forth, that they "having done great service in that mystery" as armourers. The Court instructed the Committee of war to "allow them wages of armourers from the 17th of April, 1745, to June 17th, following, they not having been paid in any other capacity for that time." At the same time an order was passed "to pay John Bell seven pounds six shillings and six pence, old tenor, on account of his sickness after his first return from Louisbourg, provided the Committee have not allowed him therefor already." The same individual probably had been wounded in an earlier war with the Indians, and twenty-four pounds were voted for his benefit.

Bemis, Edward. Nothing further is met with concerning him than is contained in the last article.

Bennet, Moses. In answer to the application of Captain Bennet, the General Court voted (August 12th, 1746), not to allow him for services in the brigantine Boston Packet, because she was sent out without the Court's authority, and at a time when there was no enemy on the coast. But it is likely the

Captain made it appear that he had authority for his voyage, for just a month later the Court voted to allow his muster roll, from the 10th of May to June 23d, following.

Bouren, Meletiah, in a petition to the General Court, it set forth, "that the Council of War, on the 25th of April, 1745, at Chapeaurouge Bay, ordered him, with William Winslow (since deceased), to receive a quantity of molasses of a prize brigantine, brought into said bay by Captain Donahew, for the use of the forces there, to the value of fifteen hundred and twenty-five pounds and fifteen shillings; that he drew upon the Committee of War in Boston for the said sum, in favor of Captain Samuel Waldo, who acted as agent to said Donahew, but the Committee refused to pay said draft to said Waldo; thereupon the said Waldo protested said draft, and has commenced an action against him, the said Bourne." Mr. Bourne belonged to Sandwich, and was the father of the Hon. Sylvanus Bourne, who died in 1763, at the age of seventy.

Buckler, Robert, was a volunteer. In answer to a petition for relief, it appears "his services and sufferings" were of more than an ordinary character, as twelve pounds and ten shillings were promptly voted him, "for his present relief."

Burn, Patrick, belonged to Wenham. With Joseph Woodward Lovett, Elisha Nevers, Joseph Allen, and Benjamin Raymond, he petitioned for an allowance on account of his "services and sufferings," August 7th, 1746. On the 6th of September following, the Committee of War were ordered to pay to the selectmen of Wenham, seven pounds and ten shillings "in full," for the use of the said Burn.

Butler, Richard, of Boston, set forth in a petition, that "he enlisted in the Cape Breton expedition, was then a servant to James Davaricks, who has since absconded, and neither instructs him in his trade, nor allows him any subsistence;" asks for wages due him while in the service. Nothing was allowed him, at least at this time, perhaps on the ground that his master had received his wages.

Buxton, Stephen, showed by a petition, that he was impressed into the service in April, 1746, and was sent home again in July following; that by the muster roll he was only allowed for that time; yet " by his wounds he was incapable of service for a long time after." He was allowed pay for nineteen weeks additional, at twenty-two shillings and six pence a week; and in March following an order passed to pay him ten pounds and thirteen shillings additional.

Carr, Richard, belonged to Newbury. He was in the desperate attack on the Island Battery, on the night of the 26th of May (1745), in which he lost two of his fingers. Five pounds were ordered to be paid him.

Cheney, William, " petitioned in behalf of himself, and company of volunteers, under the command of Captain John Ruggles, who went to Cape Breton, for further allowance." The petition was dismissed.

Choate. Mention is made of " Colonel Choate's regiment," but nothing is met with to show that it was in the expedition.

Clark, Edward. " Whereas, on the 31st of January last [1746-7], the following vote passed, namely, that Edward Clark be allowed lieutenant's wages, from May 29th, 1745, to September 30th, following, which vote is mislaid and not recorded; voted, that he be allowed," &c.

Cobb, Sylvanus. A letter is received by the Secretary of the Province, from Admiral Townsend, who is at Louisbourg, directed to his Excellency; also a journal of Sylvanus Cobb, October 11th, 1746.

Covell, William, served in Captain Doane's company. He received a hurt in his shoulder, and petitioned for some assistance on account of it. The Court gave his petition a negative; from which circumstance it may be inferred that the applicant did not receive his hurt in the service.

Crecey, Joseph, belonged to Ipswich. He petitioned for "consideration," having been employed to take care of sick soldiers at Cape Breton. Whether he went as a soldier, or what was the success of his application, does not appear.

Crosby, Josiah, sets forth in a petition, that by order of the Governor he enlisted twenty-five men for the garrison at Louisbourg; that three of them deserted, to whom he had advanced forty-four pounds, old tenor; that he had also advanced one hundred and eighty-nine pounds for billetting the men; he therefore prays for reimbursement. It was dismissed by the Court, July 25th, 1746. The matter was brought up again on the 15th of November following, and referred to the next sitting of the Court.

Dalhonde, John, was of Boston. On the 7th of August, 1746, he petitioned the General Court for remuneration "respecting his extraordinary services in the late expedition against Louisbourg." He at the same time prayed for allowance on account of the services of his servant on board the brigantine Boston Packet. The Court ordered the petitions to be dismissed. He had served as a physician, and why this summary refusal to entertain his petitions was taken is not fully explained; it seems, however, that a committee was appointed to examine the matter, who, on the 15th of August following, stated, " that although the petitioner received no warrant from the Governor to practice as a doctor in the army at Cape Breton, yet by order of General Pepperell he was improved as such ; and especially at a time when the sickness greatly prevailed in the army, and scarcely any doctors to take care of the sick ; therefore it was voted to allow him doctor's wages."

There was at the same time living in Boston, another Dr. Dalhonde, of the given name of Lawrence ; whether a relative of John, does not appear. Dr. Lawrence Dalhonde was the family physician of Thomas Hancock. He made himself rather unpopular by his opposition to innoculation of the small pox. He died on the 24th of November, of this year (1746), at the age of seventy-one. His wife, Elizabeth, was executrix. She died previous to the 6th of April, 1749, and Mr. Hugh Vans, merchant, was her executor.

Davis, Jedidiah, represented " his sufferings " in a petition of the 29th of August, 1746. No action is found taken upon it.

Davis, John, was wounded. On December 30th, five pounds were ordered to be paid him " for smart money and loss of time ;" and on the 2d of January following, another five pounds was granted, which was also " for smart money and loss of time." He remained sick a long time, in the house of Robert Thorndike. See THORNDIKE, R.

Dixwell, Bazil, died in the service at Cape Breton. He belonged to Captain Goldthwait's company, and was a lieutenant. Whether he were a descendant of the Regicide JOHN, perhaps the editor of the new edition—long promised—of Dr. Stiles's History of the Judges of Charles I, may inform the reader.*

Doane, Elisha, was Captain of a company, and was one of the first, who, at the head of his company, started for Cape Breton. On the 24th of June, 1746, he set forth in a petition

---

* Sir *Basil* Dixwell was a connection of the Judge, for whom the Lieutenant was probably named.—See Stiles's *History of the Judges*, 143.

APPENDIX.] *Sufferers in the Louisbourg Expedition.* 233

to the General Court in behalf of himself and men, that they underwent great hardship, that their wages was but five pounds per month, and "that they lost all benefit of plunder by the capitulation." Captain Doane was probably of the Eastham family, and may have been that *Elisha* Doane, born there, February 3d, 1705.—See *New Eng. Hist. and Gen. Register*, vol. VI, page 44.

Dolliber, Thomas, was of Marblehead, a fisherman. Through his agency news was obtained that the great French armada, under the Duke D'Anville, was arrived in the northern seas. He abandoned his fishing, took a Frenchman from the Isle Sables, conveyed him to Louisbourg, and through his means the news was obtained. On the 13th of November, 1746, a request for remuneration of his expenses was before the General Court. His principal claim was that he had "lost a fair of fish." The name Dolliber, with several variations, is an early one in New England. Perhaps *Dolebare* is of the same origin.

Donahew, David. This active commander is duly noticed in the body of this history. He probably belonged to Newburyport, and as early as the 27th of February, 1745, was taken into the service of the Province, with his vessel, a sloop.

Dunn, John, belonged to Barnstable, Cape Cod, and was a drum major in Col. Gorham's regiment. He claimed that he had not received his dues of the government, as set forth in a petition; but on the 25th of July, 1746, his petition was "dismissed," yet on the 9th of October following, his claim was liquidated by an allowance of two pounds and seventeen shillings.

Dyre, Joseph, was a soldier in Captain James Noble's company, and was one of those who complained of that officer's barbarous treatment of his men.

Ee

Fearne, *John*. In answer to a petition of his, January 29, 1747, ten pounds were voted him, on account of his great sufferings by sickness.

Gardner, *John*, was of Salem. On the 5th of March, 1745, he was appointed pilot of the Massachusetts frigate, Captain Edward Tyng. On the 9th of the same month a vote passed in the General Court adding two shillings a month to his pay.

Garrish, *George*, served as a blacksmith. In September (1746) he petitioned the Court for remuneration on account of having lost his tools at Louisbourg. He represented that they were stolen from him, which circumstance probably influenced the Court to throw out his claim; perhaps concluding that the government could not be holden in such cases.

Gayton, *Pierce*. He was master of a mast-ship, and was waiting here, as the mast trees could not be got ready before the end of June. His ship was a fine one, equal to a man of war of forty guns. Gov. Shirley prevailed upon him to join the expedition against Louisbourg. His ship had been taken from the French, and its name was the Bien Amié. It was now the 7th of March (1745) and although she required seventy men to make up her compliment, the Governor said she would be ready to sail the following week. In the mean time Capt. Gayton received orders from Commodore Knowles which interfered with the arrangement for the voyage to Louisbourg. On the 11th of September he petitioned the General Court, stating that he had been constrained by the justices of the county of Suffolk to give evidence concerning the murder of William Bryan and John Conner, whereby he was prevented following his business at sea. On the 15th of November following his claim was acknowledged by an allowance of "£11 5*s*. in full."

Girler, William. He seems to have been a coast pilot. On the 14th of June, 1747, a petition of his is noticed in the Court Journals, in which it is said that "he did very considerable service in piloting the transports into Sheepscot and Canso, and catching fish for the fleet." The family name of this pilot may have been Girdler. If so, this man probably originated at Marblehead.

Gorham, John. On the 8th of August, 1746, he petitioned for pay as lieutenant-colonel. Three days later, with other officers of the "whale-boat regiment, so called," prayed that some method be taken to regulate the distribution of plunder. Col. Gorham belonged to Cape Cod, and usually had many of the Cape Indians in his regiment.

Harris. Thomas Harris, of Ipswich, was allowed five pounds upon his representing that he had been at great charge in nursing one of his sons who returned sick from the expedition, and died in consequence of that sickness.

Hills, Daniel, was sick at Cape Breton. He afterward received four pounds for medicine expended in his sickness there.

Hicks, Nathaniel, was of Kittery, and was among the wounded. He afterwards petitioned for relief. Whether any was accorded, is not found.

Hoyt, Moses, was of Newberry; having petitioned for relief, on account of his services and sufferings, the court, on the same day his petition was read, voted him, "for his present relief," twelve pounds and ten shillings, July 23, 1746. See *Genealogy of the Hoyts,* by D. W. HOYT, p. 32.

Hunniwell, Roger, belonged to Scarborough. He lost his right arm at Louisbourg. On June 26, 1746, seven pounds and ten shillings were voted him for present relief. Again, in April, 1747, another £7 10s. were voted him, "and the Governor be desired to place the petitioner in one of the garrisons, and to be in the pay of the province."

Jackson, William, was captain of the cartel ship which conveyed the Louisbourg captives to France, after the surrender. His wife not hearing anything from him for above a year after he sailed from Louisbourg, petitioned the authorities for his wages. This was in January, 1746–7. Between that date and March 17th following, the captain made his appearance, and was allowed to visit the General Court, on which event the clerk made a record to this purport: " Captain William Jackson, who was sent by his excellency, the Governor, express from Louisbourg to Great Britain, in November, 1745, by order of the House, appeared on the floor, and after divers questions respecting his voyage, etc., withdrew."

Jenkins, Phillip, represented himself as a "soldier in the expedition," and that he "had many things stolen from him," for which he prayed remuneration from the government, but it does not appear that he got any.

Jordan, Henry. On the 2d of April, 1747, it was ordered that he be allowed ten pounds on account of his sufferings; and that the Governor be desired to place him in one of the garrisons, and to be in the pay of the province. He had the year before been allowed five pounds for present relief.

Jose, Francis; seems to have been an inhabitant of some part of Cape Breton when this war came on, and acted as pilot to the English ships, and was allowed wages for his services. At the same time his son was "a common soldier" in the army. He also furnished supplies, for which, August 7th, 1746, he was allowed forty pounds " in full for cattle, wood, and services."

Kelton, Jonathan, was of Dorchester, and served as armourer at the Grand Battery during the siege.

Kenny, Nathan, having received a musket ball in his thigh, "which had occasioned him great charge, trouble and pain," petitioned for recompense, and on the 10th of October, 1746, fifty shillings were allowed him.

Kinslaw, John, was a captain, and was at Louisbourg in the end of August, 1746. His pay roll was presented to the Court but was not sworn to by the captain; "and the soldiers who are alive, and the representatives of those who are dead, will be great sufferers if payment be delayed until said roll can be sworn to; therefore it was voted that the Committee of War make payment on said roll."

Leatherland, Jacob, was of Ipswich, a volunteer. He petitioned the General Court for remuneration, in the usual form, on account of his sufferings, but it was "laid on the table."

Lewis, Thomas, was of Hingham. On the 12th of November, 1746, complaint was made against him, that he had by a forged order, received part of the wages of Edward Ward, Jr., of the said Hingham, and had enlisted into the service and gone for Annapolis. An order was passed requesting the Governor to send for him, "that he may be brought to justice." Mention is made by Mr. Lincoln in his history of Hingham of a Thomas Lewis of this time in that town, but nothing of his having served in this war.

Lovett, Joseph Woodward. On August 7th, 1746, a petition from him and several others was taken up, but not acted upon till September 3d. It was then "ordered that the Committee of War allow J. W. Lovet wages for so long time as it appeared to them he was allowed subsistence."

Marsh, Jacob, belonged to Newbury, was chirurgeon's mate in Colonel Williams's regiment, and chief surgeon in Colonel

Waldo's regiment. The Court ordered, " that, on due proof of what he alleges, full chirurgeon's pay be allowed him."

March, John, was of Salisbury. For his hardships and sufferings, six pounds were voted him.

McFaden, James, petitions for reimbursement of twenty-four pounds, which he has paid his doctor since the last grant of the Court in April, 1746. On July 18th, the Committee of War were directed to pay six pounds " to whom it is due for nursing and board, and four pounds to the petitioner for his loss of time."

Nevers, Elisha, was allowed two pounds and five shillings on account of his services and sufferings, August 11th, 1746.

Noble, James, Captain, was complained of for ill treatment of his men, which seems to have amounted to barbarity, as the General Court, on hearing the testimony against him, requested the Governor " not to suffer the said James Noble to sustain a post in the public service." He was in General Samuel Waldo's regiment of Cumberland county.

Pierce, James, of Wiscasset, was a volunteer, and among the sick soldiers. His petition for aid, of June 18th, 1746, was passed over. On the 11th of November he was allowed six pounds " as a further allowance." On April 4th, 1747, four pounds were voted him, " and to be put into the hands of Josiah Pierce, for the best use of the petitioner."

Pike, Thomas, was of Newbury. He petitioned for an allowance, " showing, that on the 20th of June, 1745, he received a commission from Governor Shirley to be adjutant in Choate's regiment ; that he was before and after that, lieutenant, and performed the duty of both." But his claim was not allowed, at this time, July 19th, 1746.

Pines, Thomas, was of Boston. In the beginning of the

APPENDIX.] *Sufferers in the Louisbourg Expedition.* 239

expedition "he enlisted and went a Serjeant under Captain Samuel Rhodes, and received wages as such to October, 1745; that he continued to the 15th of May, 1746, in the service, but cannot get his wages, because Captain Rhodes has made up no muster roll."

Preble, Zebulon, of York, claimed " that his son, who served at the reduction of Louisbourg, and died in the service, had due to him wages to the amount of eight pounds fifteen shillings and one penny; that his order for that amount was returned, endorsed, 'paid William Walker, per order,' the amount for wages and bounty; whereas, the petitioner never drew such order, neither doth he know said Walker." The Committee of War was ordered to stop Walker's wages till he should make it appear that the order in question was genuine.

Prout, Ebenezer, was a commissary. On November 11th, 1746, he memorialized the government respecting his accounts.

Pynchon, Charles, a physician in the expedition, petitioned respecting his great suffering in the service, which being "committed to the gentlemen appointed upon petitions of wounded soldiers, June 12th, 1746," it was ordered that the Committee of War allow the petitioner twenty-five pounds " for his services and sufferings." He was a descendant "of the worshipful William Pynchon, of Springfield, and Dr. Allen says he died before 1789; that he was son of John, who died in 1721; if so, he was grandson of the Rev. William Hubbard, the historian.

Raymond, Benjamin, among other soldiers, petitioned for consideration for his services and sufferings, which was presented in August, 1746.

Reddington, Nathaniel, a volunteer, whose " services and sufferings," in the opinion of the War Committee, amounted to two pounds and ten shillings, which was ordered to be paid him "in full."

Rouse, John, conspicuous in this and the later French wars, was doubtless a native of Boston or its vicinity,* but who his immediate ancestors were, none of the writers who notice him appear to have had any knowledge. The name Rouse appears very early on our records. It may have, like many others, undergone changes; as *Ross, Rose*, &c. Still, there was a *John Rouse* in New England as early as 1640. William Rouse was of Boston, a goldsmith, who had a family here, and also another William, a generation later, who is styled mariner, and with several others was imprisoned under the accusation of trading with the French enemy. He might have been the ancestor, and even the father of Captain John Rouse, the subject of this article, but of that proof is wanting. It is remarkable that there is not a line in any of our biographical works respecting a man so distinguished as a naval commander as was Captain John Rous, or Rouse, as then often written.

The name Rous appears among the English baronets in 1660, and in the peerage in 1796, as Earl Stradbrok. Mention is here made of the English family, because Captain John Rouse, a native of New England, received most of his honors in Old England, as a succinct notice of him, now undertaken, will show.

Dr. Douglass thus introduces him: "In the end of July, 1744, Captain Rouse in a Boston privateer, arrived at St. Johns harbor in Newfoundland, from the Great Banks. He brought in eight French ships, with ninety thousand mud-fish. In August Captain Rouse, in consort ship, with Captain Cleves in a ship, and some small craft, and fifty marines, fitted out by the

* See Penhallow, *Indian Wars*, page 33.

British man-of-war stationed at Newfoundland, sailed in quest of the French ships that cure codfish in the northern harbors of Newfoundland. August 18th, at Fishot [Fishotte], they took five good French ships, some dried fish, and seventy tons of liver oil. Thence they proceeded to the harbors of St. Julian and Carrous. Captain Rouse hereby merited, and accordingly was made, Post or Rank Captain in the British navy." But it appears from other authentic sources that several important circumstances in the career of Captain Rouse transpired between his privateer services and his advancement to a captaincy in the British navy. When the expedition was resolved upon against Cape Breton, Governor Shirley sent for Captain Edward Tyng (who had recently succeeded the veteran Captain Cyprian Southack), and directed him to procure the largest and best ship he could find, and appointed him Commodore. To him Captain Rouse was second in command, and shared in all his operations.

After the capture of the great French ship, the Vigilant, Commodore Warren proposed to Captain Tyng to take command of her, under the rank of Post Captain; but as he was now about sixty-five years of age, he did not think it prudent to accept the office, but recommended Captain Rouse, who was thus instated in the navy, and appointed to the command of the Shirley frigate, or galley, as it was sometimes, or hitherto denominated.* After sharing in all of the hardships in the reduction of Louisbourg, Captain Rouse went to England, where, after the peace of 1748, he was appointed Captain of

* The Rev. Timothy Alden, in his account or memoir of Captain Tyng, insinuates that Captain Rouse had usurped the honor intended for his superior, which is not warranted by the facts in my possession, which are fully and correctly given in the text, from the best authorities of the time.

Ff

the Albany sloop. This command was inferior to his hitherto place, but in time of peace such exchange from larger to smaller ships were common. In 1755, however, he appears as Captain of the Success, a twenty-two gun ship, and was soon after ordered to his old field of exploits, about Nova Scotia. Here he cooperated with Colonel Monckton. A letter written at Halifax, July 18th, the same year (1755), affords an insight into some of his brilliant operations: "The French have abandoned their fort at St. Johns river, and as far as in their power demolished it. As soon as the forts on the Isthmus were taken, Captain Rous sailed from thence, with three twenty-gun ships and a sloop to look into St. John's river, where it was reported there were two French ships of thirty-six guns each. He anchored off the mouth of the river, and sent his boats to reconnoitre; they saw no ships there; but on their appearance the French burst their cannon, blew up their magazine, burned every thing they could belonging to the fort, and marched off. The next morning the Indians invited Captain Rous on shore, gave him the strongest assurances of their desire to make peace with the English; and pleaded, in their behalf, that they had refused to assist the French upon this occasion, though earnestly pressed by them." Two years later (1757), we meet with Captain Rouse in the same ship, under Admiral Holburne, who, on his arrival at the Chibouctou, or Halifax station, dispatched him for the purpose of reconnoitering the French fleet at Louisbourg. On his return he was removed into the Winchelsea of twenty-four guns. About the end of the year he returned to England, and was promoted to the Southerland, of fifty guns, and again returned to America, where he continued to signalize himself by his bravery and good conduct till after the fall of Quebec; about which time it is believed he returned to England,

APPENDIX.] *Sufferers in the Louisbourg Expedition.* 243

with greatly impaired health, and on the 3d of April following, died at Portsmouth.

Rogers, William. On January 21st, 1747, a petition from him was presented to the General Court, praying compensation, for that he had served in a double capacity at Cape Breton; namely, as commissary to a regiment and clerk to a company. The Court decided that "the time for receiving petitions was past, and consequently his was not then considered. The same was again presented, on the 21st of April following, but does not seem to have been acted upon.

Ruggles, John, was a captain in the Louisbourg expedition, and is only incidentally mentioned.

Shuttleworth, Vincent, belonged to Wrentham, Massachusetts. He was among the badly wounded, and a pension of three pounds and five shillings was voted him by the General Court previous to November 11th, 1746, at which time the same amount was ordered to be paid him yearly for life. The family name is found among the emigrants of 1635, in which year John *Shettleworth's* name is found, though Savage appears not to have met with it.

Spier, David, was of Woburn, Massachusetts, and died after the expedition, having "served during the whole siege of Louisbourg. After which he was taken sick, and sent to Boston, where he died. He was son of John Spier, of Woburn, but no mention is found of the name of SPIER in the history of that town, nor in the *New England Genealogical Dictionary.*

Stanwood, Job, was a volunteer. In August, 1746, he petitioned for consideration on account of his sufferings, and on the 14th of November following, the Court granted him "five pounds for his present relief." The Stanwoods were early at Gloucester. Job and his brother David were both in this expedition, and both wounded. Job lost his left arm, and, in 1749, was given a pension of fifteen pounds a year during life.

Strong, Elisha, was of Northampton, a volunteer. In January, 1747, "he petitioned for a further allowance, by reason of his services and sufferings. He was in Captain Hubbard's company. He was doubtless of the same stock as the late Governor Caleb Strong, the Rev. Nathan, D. D., and other highly distinguished men of the name.

Tarrant, Alexander, was "allowed for his present relief," twelve pounds and ten shillings.

Tatness, Samuel, a volunteer, petitioned, in September, 1746, "representing his sickness and sufferings," and was referred "to the gentlemen appointed for such service." The next February the Court ordered that five pounds should be paid him "in full for his sufferings and sickness." In April, 1747, Eleanor Drisdell, of Boston, brought in a bill "for boarding and nursing Samuel Tatness from June to January," seven pounds and ten shillings, which was allowed her.

Terry, John, captain of a company of grenadiers, appointed by Gen. Pepperrell, but had received only a lieutenant's pay; that he advanced a considerable sum in provisions for his company; he therefore petitioned the General Court "for an allowance." The Court referred him to their committee, appointed to examine such claims, June 7, 1746.

Thomas, William, was of Plymouth, and "under surgeon" in Captain Samuel Waldo's regiment, but was obliged to take care of Col. Gorham's regiment also. He was ordered to be paid wages as chief surgeon, by the committee of war, "provided they find that Col. Gorham's regiment had no chief surgeon, January 12, 1747.

Trayne, Joshua, was of Framingham, a volunteer. In

APPENDIX.] *Sufferers in the Louisbourg Expedition.* 245

March, 1747, he petitioned for "consideration," on account of loss of time and sickness since his return from the expedition. A Joshua Trayne, probably the same, is mentioned in the history of Framingham, who married, in 1743, Mary Nichols. He was son of John Trayne, of the same town, and was rated there in 1746 and 1752. He may not have been assessed the intermediate years in consequence of his sufferings in the expedition. Nothing is said in Barry's *History of Framingham* about his service against Cape Breton.

Turner, Abner. In October, 1746, he petitioned for compensation, setting forth, that he was at the reduction of Louisbourg, that afterwards he was shipped to carry some French prisoners to France; that upon his return he was put on shore at Philadelphia, and there was seized with the small-pox; that that cost him nine pounds and ten shillings. The Court did not, at this time, entertain his claim.

Twichel, Daniel. In March, 1747, he petitioned the government for consideration, as a soldier, wounded in the service, but in what service is not mentioned.

Tyng, Edward. A captain in the sea service, and one of the ablest commanders in the wars of his time, as will be found elsewhere detailed; as well in other works as in these pages. In the Cape Breton expedition he was in command of the Massachusetts frigate. Early in this war he memorialized the government for a "further allowance for the doctor, that he be kept in constant pay, and that he may be allowed a mate." Whereupon an order was issued, granting eight shillings a month to be added to the doctor's pay. A mate was also granted, with two pounds and ten shillings a month wages. Also a second lieutenant, with three pounds and three shillings wages per month. In February, 1746-7, he petitioned for a doctor's mate, but whether this request were granted or not, does not appear. At this time Capt. Tyng was about sixty-four years of age. He died in Boston, September 8th, 1755, aged about seventy-two. His residence was in Milk street. In 1734 he advertised for sale "A likely Negro Man, aged about twenty-two years, speaks good English, is an excellent Barber, and endowed with several other valuable qualifications." In 1736, a large tract of land was granted to "Edward Tyng of Boston, merchant, Temple Nelson and Nathaniel Alden of Boston, for themselves and others, the heirs of Col. Edward Tyng, deceased; John Nelson, Esq., deceased; and Captain John Alden, deceased; in consideration for the deceased's extraordinary services and sufferings; they having suffered a long and tedious captivity in France, the said Col. Tyng dying in a dungeon there." Hence Captain Tyng was grandson of the emigrant of the same name, who settled in Dunstable, and died there in 1681, at the age of ninety-one. His father served in Philip's war, was lieutenant to Capt. Appleton, and wounded in the Narraganset swamp fight of Dec. 19, 1675. Seven years after the death of Captain Tyng, his estate in Milk street, two brick tenements in Fleet street, and a house, warehouse, and wharf, near Windmill Point, were advertised for sale. The valuable article on the Tyng family, in *Alden's Epitaphs*, II, 328, etc., may be materially augmented from our memoranda.

Vaughan, William, was a son of Lieutenant-Governor George Vaughan of Portsmouth, New Hampshire. There has been occasion to speak of him and his agency in the previous pages of this history. He appears to have been a man of great enterprise. In 1730 and 1731, having made a purchase of a fine mill privilege at the Fresh Falls on the Damariscotta, of persons who derived their title from Mr. John Brown, proceeded to erect mills there, and soon had two double saw-mills and a gristmill in operation. After the fall of Louisbourg he went to England to obtain some reward for his extraordinary services; but, owing to some cause, he did not succeed. Perhaps, as he had no command in the expedition, his claim was disregarded. Although his services were well known to have been great, and important to the enterprise, he stood a small chance for remuneration among the hundreds of hungry army officers. He died in England in 1755. His death may have been hastened by neglect and disappointment. His brother, Elliot Vaughan, succeeded him at Damariscotta. By his will he gave Mercy, Jenny, and Mary Campbell a hundred acres of land each. Jenny Campbell became the wife of James Brown. The notice taken of William Vaughan by Dr. Douglass, undoubtedly requires considerable qualification: "A whimsical, wild projector in his own private concerns, entirely ignorant of military affairs, and of the nature of the defense or strength of a place regularly and well fortified at an immense expense; dreamt or imagined that this place might be reduced by fifteen hundred raw militia, some scaling-ladders, and a few armed small craft of New England." The same author says scaling-ladders were sent with the expedition, but were found ten feet too short; but had they been long enough, no use could have been made of them.

Villers, George, died in the service, before the 24th of June, 1746. At that date one Elizabeth Shute applied for consideration, showing that the widow of Villers was taken care of by her, and died in her house, but her claim was at that time rejected. The applicant was a widow, and resided in Boston.

Walker, George, was of Arundel; enlisted as a soldier in

the Cape Breton expedition; was sick at Boston several months. Five pounds were granted him.

Walker, William. Where he belonged is not stated in the records. All that is learned of him is given in the notice of ZEBULON PREBLE.

Walter, Nathaniel, clerk. We have before us "a memorial, shewing that in the late [Louisbourg] expedition, he had a warrant from His Excellency William Shirley, Esq., as interpreter to General Pepperrell, in which capacity he passed through hard service, in translating papers, etc., both before and after the reduction of the place." What action was taken upon this memorial, if any, does not appear. Mr. Walter was pastor of the Second Church in Roxbury. He was son of the Rev. Nehemiah Walter, and his mother was *Sara,* daughter of the Rev. INCREASE MATHER, D. D. His service in the Louisbourg expedition does not appear to have been known to his descendants of this generation.

Ward, Edward, Jr., was of Hingham. He volunteered to serve in the Louisbourg expedition. By a petition which he laid before the government of Massachusetts, it appears that one Thomas Lewis, also of Hingham, had by a forged order received a part of Ward's wages, enlisted into the service, and had gone to Annapolis. The government ordered nine pounds to be paid to Ward, and that Lewis be sent for, "that he may be brought to justice."

It is remarkable how many men of distinction served in America in this war, and that which immediately succeeded it. Commodore Anson was on his voyage round the world when France declared war against England; that voyage, so dis-

APPENDIX.] *Sufferers in the Louisbourg Expedition.* 249

astrous to hundreds who participated in it. In one of Anson's ships, the Wager, cast away on the western coast of Patagonia, was a midshipman, mentioned in the narratives of that voyage as the Hon. JOHN BYRON, then a young man. The majority of the crew of the Wager succeeded in reaching the shore of what proved to be a desolate island. Of about one hundred and eighty souls, scarce twenty ever lived to reach their homes, the greater part having died from starvation and the exposures to which for months some, and years others were subjected. Mr. Byron, with some twelve comrades, refusing to proceed with the majority of the survivors by the straits of Magellan, bent their way northward, hoping by this course to fall in with some Spanish ship which they might capture, and in it to reach an appointed rendezvous of their commodore; but their numbers soon became too much reduced to admit of the entertainment of this idea, even by their fool-hardy captain. At length but four remained alive, among whom was the captain, whose name was Cheap, and Mr. Byron. These two, by the aid of the Indians, after some months of the most excessive sufferings, arrived at a Spanish settlement on the island of Chiloe. They now became prisoners to the Spaniards, who treated them kindly, furnished them with clothing and other necessaries, and finally they got back to England, by way of France, after about five years' absence. Byron soon after resumed his place in the British navy; was made a captain in 1746. In 1757 he commanded the America, a sixty gun ship, and afterwards the Fame, a seventy-four, in which he sailed to Louisbourg, with transports conveying engineers, etc., charged with the demolition of the famous fortification there, about which the English and French had fought so desperately. While at Louisbourg he learned that several French frigates

GG

and storeships were lying in the bay of Chaleur, all of which he took or destroyed. He afterwards served under Lord Colville, and at one time under Sir Edward Hawk. He was governor of Newfoundland; then an admiral; commanded an exploring expedition round the world; served during the war of the American Revolution; manœuvred successfully with Count D'Estaing, and saved Admiral Barrington's command in the West Indies. This seems to have been among his last naval services. He married, in 1748, Sophia, daughter of John Trevanion, Esq., and died in 1786. Such was the grandfather of LORD BYRON, one of the greatest poets of any time, whose singular career and fortune have given rise to one of the most lamentable and uncalled for crusades against his reputation to be found in the annals of scandal.

APPENDIX E.

Page 120.

THE REV. JOHN NORTON.

INTRODUCTION.

TO the narrative of the Rev. John Norton these previous pages are indebted for many of the valuable facts detailed in them. After the manner of an older work, Mr. Norton entitles his " 𝔗𝔥𝔢 𝔑𝔢𝔢𝔡𝔢𝔪𝔢𝔡 𝔆𝔞𝔭𝔱𝔦𝔳𝔢, being a narrative of the taking and carrying into captivity the Reverend Mr. John Norton, when Fort Massachusetts surrendered to a large body of *French and Indians*, August 20th, 1746." " *Written by himself.*"

Mr. Norton's captivity was of one year's continuance, wanting four days. His narrative was printed in 1748, in Boston, " and sold opposite the prison." Who the printer was, or the bookseller, is not mentioned. As Daniel Fowle kept in Queen street at this time, and the prison was in that street, where the court house now is, he was probably the printer. The author was perhaps his own publisher. He appears not to have had much practice as a writer, but what is of more importance, he was evidently one of the most truthful, while the printer did not perform his part with much credit to himself, which might have been the occasion of his withholding his name to Mr. Norton's work.

Mr. Norton was born in Berlin, Connecticut, 1716; graduated at Yale College in 1737. Four years after, namely, in

1741, he was ordained in Fall Town, since Bernardston, Massachusetts, and was the first minister in that town. Owing "to the unsettled state of the times," he continued in Fall Town but about four years; the people had quite as much as they could do to maintain their families, while they were exposed to inroads of the enemy in a war already commenced. The statement of his having been settled at Deerfield in 1741, is probably incorrect. After his return from captivity he was installed pastor of the Congregational church in East Hampton, Middlesex county, Connecticut, November 30th, 1748, where he continued about thirty years, at which period he fell a victim to the small pox (March 24th, 1748).

Bernard's Town, at the time Mr. Norton preached there was, as just mentioned, called Fall Town. It was thus designated because it was granted to the soldiers, or the descendants of those soldiers who were in the fight with the Indians at the Great Falls in the Connecticut river, May 18th, 1676. While in captivity his wife applied to the government of Massachusetts for the wages due him as chaplain, and at one time received one pound sixteen shillings and six pence, then due, March 12th, 1747.

Mr. Norton was thirty years of age when taken prisoner; and though he has given us a work full of valuable facts, he evidently had had little experience in literary matters, and would have made his work much more valuable had he re-written it at a later day. But narratives of the kind of this of Mr. Norton's would not at the time of its publication, attract the attention of the reading public. His immediate friends, and the friends of those in captivity with him, were about all who would take any interest in its publication. There was no charm of composition about it. Its details are the dryest possible. Hence its circulation was of the most limited kind. This circumstance may account for its extreme scarcity, which scarcity probably extends back to within a very few years of its publication. Many of the most valuable works have been issued in small editions; a few copies only bound or stitched up to meet the first demands of friends; the rest are taken by the author into the country, perhaps in sheets, and eventually used for waste paper; or, possibly left on the printer's hands to meet a similar fate. Such cases are known to the writer.

NORTON'S REDEEMED CAPTIVE.

Mr. Norton thus begins his " Narrative," &c. [3]* " Thursday, August 14, 1746, I left Fort Shirley,† in company with Dr. [Thomas] Williams, and about fourteen of the soldiers; we went to Pelham Fort, and from thence to Captain Rice's, where we lodged that night.

"Friday, the 15th, we went from thence to Fort Massachusetts, where I designed to have tarried about a month.

"Saturday, 16th. The doctor, with fourteen men, went off for Deerfield, and left in the fort, Sergeant John Hawks,‡ with twenty soldiers, about half of them sick with bloody flux. Mr. Hawks sent a letter by the doctor to the captain, supposing that he was then at Deerfield, desiring that he would speedily send up some stores to the fort, being very short on it for ammunition, and having discovered some signs of the enemy;

---

* The figures thus enclosed denote the original pagination of Mr. Norton's work.

† In what is since the town of Heath, about eighteen miles north north west of Northampton, Mass.

‡ The same who was ambushed and wounded at Fort Massachusetts, May 9th, 1746. He had been a captive among the Indians, and was recently returned.

but the letter did not get to the captain seasonably. This day, also, two of our men being out a few miles distant from the fort, discovered the tracks of some of the enemy.

"Lord's day and Monday, 17th and 18th, we met with no disturbance, nor did we discover any enemy; but the sickness was very distressing; for though some began to amend, yet there were more taken sick. Eleven of our men were sick, and scarcely one of us in perfect health; almost every man was troubled with the griping and flux.

"Tuesday, 19th. Between eight and nine o'clock in the [4] morning, when, through the good providence of God, we were all in the fort, twenty-two men, three women, and five children, there appeared an army of French and Indians, eight or nine hundred in number, commanded by Monsieur Regand de Vaudrŭle,* who, having surrounded the fort on every side, began with hideous acclamations to rush forward upon the fort, firing incessantly upon us on every side. Mr. Hawks, our officer, ordered that we should let them come without firing at all at them, until they should approach within a suitable distance, that we might have a good prospect of doing execution.

"We suffered them to come up in a body till they were within twenty rods of us, and then we fired; upon which the enemy soon betook themselves to trees, stumps and logs, where they lay and fired incessantly upon us; some taking opportunity to run from one tree and stump to another, and so drew nearer to the fort. This they did in a very subtle manner, running so crooked that it was very difficult to shoot at them with any

---

* His real name was Pierre François Cavagnal; was born in Montreal, 8th February, 1704. He was living as late as 1770. See Morgan's *Celebrated Canadians*, 46. Rigaud de Vaudreuil. He was brother of the last French Governor of Canada, the Marquis, Pierre François de Vaudreuil-

good prospect of success, until we observed, that when they came to a stump, they would fall down; which we observing, prepared to catch them there as they fell down by the stumps; and this we did probably with success; for they soon left off this method. About this time we saw several of the enemy fall and rise no more; among which was the captain of the St. Francis Indians, who was one of the foremost, and called upon the rest to press on upon the fort. Sergeant Hawks got an opportunity to shoot him into the breast, which ended his days.*

"At the beginning of the engagement, the General sent his ensign with his standard (which he, standing [5] behind a tree about thirty rods distant from the fort, displayed), the General also walked up the hill within about forty rods of the fort, where he stood and gave his orders; but being discovered he had a shot or two fired at him; upon which he moved off; but presently after comes to his ensign, where, being discovered, he received a shot in his arm, which made him retreat with his ensign to their camp.

"The enemy still continued to fire almost incessantly upon us, and many of them crept up within a dozen rods of the fort. We were straitened for want of shot. Several of our men being newly come into the service, and for want of bullet moulds, had not prepared for any long engagement, and therefore the sergeant ordered some of our sick men to make bullets, another to run some shot, having shot moulds. This put him upon taking particular notice of the ammunition, and he found it to be very short, and therefore gave orders that we should not fire any more than we thought necessary to hold the enemy

* The name of this Chief does not appear to have been mentioned in the French reports of the expedition, nor have the English recorded it. Though the St. Francis tribe were represented at the treaties of 1735 and 1742, no names are given.

back, unless when we had a very good opportunity and fair prospect of doing execution; so that we fired but little. We had sometimes very fair shot, and had success. We saw several fall, who, we are persuaded, never rose again. We might have shot at the enemy almost any time in the day, who were in open view of the fort, within fifty or sixty rods of the same, and sometimes within forty and less; the officers sometimes walking about, sword in hand, viewing of us, and others walking back and forth as they had occasion, without molestation, for we dare not spend our ammunition upon them that were at such a distance.

"Towards evening the enemy began to use their axes and hatchets. Some were thoughtful that they were preparing ladders in order to storm the fort in the night; but afterward we found our mistake, for they were preparing faggots in order to burn it. This day they wounded two of our men, viz, John Aldrich they shot through the foot, and Jonathan Bridgman with a flesh wound the back side of his hip. When the evening came on the sergeant gave orders that all the tubs, pails, and vessels of every sort, in every room, should be filled with water, and went himself to see it done; he also looked to the doors, that they were made as fast as possible. He likewise cut a passage from one room to another, that he might put the fort into as good a posture for defense as might be, in case they should attempt to storm it. He distributed the men into the several rooms. While he was thus preparing, he kept two men in the north-west mount,* and some in the great house, the south-east corner of the fort, to watch the enemy and keep them back.

"I was in the mount all the evening; it was cloudy and very

---

* A sort of watch box in an angle or corner of the fort, on the top of the wall.

dark the beginning of the evening. The enemy kept a constant fire upon us, and, as I thought, approached nearer and in greater numbers than they had in the daytime. We had but little encouragement to fire upon the enemy, having but the light of their fire to direct us, yet we dared not wholly omit it, lest they should be emboldened to storm the fort. We fired buck-shot at them, and have reason to hope we did some execution, for the enemy complained of our shooting buck-shot at that time, which they could not have known had they not felt some of them. They continued thus to fire upon us until between eight and nine at night, then the whole army (as we supposed) surrounded the fort, and shouted, or rather yelled, with the [7] most hideous outcries, all around the fort. This they repeated three or four times. We expected they would have followed this with a storm, but were mistaken, for they directly set their watch all round the fort; and besides their watch they sent some to creep up as near the fort as they could, to observe whether any persons attempted to make their escape, to carry tidings to New England.* The body of the army then drew back to their camps; some in the swamp west of the fort, the other part to the south-east, by the river side. We then considered what was best to be done; whether to send a post down to Deerfield or not. We looked upon it very improbable, if not morally impossible, for any men to get off undiscovered; and therefore the sergeant would not lay his commands upon any to go; but he proposed it to several, desired and encouraged them as far as he thought convenient; but there was not a man willing to venture out. So the sergeant, having placed the men in every part of the fort, he

* It seems odd at this day, that but little more than a hundred years ago, one writing of a locality in Massachusetts, should refer to it as out of New England.

ordered all the sick and feeble men to get what rest they could, and not regard the enemy's acclamations, but to lie still all night, unless he should call for them. Of those that were in health, some were ordered to keep the watch, and some lay down and endeavored to get some rest; lying down in our clothes, with our arms by us. I lay down the fore part of the night. We got little or no rest, the enemy frequently raised us by their hideous outcries as though they were about to attack us. The latter part of the night I kept the watch.

"Wednesday, 20. As soon as it began to be light the enemy shouted and began to fire upon us for a few minutes, and then ceased for a little time. The serg[8]eant ordered every man to his place, and sent two men up into the watch-box. The enemy came into the field of corn to the south and south-east of the fort, and fought against that side of the fort harder than they did the day before; but unto the north-west side they did not approach so near as they had the first day, yet they kept a continual fire on that side. A number went up also into the mountain north of the fort, where they could shoot over the north side of the fort into the middle of the parade. A considerable number of the enemy also kept their axes and hatchets continually at work, preparing faggots, and their stubbing hoes and spades, etc., in order to burn the fort. About eleven o'clock, Thomas Knowlton, one of our men, being in the watch-box, was shot through the head, so that some of his brains came out, yet life remained in him for some hours.

"About twelve o'clock, the enemy desired to parley. We agreed to it, and when we came to General De Voudriule, he promised us good quarter, if we would surrender; otherwise he should endeavor to take us by force. The sergeant told him he should have an answer within two hours. We came into the fort and examined the state of it. The whole of our ammunition we did not judge to be above three or four pounds of powder, and not more lead: and, after prayers unto God for wisdom and direction, we considered our case, whether there was any probability of our being able to withstand the enemy or not; for we supposed that they would not leave us till they had made a vigorous attempt upon us; and if they did, we knew our ammunition would be spent in a few minutes time, and then we should be obliged [9] to lay at their mercy. Had we all been in health, or had there been only those eight of us that were in health, I believe every man would willingly have stood it out to the last. For my part I should; but we heard, that if we were taken by violence, the sick, the wounded, and the women, would most, if not all of them, die by the hands of the savages; therefore our officer concluded to surrender on the best terms he could get, which were,

"I. That we should be all prisoners to the French; the general promising that the savages should have nothing to do with any of us.

"II. That the children should all live with their parents during the time of their captivity.

"III. That we should all have the privilege of being exchanged the first opportunity that presented.

"Besides these particulars, the general promised that all the prisoners should have all christian care and charity exercised toward them; that those who were weak and unable to travel, should be carried in their journey; that we should all be allowed to keep our clothing; and that we might leave a few lines to inform our friends what was become of us.*

"About three of the clock we admitted the general and a number of his officers into the fort. Upon which he set up his standard. The gate was not opened to the rest. The gentlemen spake comfortably to our people; and on our petition that the dead corpse might not be abused, but buried. They said that it should be buried. But the Indians seeing that they were shut out, soon fell to pulling out the underpinning of the fort, and crept into it, opened the gates, so that the parade was quickly full. They [10] shouted as soon as they saw the blood of the dead corpse under the watch-box; but the French kept them down for some time, and did not suffer them to meddle with it. After some time the Indians seemed to be in a ruffle; and presently rushed up into the watch-box, brought down the dead corpse, carried it out of the fort, scalped it, and cut off the head and arms. A young Frenchman took one of the arms and flayed it, roasted the flesh, and offered some of it to Daniel Smeed, one of the prisoners, to eat, but he refused it. The Frenchman dressed the skin of the arm (as we afterwards heard) and made a tobacco pouch of it.† After they had plundered the fort, they set it on fire, and led us out to their camp.

"We had been at their camp but a little time, when Mons. Doty, the general's interpreter, called me aside, and desired me

---

* Mr. Norton accordingly wrote a brief letter, which he placed upon the well crotch. It was afterwards found by the English. Its contents are given in the history of this war, page 120.

† It was no uncommon thing for the Indians to make use of the skin of their enemies in this way; but instances of the white people imitating them are rare. It is probably true that some of the Kentuckians, in the war of 1812, were guilty of such acts, after General Harrison's victory of the Thames, and perhaps at other times.

to speak to our soldiers, and persuade them to go with the Indians; for he said the Indians were desirous that some of them should go with them; and said that Sergeant Hawks, myself, and the families, should go with the French officers. I answered him, that it was contrary to our agreement, and the general's promise; and would be to throw away the lives of some of our men who were sick and wounded. He said, no; but the Indians would be kind to them; and though they were all prisoners to the French, yet he hoped some of them would be willing to go with the Indians.

"We spoke to Sergeant Hawks, and he urged it upon him. We proposed it to some of our men who were in health, whether they were willing to go or not, but they were utterly unwilling. I returned to Doty, and told him that we should by no means consent that any of our men should go with the Indians. [11] We took the General to be a man of honor, and we hoped to find him so. We knew that it was the manner of the Indians to abuse their prisoners, and sometimes to kill those that failed in traveling, and carrying packs, which we knew that some of our men could not do; and we thought it but little better for the General to deliver them to the Indians than it would be to abuse them himself; and had I thought that the general would have delivered any of our men to the savages, I should have strenuously opposed the surrender of the fort, for I had rather have died in fight, than to see any of our men killed while we had no opportunity to resist. He said that the general would see that they should not be abused; and he did not like it that I was so jealous and afraid. I told him I was not the officer, but as he spake to me, so I had freely spoken my mind, and discharged my duty in it; and he had no reason to be offended, and I hoped the general would not insist on this thing, but would make good his promise to all the prisoners. He went to the general, and after a little time the officers came and took away John Perry and his wife, and all the soldiers but Sergeant Hawks, John Smeed, and Moses Scott, and their families, and distributed them among the Indians. Some French officers took the care of the families, namely, Smeed's and Scott's; and Mons. Demuy* took me with him, and M. St. Luc Lacorn† took Sergeant Hawks with him; and so we reposed that night, having a strong guard set over us.

"Thursday, 21. In the morning I obtained liberty to go to the place of the fort, and set up a letter, which I did, with a Frenchman and some Indians in company. I nailed the letter on the west post. This [12] morning I saw Josiah Reed, who was very weak and feeble by reason of his long and tedious sickness. I interceded with the general for him, that he would not send him with the Indians, but could not prevail. I also interceded with the general for John Aldrich, who, being wounded in the foot, was not able to travel; but the interpreter told me they must go with the Indians, but they should not be hurt; and that they had canoes a little down the river, in which the weak and feeble should be carried. We then put up our things, and set on our march for Crown Point, going down the river in Hoosuck road. I was toward the front, and within about half a mile I overtook John Perry's wife; I passed her. M. Demuy traveling apace. I spoke with her, and asked her how she did? She told me that her strength failed her in traveling so fast. I told her God was able to strengthen her.

---

* His name is variously written in the French accounts, as De Muy, De Muyes, Dumui, etc.; he was a lieutenant in much active service.

† Pierre de Chapt La Corne. He was constantly employed till the fall of Canada, and performed many exploits against the English.

In him she must put her trust, and I hoped she was ready for whatever God had to call her to. I had opportunity to say no more. We went about four miles to the place where the army encamped the night before they came upon us. Here I overtook neighbor Perry, which surprised me, for I thought he had been behind me with the French, but he was with the Indians. I asked him after his health. He said that he was better than he had been. I inquired after his wife. He said he did not know where she was, but was somewhere with the Indians; which surprised me very much; for I thought till then she was with the French.

"Here we sat down for a considerable time. My heart was filled with sorrow, expecting that many of our weak and feeble people would fall by the merciless hands of the enemy. And as I frequently heard the [13] savages shouting and yelling, trembled, concluding that they then murdered some of our people. And this was my only comfort, that they could do nothing against us, but what God in his holy providence permitted them; but was filled with admiration when I saw all the prisoners come up with us, and John Aldrich carried upon the back of his Indian master. We set out again, and had gone but a little way before we came up with Josiah Reed, who gave out. I expected they would have knocked him on the head and killed him, but an Indian carried him on his back. We made several stops, and after we had traveled about eight miles we made a considerable stay, where we refreshed ourselves, and I had an opportunity to speak to several of the prisoners; especially John Smeed, and his wife, who, being near her time, was filled with admiration at the goodness of God in strengthening her to travel so far.

"I saw John Perry's wife. She complained that she was

almost ready to give out. She complained also of the Indian that she went with, that he threatened her. I talked with a French officer, and he said that she need not fear, for he would not be allowed to hurt her. Mons. Demuy, with a number of men, set out before the army, so I took my leave of her, fearing I should never see her more. After this Sergeant Hawks went to the general and represented her case to him. So he went and talked to the Indians, and he was kind to her after this. After we had traveled round the fields, I thought he was about to leave the river, which increased my fears. But I found out the reason; for they only went to look some buildings to plunder, and burn them. A little before sunset we arrived at Vandeverickes place, where we found [14] some of the army, who had arrived before us, but most of them were still behind; and I had the comfort to see the greatest part of the prisoners come up: God having wonderfully strengthened many who were weak; the French carrying the women. There were some few that tarried behind about two miles, where Mrs. Sneed was taken in travail: And some of the French made a seat for her to sit upon, and brought her to the camp, where, about ten o'clock, she was graciously delivered of a daughter, and was remarkably well. The child also was well. But this night Josiah Reed, being very ill, either died of his illness, or else was killed by the enemy; which, I could never certainly know, but I fear he was murdered.*

" Friday, 22. This morning I baptised John Smeed's child. He called its name CAPTIVITY. The French then made a frame like a bier, and laid a buck skin and bear skin upon it,

---

* It might not have been perfectly clear to Mr. Norton when he wrote the above, but it was made clear after the return of the captives, that the man died of his malady. No captives were probably ever treated better under similar circumstances.

and laid Mrs. Smeed, with her infant, thereon; and so two men at a time carried them. They also carried Moses Scott's wife and two children, and another of Smeed's children. The Indians also carried in their canoes, Br. Simon and John Aldrich and Perry's wife, down the river about ten miles.

"We had remarkable smiles of Providence. Our men that had been sick, grew better and recovered strength. The enemy killed some cattle which they found in the meadow; so that we had plenty of fresh provisions and broth, which was very beneficial to the sick. I then expressed a concern for the feeble people, understanding that we were to leave the river, and travel through the wilderness near sixty miles; but Mons. Demuy told me I need not fear, for the general had promised those Indians a reward who [15] had the care of the feeble persons, if they would be kind and carry them through the journey.

"This night I visited most of the prisoners. This night, also, died two Indians of their wounds. The enemy had got four horses.

"Saturday, 23. This morning the general sent off an officer with some men to carry news to Canada. This day we left the river and traveled in the wilderness, in something of a path, and good traveling for the wilderness, something east of north, about fifteen miles; the French still carrying Smeed's and Scott's wives and children; the Indians finding horses for brothers Simon and John Aldrich. Perry being released from his pack, was allowed to help his wife, and carry her when she was weary. About three in the afternoon they were alarmed by discovering the tracts of a scout from Saratoga. This put them into a considerable ruffle, fearing that there might be an army after them. But I presumed that they need not be concerned about it. The body of the army lodged between two ponds, but part, with a number of the prisoners, were sent forward about two miles, till they crossed Sarratago river;* it is there twenty rods wide, but shallow water. This night also died two more Indians of their wounds.

"Lord's day, 24. This day we set out in the morning and came to Sarratago river, crossed it, and came to our company, which had been before us. Here we came to a rich piece of meadow ground, and traveled in it about five miles. We had good traveling this day. We crossed several pieces of good meadow land. We went about eighteen [16] miles. John Perry's wife performed this day's journey without help from any. Our sick and feeble persons were remarkably preserved to-day; for about two o'clock in the afternoon, there fell a very heavy shower of rain, which wet us through all our clothes. Mrs. Smeed was as wet as any of us, and it being the third day after her delivery, we were concerned about the event; but through the good providence of God, she never perceived any harm by it, nor did any other person but Miriam, the wife of Moses Scot, who hereby catched a grievous cold. This night we lodged in the meadow, where was a run of water, which makes a part of Wood Creek.

"Monday, 25. This morning we set out and traveled about eleven miles. We had something rough traveling to-day. We quickly left the small stream we lodged by at our right hand to the east of us, and, traveling a few miles over some small hills and ledges, came to a stream running from east to west,†

---

* This was doubtless the Hudson river, but the place of crossing is difficult to be ascertained. The *two ponds* do not appear on any maps in the editor's possession. *Ed.*

† Hence they were at a stream which falls into Lake George; having its rise in the vicinity of Wood Creek; the latter having its rise in Kingsbury, near the Hudson. The Indian name of Lake

about two or three rods in width, and about two feet deep. We crossed it, our general course being north. We traveled about two or three miles farther and came to a stream running from south-west to north-east, about six rods in width, which we crossed. And this stream (which we suppose to be Wood Creek*), according to the best of my remembrance, and according to the short minute that I made of this day's travel, we left at our right hand to the east of us; but Sergeant Hawks thinks I am mistaken, and that we crossed it again, and left it at the left hand, west of us. I won't be certain, but I cannot persuade myself that [17] I am mistaken.† The French and Indians helping our feeble people, we all arrived well at our camp, which was by a couple of ponds. Some few who were before us went to the drowned land.‡

"Tuesday, 26. This day we took our journey. Our course in the morning something west of north. In traveling about three or four miles we came to a mountain, a steep ascent, about eighty or one hundred rods, but not rocky. After we passed this mountain, our course was about west, five or six miles, till we came to the drowned lands. When we came to the canoes, the stream ran from north-east to south-west.§ We embarked about two o'clock; the stream quickly turned

George is *Caniad-eri-oit*, signifying *the tail of the lake*. It is the *Lac du Sacrement* of the French. Wood Creek the Indians called *Ossavages. Ed.*

* No doubt that *branch* of Wood Creek which falls into the main stream at what is since Fort Anne — the summit level of the Champlain canal. *Ed.*

† Their difficulty seems to have been in mistaking a *branch* for the *real* Wood Creek. *Ed.*

‡ These extend some three miles along South River on the east side, beginning near Lake Champlain. The Indians call them *Ond-cri-que-gon*, or the conflux of waters. *Bassier's Map*, drawn by order of Gen. Amherst, 1762. *Ed.*

§ East Creek corresponds to this; now called Pawlet river, I suppose, *which has its rise in what is Dorset, Vermont. Ed.*

and ran to the north. We sailed about eighteen or twenty miles that night, and encamped on the east side of the water.

"Wednesday, 23. [27th.] We embarked about nine o'clock, and sailed to Crown Point,* something better than twenty miles. Some of the army went in the night before, and some before the body of the army. The sails were pulled down, and the canoes brought up abreast, and passed by the fort over to the north-east point, saluting the fort with three volleys, as we passed by it. The fort returning the salute by the discharge of the cannon. This was about twelve o'clock. Here we tarried till the 4th of September. I lodged in an house on the north-east point. We all arrived better in health than when we were first taken.

"Thursday, 28. This day I was invited by Monsieur Demuy to go over and see the fort, which I did. It is something an irregular form, having five sides [18] to it; the ramparts twenty feet thick, the breast work two feet and half; the whole about twenty feet high. There were twenty-one or twenty-two guns upon the wall; some four and six pounders, and there may be some as large as nine pounders. The citadel an octagon built, three stories high, fifty or sixty feet diameter, built with stone laid in lime, the wall six or seven feet thick, arched over the second and third stories for bomb proof. In the chambers nine or ten guns; some of them may be nine pounders, and I believe none less than six, and near twenty patararoes.† But as my time was short I cannot be very par-

---

* The French built a fort there in 1721, which they named Fort St. Frederic. The Indians gave that spot the name of *Tek-ya-dough-nigarigee*, which signifies two points opposite to each other. *Bassier, ibidem. Ed.*

† How much of a *gun* a *patararoe* was, it would have been well if the author had informed us, as we may travel from Blount to Webster without finding out. Perhaps derived from the Spanish *petardo*, or, *pataremo. Editor.*

ticular. They have stores of small arms, as blunderbusses, pistols and muskets. This night proved very cold and stormy.

"Friday, 29. This morning Smeed's and Scot's families were brought out of their tents into the house, that they might be more comfortable. It rained and was very cold all the day, and at night the wind was very high.

"Saturday the 30th was something warmer.

"Lord's day, 31. We had the liberty of worshiping God together in a room by ourselves. This day, about twelve o'clock, the enemy who went off from us from Hoosuck, the morning after we were taken, returned, and brought in six scalps, viz, Samuel Allen, Eleazer Hawks, Jun., two Amsdels, all of Deerfield; Adonijah Gillet of Colchester, Constant Bliss of Hebron, and one captive, viz., Samuel Allen, son to him who was killed. He was taken with his father and Ealeazer Hawks. The Amsdells and Gillet were killed in Deerfield South Meadow, August 25th. The Indians also acknowledged they lost one man there.* This lad [19] told us they had not then heard in Deerfield of their taking fort Massachusetts. A young Hatacook † Indian was his master, and carried him to St. Francois.

"Monday, Sept. 1. Tuesday, 2. Wednesday, 3. We tarried still at Crown Point. The weather was something lowry, but warm. I lived with the general and about half a dozen more officers, who lodged in the same house. Our diet was very good, it being chiefly fresh meat and broth, which was a great benefit to me. We had also plenty of Bourdeaux wine, which being of an astringent nature, was a great kindness to me (having at that time something of the griping and bloody

---

* See *History of the Five Years War*, pp. 125, 126. *Ed.* † Perhaps a misprint for *Scattacook*. *Editor.*

flux). While we lay here, we wrote a letter to the Hon. John Stoddard, Esq., at Northampton, to give him a particular account of our fight and surrender; as also some other private letters; the French gentlemen giving us encouragement that they would send them down by some of their scouts to some part of our frontiers, and leave them so that they should be found; but I have not heard of them since, and conclude that they destroyed them.*

"Thursday, 4. We embarked for Canada about ten o'clock, and sailed about fifteen miles. Our course, I judged to be north, about 10° east, which I take to be the general course from Crown Point to Champlain. Towards night we turned into a cove, the east side of the lake, and encamped, having the land upon the south-west, south and east of us. Here we were to wait for General De Vaudriŭle, whom we left at Crown Point, and expected would come to us this night or in the morning; but the night proved very stormy.

[20] "Friday, 5. The wind blowing hard from the north, and some rain, we lay by to-day.

"Saturday, 6. About nine o'clock this morning the general came up with us; then we embarked and sailed with a pretty good wind the bigger part of the day. Towards night we saw a few houses on the west side of the lake, but I suppose that they were deserted. We sailed at least three score miles this day. We came to where the lake was but a few miles in width, and encamped on the east shore, where there was a windmill and a few houses, but were all deserted.†

---

* One certainly found its way to the English, and was seen by Deacon Wright. See *N. E. Hist. and Gen. Reg.*, II, 210. *Editor.*

† No doubt the place afterwards called Windmill Point by the English, and not far from the mouth of Onion river. *Editor.*

Lord's day, 7. We rose early and set sail as soon as it was fair day-light, having a good wind, but the wind fell about eight o'clock, that they were obliged to ply their paddles. When we came to the end of the lake, about eleven o'clock, and were entering Champlain * river, we met a boat with three men in it, who brought a packet of letters for the officers in the army. They gave one to Mons. Demuy. After reading the letter he told me the news he had by them, viz., that there were a number of ships arrived from France to Quebec, who had brought them plenty of stores; that they came in company with a fleet of forty large men of war from the Brest and Toulon squadron; and gave the following account; that the English fleet having blocked up the Brest squadron in the harbor, the admiral of the Brest squadron wrote to the admiral of the Toulon and Rochfort squadrons to come to his assistance; who, coming on the back of the English fleet, and the Brest squadron issuing out at the same time against them, there ensued a terrible [21] fight, in which the French prevailed, and sunk one-half of the English ships, and put the rest to flight, and then they sailed for North America;† that the King sent with them twelve merchant

---

* *Chambly* or *Chamblee* river is undoubtedly meant; called also *Richelieu*, and *Sorel*, by the French. Further on the same error is noted, where the author speaks of Champlain fort. He did not distinguish between *Champlain* and *Chamblee*. *Ed.*

† There appears to have been absolutely nothing out of which this great fabrication was made. It refers to the mighty fleet under the Duc D'Anville, which was then in mid ocean, it having left Brest on the 22d of June (1746), but did not appear on the New England coast until the beginning of September; and then in too shattered a condition to be feared. His fleet of men of war and transports amounted to about ninety-seven sail; fourteen were ships of war, with three thousand five hundred troops. His fleet was watched by the English, and some of his ships taken. Capt. Leke took one of sixty-four guns; Saumarez one of sixty-four; Boscawen one of fifty, and so forth. The other French squadron referred to was probably that of M. De Tourmell. Saumarez was with Anson in his late voyage round the world. *Ed.*

ships with stores of ammunition, clothing, wine, and brandy, and a thousand soldiers to strengthen Canada; that the men of war were divided into two fleets, one of which did now block up Louisbourg, and were fighting against it, and the other part of the fleet was gone for Boston. He said their King was very angry with New England for their taking Cape Breton; and it was probable he would bring them into subjection. He told me also that they brought news that Edward Stuart, the Pretender's youngest son, was in the North of England, and had a powerful army; and that great numbers of English resorted to him daily,* and it was probable he would prevail to dethrone King George. I told him that, as for this and the fight at sea, I had good reason to think they were false, for I had news from England since the Brest fleet had sailed out, and there was no account of these things, but the contrary. He told me also that Prince William, the Duke of Cumberland,† was killed in battle at Culloden-Muir, and that he was the only person of the House of Hanover which the English nation loved; so that although the King's army got the victory, yet it was a loss to his interest; for the Duke being dead, the English nation would revolt from the House of Hanover, being weary of it, and turn to the House of Stuart. But I told him that the Duke of Cumberland was yet alive, and as he had been a scourge and terror to the King's enemies, so we had reason to hope he would still be. He grew warm in his debate, called the King [22] a usurper, the nation in bringing of him in, Cromwell's faction, and many

---

* This, though guess-work, was much nearer the real state of the case than the other part of the story. They probably had heard of the defeats of the King's men at Falkirk Moor, Inverness, etc. *Editor.*

† William Augustus, brother of George II. He died *sine prole*, 1765. He put down the Pretender, but showed himself quite as much of a barbarian as those whom he conquered. *Ed.*

other things, upon which we had a considerable debate, until he grew more mild and began to flatter; and told me what an amiable man the Pretender was, and what good times it would be if he came to the throne of England; giving free liberty of conscience to all his subjects; and he did not doubt but that they would return to the church of Rome, which was the true church. Our children, he believed, would come to a· good union in religion.

"We went on shore at the first house, about three miles above the fort,* where they were called together, and said their prayers; and as soon as they had done, Mons. Dumuy read his letter. Upon which they all shouted, crying, Vive le Roy: q. d. Let the King live. Upon which several of the young men came laughing to me, and by signs endeavored to inform me what the news was. I concluded that these fine tales were framed and sent to meet the army, in order to keep up the courage of the common people and of the Indians, who seemed to repent of their engaging in the war, and to grow very weary of it. Though I found afterwards that the Brest fleet was actually come over, with a design against New England.

"From thence we traveled down to Champlain,† where the gentlemen set up their tents, and we had great numbers to visit us of both sexes. There I expected we should have tarried that night. But a little before the sun setting, M. Dumuy came and ordered his canoe's company to embark, and go down the river; and told me I must go with them, and whatever I stood in need of, his people would [23] give me: And indeed I wanted nothing; having good fresh provisions and plenty of wine to drink; but was something surprised at this sudden

* *Chamblee*, or perhaps more probable, Fort St. John. † Chamblee. The author perhaps had no maps to refer to.

remove, and could never know the reason of it, unless it was this, viz, some of the French and Indians going out from Crown Point, while I lay there, fell on a number of our men near Saratago; had killed some and taken some prisoners, and were come to Champlain with one of them; and they wanted to get what news from him they could, and so chose to get me out of the way, and some others, lest we might give him a caution; and he really wanted a caution, for he told them that which he had better have kept to himself, viz, the miserable circumstances of Sarrtago fort.*

"We sailed down the river about three miles, and lodged at a poor man's house, who, according to his ability, was courteous to me. I lodged with him in his own bed, which was the first bed I had lodged in since my captivity; and though it was a hard bed, and destitute of linnen, yet it was very comfortable to me.

"Monday, 8. This morning there came an Englishman to see me; his name Littlefield. He was taken a lad from Piscataqua, and so continued with the French and lived, having a family at Champlain.† We had a considerable discourse together. About eight o'clock we embarked; some canoes passing down the river on the opposite side. We sailed over the river and met with Mons. Dumuy and took him in. We sailed down the river about fifteen miles and dined with a priest. The country on Champlain ‡ river appeared very poor; it being cold sour land. It is inhabited on each side, but the buildings are [24] generally but poor huts. This day Mons. Dumuy

---

* This affair is mentioned in the *Particular History of the Five Years War*, page 127.

† Persons of the name of Littlefield were great sufferers in the earlier Indian wars. See *Penhallow, Indian Wars*, pp. 44, 47, 71.

‡ Chamblee. *Ed.*

tells me another piece of news, viz, 'that one of their men of war had taken an English man of war near Louisbourg, after a whole day's engagement; that the blood was midleg deep upon the Englishmen's deck when he surrendered.' I told him they fought courageously. He said, 'True, but they were taken notwithstanding.' He said 'they had taken three hundred and twenty men out of her, who were coming up to Quebec, where I should meet them.' This was nothing but the Albany sloop, one of the men of war's tenders, which Governor Knowles sent with a packet from Louisbourg for Boston. There were but seventy men in her. She was taken by a French man of war near Jebucta. About two o'clock it began to rain, and continued a cold rain all the rest of the day. We sailed down the river between thirty and forty miles, and then carried over our canoes and packs across the land to St. Lawrence, which was about three miles; and we came to it above Lozel,* and there we lodged that night, in a French house.

"Tuesday, 9. This morning being something lowery, we did not set out very early. The wind was northeasterly and pretty high. About nine o'clock we set sail up the river for Montreal. It was good sailing. We dined at a French gentleman's house on the eastern shore. There was an Irish doctor came and dined with us — his name O'Sullivan. He pretended a great deal of respect for me, and compassion towards all the prisoners; a great deal of friendship to the English nation, and especially for the House of Hanover; and he inquired after the state of Scotland, and pretended to rejoice that the Duke of [25] Cumberland had got such a victory over the Pretender and the rebels. But I presently found he grew weary in hearing the particulars; and therefore to mortify him

* *Sorrel* is doubtless the place meant. The outlet of Lake Champlain. *Ed.*

the more, I told him all that I could;* then we set sail and went within about five miles of Mount Real. The weather was something tedious, and it rained in the afternoon.

"Wednesday, 10. This morning it rained very hard till near ten o'clock, about which time the general and some others passed by us, and we embarked directly upon it, and arrived at Mount-Real about twelve o'clock.

"Mons. Demuy took me to the Governors. He said but little to me. He only told me, that for the time I tarried at Mount-Real, I should keep at Mons. Demuy's, but that after a few days he must send me with the rest of the prisoners, to Quebec. I went with Mons. Demuy, and was courteously entertained by him for the time I tarried at Mount-Real. In the afternoon came an Englishwoman to visit me. She was, I judged, between sixty and seventy years of age. She was taken when a child from Merrimack-River. Her name Hannah Rie. She had been married to a Frenchman, by whom she had four children, three sons and one daughter. Her daughter was married and had several children, and came to see me. I saw also one of her sons. She had been a widow about fourteen years, but was under very comfortable circumstances. There was another Englishwoman came to see me, who was taken from the eastward, but I have forgot both her name and place where she was taken from.

"Friday [Thursday], 11. This day I tarried at Mons. Demuy's, where the Major of the town visited me. He told [26] me that he married an Englishwoman whose name was Storer.† She was taken when a child by Indians, from Pisca-

---

* The author appears to have suspected Dr. O'Sullivan's sincerity with no good reason, judging from anything which he tells us. *Editor.*

† Mention was often made of children being carried off by the Indians, without any family being named; as in this case: "1710. This summer, four

taqua; that one of his sons was down at the taking of us. Mrs. St. La Germine, one of his wife's cousins, who was also taken with her, came with the major, and was able to discourse in the English tongue. She told me that the Rev. Mr. Storer* of Watertown was her brother, and that she wanted to hear from her friends; but I was not acquainted with any of them.

"Friday, 12. This day, about two o'clock in the afternoon, we embarked in boats, and set sail for Quebec, and sailed down the river about five leagues. There were all that were taken with me but six men who were yet with the Indians, and John Perry's wife, who was at the Three-Rivers. There were also four Dutch with us, who were taken near Sarratago. We lodged in a house upon the north-west side of the St. Lawrence's river.

"Saturday, 13. This day we had a fair wind, and sailed down the river twenty-five leagues, when we arrived at the Three Rivers. We went into an inn. The general and some others of the gentlemen which went down with us, presently went out to the Governors, leaving only their soldiers to guard us. And after a little time the Governor sent for Sergeant Hawks and me to come and sup with him. Accordingly we went, and were courteously and sumptuously entertained by him; and while we sat at supper the gentlemen fell into discourse about the wars, and about the wounds they had received. The general's wound was discoursed upon, and the Governor desired Sergeant Hawks to show his scars, which he did. The

children are taken at Exeter while at play." *Belknap (Farmer's edition),* 178. Ed.

* The Rev. Seth Storer was ordained at W., 22 July, 1724. *Francis,* 78. The author speaks of notes in Mr. Storer's old Almanacs, which he had seen. *Three Discourses,* 12. He died Nov. 27, 1774, æ. 72. *A. B. Fuller's Record.* He was born in Saco, the son of Col. Joseph Storer. *Allen.* Benjamin Storer was killed at Wells, April 12, 1677. *Hubbard.* Editor.

Gover[27]nor then informed us of a fight he had been in at sea in former wars, in which he received fifteen wounds, and he shewed us several scars. This I thought was a very remarkable thing, that he should receive so many wounds, and yet have his life spared. This night John Perry's wife was also brought to us, and added to our number.

"Lord's day, 14. We set sail, but received little help from the wind. The soldiers were obliged to row the greatest part of the day; but at night, the tide favoring of us, we sailed till two or three o'clock in the morning. We sailed in the day and night twenty-three leagues. Then we went on shore the north-west side of the river, and lodged at a house in a small village.

"Monday, 15. This day we sailed seven leagues and came to Quebec. We were landed at the east point of the town, where St. Lawrence meets with Loretto,* and were conducted up by a number of soldiers through the lower town to the Governor General's,† where I was taken into his private room, and he desired me to tell him what news we had in New England. I told him of considerable news we had from Europe concerning the Duke of Cumberland's victory over the rebels. He seemed to have a great mind to persuade me that the Duke was killed, but I told him he was alive and well. I told him of several other pieces of news, but none very good for the French. He told me he had heard that we designed an expedition against Canada. He asked what there was in it. I told

---

* A small village of Christian Indians, three leagues north-east of Quebec. It has its name from a chapel built according to the model of the Santa Casa at Loretto in Italy; from which an image of the Holy Virgin has been sent to the converts here, resembling that in the famous Italian sanctuary. These converts are Hurons. *Morse. Ed.*

† Roland Michel Barrin, Count de la Galissonière was at this time Governor of New France. *Ed.*

him that I lived at a great distance from Boston, and could say but little about it. I had heard that his Majesty had sent over to some of the governors in America, that he had thoughts of an ex[28]pedition against Canada, and would have them in readiness to assist him, in case he should send a fleet over. He inquired what it was that had put it by. Something, he said, was the matter. I told him I could not tell; so he seemed to be pretty easy.

"After this I was conducted to the Lord Intendants, who inquired also after news, both of me and Sergeant Hawks; after which he gave us a glass of wine; then we were conducted to the prisoner's house, which is a guard-house standing by a battery towards the south-west end of the town, about one hundred and fifty feet in length, and twenty in width, and two stories high; and we made to the number of one hundred and five prisoners. Here we had the free liberty of the exercise of our religion together, which was matter of comfort to us in our affliction. Sergeant Hawks and myself were put into the Captain's room, where we found three English masters of vessels, viz, Mr. William Chapman of Maryland, Mr. James Southerland* of Cape Cod, and Capt. William Pote† of Casco Bay, who had all been prisoners near sixteen months.

"Tuesday, 16. This day there came some gentlemen to see me, among whom was Mr. Joseph Portois, who understands the English tongue, and Mr. Pais, who, Mr. Portois told me, was his kinsman, and that he was a protestant, and came

---

* The name of Southerland or Sutherland is of rare occurrence in New England records. It occurs but twice in the twenty-three volumes of the *New Eng. Hist. and Gen. Register*, and then with no reference to a Cape Cod residence. *Ed.*

† He belonged to Portland; went there from Marblehead; had seven sons; built the two story house near Woodford's Corner on the old road from Portland. See Willis, *Portland*, 637, where other interesting particulars may be found. *Ed.*

on purpose to see me, and to shew me a kindness. He gave me twenty-four livres in cash. From this time to the 23d, there was nothing remarkable happened, only this : — that the jesuits and some unknown gentlemen, understanding I was short on it for clothing, sent me several shirts, a good winter coat, some caps, a pair of stockings, and a few handkerchiefs, which were very acceptable.

[29] " Tuesday, 23. Capt. William Pote was taken ill with the fever and flux. Jacob Reed was also taken with the same. This day came into prison two of our men who had been with the Indians, viz, David Warren, and Phinehas Forbush, who informed that John Aldrich was in the hospital at Mount-Real. They informed us, also, concerning some other prisoners who were taken from New England, and with the Indians.

" Wednesday, 24. There came unto prison forty-three new prisoners, who were taken at sea by a couple of French men of war. Among whom was Mr. William Lambert, master of the Billinder,* one of the men of war's tenders, who was taken near Jebucta, as she was going from Louisbourg to Boston, and Zephaniah Pinkham, master of a whaling sloop from Nantucket ; and John Phillips, master of a fishing schooner from Marblehead.

" Thursday and Friday, 25, 26. There came in about seventy-four prisoners, all taken at sea by the aforesaid men of war ; among whom were several masters of vessels. This day † there also came in Jacob Shepherd, who was taken with me, and had been with the Indians, and one widow Briant, taken the spring before, near Casco Bay. There was nothing further

---

* Properly *Bylander*. A coasting vessel, so named as expressive of its *alongshore* use. I do not know why it is not in the dictionaries. *Ed.*

† October 1, Jacob Shepard, of Westborough, taken at Hoosuck, was brought to prison. October 3, Jonathan Batherick was brought to prison. *How*, 19. *Ed.*

remarkable in this month; so that we were by this time increased to the number of two hundred and twenty-six.

"Lord's day, October 5. There came in seventeen prisoners, viz, three of our men, Nathaniel Hitchcock, Stephen Scot, and John Aldrich; two taken by Indians at the Eastward, viz, Richard Stubs,* and Pike Gordon; and twelve from the Bay Verde.

"Lord's day, 12. There came twenty-four men taken at sea by the Lazora and Le Castore men of war.

[30] "Wednesday, 22. I sent a petition to his lordship the General of Canada or New France, to permit me to go home to New England, upon a parole of honor, setting me a suitable time, and I would return again to him; but I could not prevail.

"Thursday, 23. Edward Cloutman and Robert Dunbar, two prisoners, broke prison and made their escape. But it was found out the next morning, and we were upon it threatened to be confined to our rooms, but this threatening was never executed; the only consequent in respect to us was to have a stricter guard kept about us; but they sent out a number of men in pursuit after them.†

"Friday, 31. Mr. Phillips and Mr. Pinkham, with about a dozen of their men, went out from us in order to return home; but they went by the way of the West Indies.‡

"Here I shall speak of the sickness that prevailed among the prisoners. It had generally been very healthy in the prison before this fall; for though there had been some prisoners there sixteen months, and about fifty nine months, yet there had but

* Taken at New Casco. *Ibidem.* Oct. 19. Six seamen are brought to prison. Oct. 20. Jacob Read died. *Ibidem.*

† Oct. 27. A man was brought to prison, and says the Indians took five more, and brought ten scalps to Montreal. *How,* 19.

‡ They may have been exchanged. The author seems not to have known on what terms they went away. *Ed.*

two died; the first, Lawrence Platter.* He was taken at Sarratago, Nov. 17, 1745, and died the winter following.

—— Johnes,† taken at Contoocook in the summer, 1746, and died in August following.

"But our people who were taken at sea by the two French men of war, viz, the Lazora and Le Castore, found a very mortal epidemical fever raged among the French on board their ships, of which many of them died. The prisoners took the infection, and a greater part of them were sick while they lay [31] in Jebucta ‡ harbor; yet but one or two of them died of it. And when they set out from thence for Menis, some of them were sick, and some they left sick at Menis when they set out for Canada. Some of them were taken with the distemper upon their passage to Canada, and so brought the infection into the prison; and the fever being epidemical, soon spread itself into the prisons to our great distress.

"Those who brought it into the prison mostly recovered, and so there were many others that had it and recovered; but the recovery of some was but for a time,—many of them relapsed and died. It put me in mind of that text, Jude, ver. 5, '*I will therefore put you in remembrance, tho' ye once knew this, how that the Lord having saved the people out of the Land of Egypt, afterwards destroyed them that believe not.*' Not that I have any reason to think ill of those upon whom the sickness fell, and who died with it. Many of them, I hope, were truly pious and godly persons. I thought we might very properly take up the Lamentation of Jeremiah, Lam. 1, 18. '*The Lord is*

---

* *Plaffer* is probably the name intended. See *Particular History*, 86, 87, where will be found an account of the depredation in which he was taken. *Ed.*

† Thomas Jones. See *Ibidem*, 95. *Ed.*

‡ Chebucto, a bay and harbor on the S. S. E. coast of Nova Scotia. Near its head, on the west side, is Halifax, settled by the English in 1749. See Morse, *Gazetteer*, ed. 1797, art. CHEBUCTO. *Ed.*

APPENDIX.] *Norton's Redeemed Captive.* 283

righteous, for I have rebelled against his commandment. Hear I *pray for you, all people, and behold my sorrow. My virgins and my young men are gone into captivity.'* Ver. 20. '*Abroad the sword devoureth, at home there is death.*'

"Monday, 20. Jacob Reed died. He was taken at Gorham-Town, near Casco Bay, April 19, 1746.*

"November 1. This day died John Reed, son to Jacob Reed, deceased. He had been a soldier in Annapolis, and was taken near the fort by some Indians, May 9, 1745.

"Nov. 10. Died one —— Davis,† a soldier belonging [32] to the King's forces at Louisbourg. He was taken on the island of St. John's, July 10th, 1746.

"Nov. 13. Died John Bingham. He belonged to Philadelphia, and was taken at sea, May 22, 1745.

"Nov. 17, died Nathan Eames.‡ He belonged to Marlborough in the province of the Massachusetts Bay, was taken with me at Fort Massachusetts, August 20, 1746.

"Nov. 18. Died at night, Andrew Sconce. He was taken near Albany, August 17th, 1747.

"Nov. 20. Died John Grote of Shenectada. He was taken April 27th, 1746.§

"About this time‖ there came into prison two men who were taken at Sheepscot in the eastward. Their names Robert Adams and John McNeer. They were taken October 20th.

---

* See *Particular History*, etc., page 90. *Editor.*

† John Davis, and he died Nov. 9. *How*, 19.

‡ He was doubtless a descendant of Thomas Eames of Sudbury, who was so great a sufferer in Philip's war. Barry (in his *Framingham*) has no *Nathan*, but a *Nathaniel*, who died, he says, Jan. 1st, 1746. *Ed.*

§ On the same day, Mr. Norton married the two captives, Leonard Lydle and Mrs. Sarah Briant. His reason for not mentioning it in his narrative may be conjectured. *Ed.*

‖ November 19th. *How*, 19.

They informed that one of their neighbors, named Anderson, was then killed.*

"The sickness increasing and spreading itself so greatly, we sent a very humble petition to his Lordship, the Governor General, intreating that the sick might be removed out of the hospital, least the whole prison should be infected; but he refused to send our people to the hospital, for they told us that their hospital was full of their own sick; yet he did not wholly neglect our petition, but ordered that one of the most convenient rooms in the prison should be assigned for the sick, where they should all be carried, and have their attendance, and this was directly done, and the sick were all brought in.†

"Nov. 24. Died John Bradshaw. He belonged to Capt. Donahew. He was taken when Capt. Donahew was killed at Canso, June 29th, 1745. He was wounded when taken, but recovered of his wounds; soon fell into a consumptive way, and died of it.

[33] "Nov. 28. Died Jonathan Dunham. He was taken with Capt. Pote near Annapolis, May 17th, 1745. He died after eight or ten days sickness.

"Nov. 29. Died William Bagley.‡ He was master of a vessel taken at sea, May 29th, 1746.

"December 1. Died Gratis Vanderveriske, after a tedious sickness of six or seven weeks. He belonged to Sarratago, was taken by the enemy, November 17th, 1745.

"Dec. 6. Died Pike Gordon. He was taken from Biddeford, September 5th, 1746; was sick eleven days, and all the time deprived of his reason.

---

* Nov. 22. The abovesaid Anderson's uncle was brought to prison. *How*, 19.

† Jonathan Dunham died. *How*, 20.

‡ *How* has this under the same date: "Capt. Bailey of Almsbury died." *Bagley* is probably the right name.

"Dec. 7. Died Martha Quaquinbush, a girl taken at Sarratago, Nov. 17th, 1745. She had a long and tedious sickness; what it was is uncertain.*

"Dec. 11. Died Mirriam the wife of Moses Scott. She was taken with me at Fort Massachusetts. She got a cold in her journey, which proved fatal, her circumstances being peculiar. She was never well after our arrival at Canada, but wasted away to a mere skeleton, and lost the use of her limbs.

"Dec. 15. Died John Boon. He was taken at sea, May 1st,† 1746. He died of a consumption; belonged to Devonshire in England.

"Dec. 18. Died Mary Woodwell, wife to David Woodwell,‡ of New Hopkinton on Merrimack river. She lay in a burning fever about a fortnight. She was taken captive, April 27th, 1746.

"Dec. 23. Died Rebecca the wife of John Perry. She was taken with me at Fort Massachusetts, August 20th, 1746. Her illness was different from all the rest. She had little or no fever; had a cold, and was exercised with wrecking pains until she died.

"Dec. 24. I was taken with the distemper; was seized with a very grievous pain in the head and back [34] and a fever; but I let blood in the morning, and took a good potion of physic, and in a few days another; so that I soon recovered again.

"Dec. 26. Died Wm. Daily of New York. He belonged to Capt. Rouse's ship, and was taken upon St. John's Island, July 10th, 1746. He had a very long and tedious sickness;

---

* She was ten years of age. *How.*

† One of Capt. Robertson's lieutenants died. *How.*

‡ See *Particular History*, etc., p. 92, where will be found some particulars of her singular vicisitudes of fortune.

several times he seemed to be in a way to recover; but took relapses, till he was worn out. He swelled in his neck and side of his face, and mortified.

"January 2, 1746–7. Died Thomas Atkinson of Lancashire in England; was taken at sea, May, 1745; his sickness very tedious about eight or nine days before his death.

"Jan. 3. Died Jonathan Hogadorn. He belonged to the county of Albany, and was taken on a scout near Fort Ann, Nov. 16th, 1745; had a long and tedious sickness of more than two months continuance.*

"The sickness thus increasing, there were many taken sick, which I do n't pretend to mention. The sickness also got into the prison-keeper's family. He lost a daughter by it, the 4th instant. Upon this the Governor ordered a house to be provided for the sick, where they were all carried the 12th instant, about twenty in number, with three men to attend them; and after this, when any were taken sick, they were carried out to this house.

"Jan. 12. Died at night, Francis† Andrews, of Cape Ann. He was taken at sea, June 24, 1746, and died of the bloody flux, after a tedious spell of it.

"Jan. 15. Died at night, Jacob Bagley,‡ of Newbury, after about two days sickness. He was taken at sea, May 26th, 1746.

"Jan. 27. Died Guyart Brabbon,§ of Maryland, after ten weeks sickness; taken at sea, May 22d, 1745.

---

* Jan. 4. The Rev. Mr. Norton was so far recovered from sickness that he preached two discourses from Psal. 60, 11.

† *How*, p. 20, gives the name *Phineas* Andrews.

‡ *How, ibidem,* gives the fact thus: Jacob *Baley,* brother of Capt. Bailey aforesaid, died.

§ Giat Braban, Capt. Chapman's carpenter. *Ibidem.*

[35] "Jan. 23. Died Samuel Lovet, after near a month's sickness. He was taken with me.*

"Feb. 11. Died in the morning, Moses Scot, son to Moses Scot. He was a child of about two years old, and died with the consumption. In the afternoon died Wm. Galbaoth,† a Scots-man. He was taken at sea, April 4th, 1746; was sick about a month before he died.

"About this time I had another turn of illness. I had a grievous pain in my head and back. The doctor blooded me, and advised me to go to the hospital; for, he said, I was going to have the distemper, but, by careful living, I soon recovered, and escaped the distemper.

"Feb. 23. Died Richard Bennet. He belonged to Capt. Rouse's ship, and was taken at the island St. Jon's, July 10th, 1746. He belonged to the Jerseys, and had a long and tedious sickness.

"Feb. 24. Died Michael Dogan, an Irishman. He listed at Philadelphia, a soldier for Louisbourg, and was taken in his passage by a French man of war. He had been sick, and recovered, but took a relapse the 20th instant.

"March, 1747. The fore part of this month our people were generally better in health than they had been, and we were in hopes the distemper would abate; yet there was a number sick.

"March 5. We had news from Nova Scotia, that the French, under the command of Mons. Ramsey, had fallen

---

* He was son of Major Lovet of Mendon. *How*, 20.

† Printed *Garwafs* in *How*, p. 20. Feb. 15. My nephew, Daniel How, and six more were brought down from Montreal to Quebec, viz., John Sunderland, John Smith, Richard Smith, William Scot, Philip Scofil, and Benj. Tainter, son to Lieut. Tainter of Westborough. *How*, 20-1.

upon an English army at Minis, had killed one hundred and thirty-three, and had taken four hundred prisoners; but the truth I suppose was, that they had killed about seventy, and taken about as many more.

"March 18. Died Thomas Magra, an Irishman. He was taken in the Billinder. His sickness was very short.

[36] "March 21. Died John Fort, servant, a Dutchman. He was taken on a scout near Fort Ann, November 16th, 1745. He died of a consumption. The same day died Samuel Goodman of South Hadley. He was taken with me at Fort Massachusetts, and died of the scurvy.

"March 29. Died Mary, the wife of John Smeed, after a tedious sickness of about eight weeks; was taken with me.

"April 7. Died John Smeed, Jun. He was taken with me at Fort Massachusetts. He was seized with the distemper in October last, and was bad for a time, and then recovered in some good measure, and after a little time relapsed, and as he did several times, till at last he fell into a consumption, of which he died.

"April 8. Died Philip Scaffield. He belonged to Pennsylvania soldiers, was taken near Albany, October, 1746. His sickness was short, but his fever very violent.

"April 10. Died John Jordan, master of a vessel taken at sea, June 1st, 1746. He came sick into prison, but seemed to recover; and so had frequent relapses till he died. He belonged to the Bay government.

"The same day died Antonio, a Portuguese. He was taken in the English service, and so always kept confined. His sickness was short.

"April 12. Died Amos Pratt. He was taken with me. He had a hard turn of the Fever in November and December, but recovered; was taken again the latter end of March, and so continued till he died.

"April 13. Died Timothy Cummings. He was taken near George's fort, where he belonged, May 22d, 1746. His sickness was short but very tedious.

"April 16. Died John Dill. He belonged to Nantaskett; was mate of a sloop, and taken at sea, near Jebucta, May 29th, 1746. His sickness was upon him about ten days before his death.

[37] "April 17. Died Samuel Evans of Newbury. He was taken at sea with Capt. William Bagley. He had a fortnight's sickness.

"April 18. Died Samuel Vaughn,* one of Capt. Rouse's men, taken at St. John's, July 10th, 1746. He belonged to Plymouth in New England. He was sick about eight days before his death.

"April 27. Died Joseph Denning of Cape Ann, master of a fishing schooner, taken at sea, June 24th, 1746. He was exercised with purging the greatest part of the winter, and was worn out with it and died.

"April 30. Died Susanna Mc Cartees, infant child.

"The 28th of this instant, when the prisoners were all confined in their rooms, but one or two in the lower room cooking the pot, the prison house took fire. It began on the ridge. We supposed that it catched by sparks lighting upon it. It being very dry, and something windy, it soon spread upon the house, and we could not come at it, having no ladder, to quench it. There were no lives lost, but many lost their bedding and clothing.

"We were conducted by a strong guard to the governor's

---

* Printed in *How's Narrative*, page 21, *Venhon*.

yard, where we were kept till near night, when we were conducted to the back of the town to the old wall, in a bow of which they had set up some plank tents something like sheep's pens. We had boards flung down to lay our beds upon, but the tents generally leaked so much in wet weather, that none of us could lie dry, and had much wet weather this month.

"The gentlemen of our room sent in a petition the beginning of May, that they might be removed to some more convenient place. Upon which we had a house built for us in the prisoner's yard, about twenty feet square, into which we were removed the 23d instant. This was something more comfortable than the tents. In this yard we were confined, having the wall behind it and at each end, and the fort side picketed in, and a guard of about twenty men to keep us in both by day and night.

"N. B. I should have observed that several prisoners were brought into prison before this; as Feb. 15th, there came in seven men from Mount-Real, taken the summer before. [38] In March there came into prison a Dutchman from Schanectada, and a woman from Saratago.

"April 26th, there came into prison, three persons taken some time before at Saratago, and Jonathan Williamson, taken at Wiscassett, at the eastward, April 13th, 1747.*

* Probably an error, and should be 1746, unless this was the second time Williamson was a captive. His place was at Broad Bay, and Smith says —*Journal*, 42 — news came to Falmouth, May 21 (1746) that "the Indians had burnt all the houses at Broad Bay." Sullivan says, page 168, that he returned out of captivity the next year (1748). Williamson lived at Broad Bay, and was doubtless taken when the place was destroyed. If he were taken on the 13th of April, and delivered at Quebec on the 26th following, it was rather a short time (thirteen days) in which to take him through the wilderness, judging from what is stated respecting the tedious journeyings of Indian captives of that time. Nehemiah How also records the arrival of Williamson, and How died May 25th following; hence this reduces the journey to twelve days, if Williamson was taken in 1747. Circumstances seem to authorize the correction we have made. *Editor*.

APPENDIX.] *Norton's Redeemed Captive.* 291

" May 9. Died Sarah, the relict of Wm. Bryant. She was taken at Gorham Town, near Casco Bay, April 19th, 1746. Her husband and four of her children were then killed; one escaping. She was taken sick the 1st of May.

" May 13. Died Daniel Smeed, a young man. He was taken with me, and was son to John Smeed. He was first taken sick in November, and by frequent relapses was worn out, and fell into a purging, by which he wasted away and died.

" May 14. Came into prison John Larmon, taken at Damascota, in the eastward, by eleven Indians, April 27th, 1747, and informed that his wife and daughter were killed by them.

" May 15. Died in the morning Christian Tedder,* of Schenectada, taken May 7th, 1746. He was taken sick about the beginning of this month.

" The same day died Mr. Hezekiah Huntington, son to Col. Huntington of Norwich in Connecticut. He was taken at sea, June 28th, 1746. He was well beloved and much lamented by all sober religious persons.†

" This day also died Joseph Gray of Maryland. He was taken by sea, May 22d, 1745. A likely young man. Thus we had three likely young men taken from us in one day.

" May 17. Died Captivity Smeed, an infant about nine months old, daughter to John Smeed.

" May 18. Died Samuel Martin of Lebanon in Connecticut; a likely young man, taken at sea. His sickness short.

" This day there came into Quebec, a schooner and sloop from Martineco. In their passage they took a sloop bound from Philadelphia to Antigua, and brought in four of her men. This day came up three prisoners from Bay Verde, viz., George

---

* *How* has the name *Fether.* † See *Particular History*, p. 97. *Ed.*

Schavolani, Zechariah Hubbard, and a Negro, and three from the frontiers of New England.

"May 19. Died Samuel Burbank, of New Hopkinson, an old man, taken April 22d, 1746.* The same day died Abraham Fort, son to John Fort, deceased, taken near Fort Ann, November 16th, 1745.

[39] "May 20. I was taken ill with a grievous pain in my head, and a sore eye, that I was almost blind with it. The 21st I yielded to be sick. Capt. Roberts and Capt. Williams were also both of them very sick, being taken a few days before me. This day I was blooded, having something of the fever. The 23d I was blooded again; the doctor also gave me a bottle of eye-water, and advised me not to be concerned about the fever. I was sensible they did not apprehend how ill I was. I intreated of him to give me a potion of physic, which he did, the 25th, and it worked very well. In the night I fell into a sweat, and was in hopes it would go off, but I was sadly disappointed, for I grew worse the next day. My reason departed from me, and returned not, until the 14th of June. Part of this time I was given over by every one that saw me. I had the nervous fever, and was very much convulsed. I was exceeding low and weak when I first came to myself, but I recovered strength as soon as could be expected; for, by the 24th of June, I got out, and went into the chamber.

"May 21. Died Robert Williams. He belonged to England, and was taken at sea.

"May 22. Died Nathaniel Hitchcock of Brimfield. He was taken with me.

---

* See *Particular History*, page 92, where the circumstances of the attack on Hopkinton are detailed. "At the same time [the death of Mr. Burbank happened] died two children, who were put out to the French to nurse." *How*, 22. May 19, he mentions receiving a letter from Major Willard, which is his last entry. *Editor*.

"May 25. Died Mr. Nehemiah How, of No. 2, aged about fifty-six; taken at Great Meadow, October 11th, 1745.*

"May 26. Died Jacob Quaquinbush, and Isaac his son, both taken at Sarathtoga, November 17th, 1745.

"May 30. Died Jacob Shepherd, a pious young man, well beloved and much lamented. He was taken with me.

"June 3. Died Robert David Roberts of Dartmouth, in England, master of a snow, taken at sea, May 1st, 1746.

"June 10. Died John Pitman of Marblehead, of the scurvy, taken at sea, May 27th, 1747.

"June 12. Died Abraham De Grave of Sechanectada, taken Oct., 1746.

"June 17. Died Samuel Stacy, taken at Menis, Feb., 1746, 7.

"June 20. Died William Nason of Casco Bay, taken at Menis, February, 1746, 7.

"June 30. Died Matthew Loring, taken at sea, May 29th, 1746.

[40] "This month there came into prison several prisoners; first, there were three prisoners brought from Mont Real, two of which were taken at Sarratoga, Feb. 22d, 1746, and one from Canterhook, April 10th, 1747. One man killed; at the same time a woman and child captivated with him.

"June 5. Came in two men taken at Pemaquid. There were twelve men killed when they were taken.

"June 11. We had an account from the French, that they had taken a number of Indians and Dutch, who had first done some mischief in Canada. There was about fifty in the whole scout, and they had taken about ten or twelve of them in this

---

* An account of his captivity was published in 1748, and republished in *Drake's* *Collection of Indian Captivities*, 1839. See, also, *Particular History*, 85.   *Ed.*

month. There came also thirty-six prisoners from Nova Scotia, most of which were taken at Menis, February, 1746, 7.

"July 2. Died Archibald Gartrage, a child, and son to Charles Gartrage, aged nine months.

"July 4. Died William Prindle, a Louisbourg soldier, a New England man originally, taken at St. John's, July 10th, 1746.

"July 11. Died Corporal William Norwood. He belonged to his Majesty's troops which came from Gibraltar to Louisbourg, taken at St. John's, July 10th, 1746.

"July 16. Died James Doyl. He was taken at sea, May 29th, 1746.

"The same day died Phinehas Forbush, of Westboro', taken at Fort Massachusetts with me. He was a very likely man.

"July 21. Died Jonathan Brigman, of Sunderland. He was taken with me at Fort Massachusetts.

"July 25. We came on board the ship Verd Le Grace,* which the governor of Canada sent with a flag of truce to Boston. The 27th we set sail for New England, at ten in the morning. August 1st we came in sight of Cape Breton Island.

"August 11. Died on board our flag of truce, Nicholas Burt. He belonged to the West of England, and was taken at sea, May 1st, 1746. Died in captivity, in all, seventy-three.

"August 16. We arrived at Boston. The sick and infirm were taken to the hospital. Col. Winslow† sent to me and

---

* The ship Vierge-de-Grace [Handsome Virgin], Captain Larregni. See *N. Y. Col. Docs.*, X, 118. *Ed.*

† Probably John Winslow, of the fourth generation from Governor Winslow of the Mayflower. He was in the calamitous Cuba expedition of 1740; in the Nova Scotia expedition of 1755, and general and commander-in-chief at Fort William, 1756; councillor of the Province, etc., etc.; died in Hingham, 1774, aged seventy-two. In the *News-Letter* of 5 June, 1760, is this notice: "In Capt. Watts came passenger General Winslow, who was welcomed ashore and congratulated by a great number of people, upon his return to his native country." *Editor.*

desired me to come and tarry with him while I continued in Boston. I thankfully accepted it, and was courteously entertained. This was a day of great joy and gladness to me. May I never forget the many great and repeated mercies of God towards me."

END OF THE REDEEMED CAPTIVE.

POSTSCRIPT.—In the account of CAPT. ROUSE, given *ante*, pages 240–3 — in noticing the antiquity of the name of Rouse — the following interesting facts would not have been inappropriate. In one of the first voyages made into the West Indies by Capt. FRANCIS DRAKE, namely, in the year 1572, he met there one Capt. ROUSE. In the first published account of that voyage the name is spelt *Rause;* and in a later edition, sometimes *Rause* and sometimes Rawse. These spellings might lead one to suppose the original may have been *Ross*. But Sir William Davenant, who lived near Sir Francis Drake's time, and wrote a play which he entitled the *History of Sir Francis Drake*, in which he introduces Drake's companions, uniformly writes the name of this one, *Rouse*. Hence it is presumed that *Ross* and *Rouse* are distinct names; and that Drake's companion was *Rouse*, and not *Ross*. Davenant printed his play in 1659, "Represented daily at the *Cockpit* in *Drury-Lane* at Three Afternoon Punctually." Perhaps some American *Rouse* may find himself a descendant of the old freebooter of 1572; if so he may derive satisfaction in this note, if not in his progenitor.

APPENDIX F.

Page 160.

THE following observations and criticisms on the affairs of the period of this war, admirably exhibit the condition of the country, the circumstances of the people, and the impressions upon their minds as to the conduct of their rulers. They are extracted from the close of Mr. Doolittle's *Memoirs*, as well an act of justice to him as for the reasons before stated. It should be remembered they were written before the war had fairly closed.

"The following remarks are easy and natural from the preceding history:

"1st. What a great difference there is between our managing a war and our enemies. The most we do is to defend ourselves at home; but they are for an offensive war. And it is true if they have any they must have this; for a defensive war they can have none with us: for not a man of ours has seen a French settlement all this war, except such as were carried captive or went with a flag of truce.

"2dly. It is a rare thing we can obtain an Indian scalp, let us do what spoil we will upon them; so careful are they to carry off and conceal their dead. For at Fort Massachusetts, where, it is probable, near sixty * have been killed, never have been found more than three scalps, which shows us that our

---

* The number killed at the siege and died of their wounds. It seems incredibly large, too, in view of what was said by the English at the time. But the besiegers showed uncommon daring, and were numerous.

men will not venture out after the enemy on any scalping act whatsoever. Our men will not venture their lives and service, on such uncertain encouragements; * if they should be much greater than ever they have been. The like is demonstrated at Number Four, where they have killed so many of the enemy, never a scalp could be recovered.†

"3dly. We may observe, of how much importance the enemy judge those two forts, at Number Four, and Hoosuck, to be to us. Hence their repeated endeavors to destroy them; which they would not do, were they not advantageous to us, and in their way in coming upon us. And it shows how much it must encourage our enemies for us to give up either of them.

"4thly. We may observe, how safely the enemy can draw off when they have done mischief. I think but one instance ‡ has there been all this war of our pursuing and overtaking the enemy to do any spoil on them, and there are many reasons for it : One is, that no body may move till an account is sent to the chief colonel ; and then men must be mustered, which takes so long a time that there is no possibility of our taking them. Another reason is, that we never have men near, equipped to pursue them in the woods ; and when they have gone a few miles in the woods, they are discouraged and return home.

"5thly. It is observable, that the continual changing of schemes renders all measures for the war unsuccessful. Before any one single scheme is tried, it is flung up, and nothing ever

---

* As the bounty offered by the government for scalps. *Ed.*

† Because the defenders in the garrison durst not venture out for fear of being cut off by some in ambush, as they had too often experience. *Ed.*

‡ The author probably has reference to Capt. Melvin's expedition; or perhaps to that of the Mohawks, of November, 1746. However much the English were accustomed to the woods, the Indians were far more at home there. *Ed.*

prosecuted to advantage: There is scarcely any one scheme of more than six months continuance.

"6thly. We may observe, that when the Province have voted any number of men for a particular service, by that time the commissary can furnish the men with their provisions, their time is expired; and this was the case the summer past:* it took the greater part of the summer to supply the garrisons with provisions; they were so scarce: And the soldiers who were designed as scouts towards Crown Point, were a good part of their time employed in guarding provisions to the forts.

"7thly. It is observable to all who know the state of these frontiers, that there is not due provision made to furnish the men out on any occasion after the enemy. There is neither bread nor meat, shoes, blankets, etc., that a number of men may take on any sudden occasion. They have their bread to bake, their meat to cook, and other things to get, when they should be on their march:† And so long as this is the case the enemy never need fear our annoying them when they have distressed us.

"8thly. It is observable, that all this war we have never kept men in the woods towards Crown Point, to discover their large bodies coming down upon us, and give notice of an approaching enemy: So that they came securely, week after week, upon us; yea, we have since found that the enemy have camped several months within thirty or forty miles of Fort Dummer.

"9thly. Another thing observable, is the great temptation soldiers have to be unfaithful in the service. For there is no distinction made, as to their wages, between a soldier in an old town, one in a garrison, and one marching in the woods; who

---

* The summer of 1748. *Ed.*
† This was specially the case when so many men were lost on the 4th of May, 1746. See Potter's *Manchester*, 221. *Ed.*

when he is in the woods, wears out as many clothes as his wages will procure, besides all his hardships and sufferings. Soldiers therefore choose to lodge in the garrison; and think hard if they must be kept in the woods, when others have as much pay in old towns, who eat and lodge well.*

"10thly. We differ much from the French with respect to the war. They will not give men commissions, 'till they have been out in the war and done some spoil on their enemies. If the like method was practiced with us, there would be fewer commissions; and more, it is probable, would be done on the enemy, in order to obtain them. But so long as no regard is had to this in promoting of men, we cannot expect men will exert themselves as they ought to do.

"11thly. The reader may observe, how much the people in the western frontiers must be distressed by the war, and how falsely they judge, who think the war is an advantage to them. Their case is most distressing. The repeated alarms take them off from their business, day after day, for forty or fifty miles together; and the reader is to observe, that in the preceding history, there is mention of great number of times of the enemy being seen and shot at, both in the night and day time; and of their setting open gates, and turning creatures into fields to devour crops. It was not the design of the author to give you an account of the people's losses, but of the mischief done. If any envy the inhabitants in the frontiers their portion, they may come and take their lot with them.

---

* Wages in those days were very small. A common soldier had about £1 5s. a month; a sergeant, £1 12s.; a corporal, £1 8s.; a captain, £4 10s.; a major, £8 10s.; colonel, £10; brigadier-general, £15; a surgeon, £4 10s.; a surgeon-general, £5; clerk, £1 12s.; chaplain, £4 10s.; captain of artillery, £9; lieut. of artillery, £4 10s.; gunners, £2. This list of wages was made up with reference to the Louisbourg expedition, and was somewhat modified subsequently. *Ed.*

" 12thly. It ought to be observed, that great injustice is done the inhabitants in the frontiers, in pressing them out of their business into the Province service, either to follow the enemy or convoy stores, and not rewarding them suitably. They are sent out day after day, with their horses, and have not half so much per day as they must give a man to labor for them in the mean time.

" Lastly, we may observe, that in this war, as we increased in our number of men in our forts or scouts, the enemy have increased their numbers; and the longer the war continues, the oftener they come, and the more bold they grew; which shows us what we must expect, if the war breaks out anew; especially at this time, when there is no provision made for men in our frontiers."

END.

---

* If the people on the frontiers supplied the contractors with certain articles, those able to supply them doubtless were benefited. Those away from the frontiers probably grumbled because they had not an opportunity to profit by the war. There can be no such thing as an equality of burthens in war. *Ed.*

INDEX.

ABANAQUES, of St. Francis, 34, 36–38, 89, 111, 127, 148, 151.
Abbot, ——, killed, 171.
Abercrombie, James, 25.
Acadie, origin of name, 51.
Adams, Robert, a captive, 132, 283.
Aix la Chapelle, treaty of, 172.
Albany, in peril, 27, 28, 37, 39; Indian conference at, 53, 63, 84, 113; men killed near, 98.
Alden, Timothy, 211, 241, 246.
Aldrich, John, a captive, 119, 256, 262; carried on Indian's back, 263.
Alexander, Capt., shoots a Frenchman, 152.
Algonkins, join the French, 36, 39, 41, 89.
Allen, Benjamin, 227; Elijah, killed, 101; Joseph, *ib.*, 229.
Allen, Samuel, 93, 126, 153.
Allen, William, 12, 15.
Allen, Zebulon, captured, 146.
American Magazine, 47, 48, 58.
Ames, Jacob, severe fight, 156, 157.
Amherst, Jeffery, Gen., 25, 210.
Amrusus, husband of Eunice Williams, 86.
Amsden, Oliver, killed, 125.
Amsden, Simeon, killed, 125.
Anderson, James, captured, 84; killed, 132, 284.
Anderson, Samuel, captured, 84.
Anderson, John, captured, 154.
Andrews, ——, wounded, 155; Francis, dies, 286.
Anson, George, Com., 154, 248, 249, 271.
Annapolis, attempted, 55; relieved, 57.

Antonio, ——, dies in prison, 288.
Argall, S., expedition to Canada, 51.
Armadas, notice of, 129.
Arresuguntoocooks, treaty with, 176.
Ashley, Jonathan, 11.
Ashuelot, since Keene, 78, 93, 96, 115; attacked, 143, 149, 150.
Askmacourse, harbor, 66.
Athol, man killed at, 117; Indian name, *ibidem*
Atkinson, Theodore, 176; Thomas, dies, 286.
Attenkins, number of, 34, 37.
Auchmuty, Robert, 22; Samuel, Sir, 22, 23.
Aussaado, a Weweenock chief, 176.
Avery, ——, captured, 158; Oliver, wounded, 153.
Avery's Garrison, some killed at, 158.

BABCOCK, John, captured, 157.
Bacon, Quartermaster, wounded, 101; Ebenezer, wounded, 227.
Bagley, Jacob, dies in prison, 286.
Bagley, William, dies in prison, 284.
Baker, James, killed, 109.
Ball, ——, killed, 158.
Bancroft, George, 16.
Bane, David, 227; Joseph, *ibidem*. See BEANE.
Barber, John W., cited, 11.
Baron, Timothy, a soldier, 228.
Barrington, Samuel, Admiral, 250.
Bassiere, should be Brassier, which see.
Batherick, Jonathan, a captive, 280.
Beaman, John, captured, 109, 110.
Bean, or Beane, John, killed, 116; Steven, Thomas, 228.

Index.

Beard, Robert, killed, 149.
Beatson, R., cited, 47.
Beauharnois, M. de, 33, 76.
Becket, ——, Captain, 66, 67.
Bedford, men ambushed there, 88.
Belden, Aaron, killed, 171.
Belknap, J., cited, 109, 215, 277.
Bell, John, armourer, 228.
Bemis, Edward, armourer, 228.
Bennet, Moses, Captain, 228; Richard, 113; dies in prison, 287.
Berry, Thomas, at Indian conference, 63.
Berwick, people killed at, 159, 160.
Bickford, William, killed, 163.
Biggs, William, cited, 207.
Billings, ——, killed, 168.
Bingham, John, dies, 283.
Blachford, Benjamin, a captive, 178.
Blake, Nathan, taken, 93; ransomed, 153.
Blanchard, William, taken, 163.
Bliss, Constant, killed, 124, 126.
Blodget, ——, killed, 166.
Bollan, William, 29.
Bolton, William, a captive, 150.
Book of the Indians, reference to, 133.
Boon, John, dies in prison, 285.
Boovee, Peter, captured, 151.
Boscawen, Edward, Admiral, 154, 201.
Boularderie, M., defeated, 214.
Bouquet, Henry, Col., cited, 133.
Bourne, Melatiah, Sylvanus, 229.
Boynton, John, killed, 149.
Brabbon, Guyart, dies in prison, 286.
Bradbury, Jabez, Capt., 79, 80, 99, 151; Nathan, killed, 151.
Braddock, Edward, Gen., 21, 25, 29.
Bradley, Jonathan, killed, 116; Samuel, *ibidem.*
Bradshaw, John, killed, 76; one dies, 284.
Bradt, ——, Capt., 142; John A., killed, 170.
Brainerd, David, death of, 151.
Brassier, William, his map, 267.
Breda, treaty of, 51.
Bret, Piercy, Capt., 154.
Briant, William, killed, 90; Sarah, 280, dies in captivity, 291.
Bridgman's Fort, attacked, 109; burnt, 153.
Bridgman, Jonathan, 119; wounded, 256; dies, 294; Thomas, 11.

Broad Bay, depredation at, 99.
Brown, John, wounded, 142; Josiah, Capt., 105; Timothy, 96.
Brunswick, men killed near, 80.
Bryan, William, murder of, 234.
Buck, John, wounded, 96.
Buckler, Robert, soldier, 229.
Bull, Edward, 145; Nathaniel, killed, *ibidem.*
Bullard, John, killed, 93.
Bunten, ——, killed, 88.
Buntin, Robert, and son, taken, 158.
Burbank, Samuel, taken, 92; dies, 93, 292.
Burn, Patrick, a soldier, 229.
Burnet, William, built Fort Oswego, 52.
Burnet, or Burnel, killed, 159.
Burnet's Field, surprise at, 148.
Burns, Robert, escape of, 88.
Burt, Asahel, killed, 143; Nicholas, dies, 294.
Butler, Caleb, cited, 157.
Butler, Richard, of Boston, 229.
Butler, Walter, exploit of, 138–40.
Burton, Stephen, wounded, 110, 230.
Byron, John, adventures of, 249, 250.

CABOT, pretended discovery of, 188.
Cæsar, a saying of, 52.
Cacknawages, number of, 34.
Cadaraqui, Lake Ontario, 65.
Caldwell, George, killed, 145.
Calmady, Warwick, Capt., 184, 209.
Canada, population of, 34; belonged to the French, 50; condition of, 65.
Canajohara Indian killed, 144.
Canceau, or Canso, captured, 23, 198; by the French, 54; great rejoicing in France, 57; Gut of, described, 42, 200.
Cape Breton, importance of, 6; belonged originally to England, 88.
Cape Cod Indian, feat of one, 216.
Cape Sable Indians, 43; war declared against, 61, 82; some taken, 77; infection among, 132.
Captives, return of some, 172.
Carqueville, Sieur de, exploit of, 40.
Carr, James, killed, 158; Richard, wounded, 230.
Carrying-place, at Wood Creek, 91.
Carthagena, disastrous expedition, 195.

Index. 303

Caskebee, Casco Bay, 179.
Chandler, ——, killed, 168.
Chapeau-Rouge Bay, 206, 214.
Chapin, Elisha, exploit, 160, 162.
Chapman, William, a prisoner, 279, 286.
Charlestown, why so named, 142.
Charlevoix, P., cited, 42, 43, 188.
Chatelain, Lieut., exploit of, 111.
Cheaole, Edward, a captive, 179, 180.
Cheap, David, Capt., cast away, 249.
Chebucto, its locality, 282.
Cheney, William, a soldier, 230.
Chester, man killed there, 88.
Chew, Lieut., fight and loss, 147, 170.
Choate, John, 63, 176, 230.
Clark, Edward, Lieutenant, 230; Elijah, killed, 150; George, killed, 145; Matthew, killed, 97.
Clermont, M., at siege of Annapolis, 55, 57.
Clesson, ——, Capt., at Deerfield, 126.
Cleves, ——, Capt., voyage, 240.
Clinton, De Wit, 62.
Clinton, George, Gov., 34, 62, 65, 66, 69, 82, 113, 178.
Clinton, Peter, a captive, 178.
Cloutman, Edward, a captive, 90, 91; escapes, 281.
Cobb, Sylvanus, journal of, 230.
Coffin, ——, Capt., 173.
Colbe, Timothy, a captive, 178.
Colerain, men killed at, 97; fort, 104, 137, 138.
Colman, Benjamin, 30; dies, 150.
Colson, Timothy, a captive, 178.
Colville, Alexander, Lord, 250.
Concord, men surprised and killed, 116.
Conde, Adam, killed, 170.
Conessetagoes, number of, 34.
Connecticut, in the Louisbourg expedition, 28, 69, 84, 198; population, 35.
Conner, Francis, a captive, 170, 178; John, killed, 234.
Contoocook, attacked, 95, 116.
Cook, Elisha, killed, 95; Thomas, 96.
Cooper, Boyce, captured, 81; Moses, killed, 156.
Corbett, Jesse, drowned, 92.
Corlaer's Creek, 38, 39.
Corne, St. Luc de la, at Fort Massachusetts, 36.

Cornwall, Frederick, Capt., 212.
Cotton, Rowland, Secretary, 107.
Covell, William, wounded, 231.
Cox, John, Capt., killed, 145; Joseph, killed, 146.
Crecy, Joseph, a soldier, 231.
Creighton, David, killed, 81.
Crisson, Thomas, captured, 168.
Cromwell, Oliver, 51, 272.
Crosby, Josiah, petitioner, 231.
Crown Point expedition frustrated, 27; French magazine, 28; Fort St. Frederick, 36; seized by the French, 52, 53; some Mohawks assault, 124.
Croxford, William, killed, 173.
Cumberland, Duke of, victorious, 272, 275, 278.
Cummings, Timothy, captured, 100; dies, 289.

DAILY, William, a prisoner, 113; dies, 285.
Dalhonde, John, physician, 231, 232.
Damariscotta, people killed at, 143, 144.
Darling, Lieut., 169; killed, 170.
Davarisks, James, deserter, 229.
David, Capt. [Donahew?], 42, 43.
Davis, ——, Capt., 113, 173; Jedidiah, 232; John, wounded, 100, 232; dies, 283.
D'Anville, Duc, disaster of, 154, 271.
Debeline, Mons., defeat of, 140–2.
Deerfield, attack on, 125, 126.
D'Estaing, Count, 250.
Desabrevois, Capt., 36.
De Graaf, Klas A., killed, 190; Abraham, dies, 293.
Delancy, James, 26.
Demuy, Mons., Lieut., 40, 262, 264, 268, 271, 273, 274, 276.
Denning, Joseph, dies in prison, 289.
Diary of depredations, 6, 107–74.
Dickinson, Nathaniel, dies, 143.
Dill, John, dies in captivity, 289.
Dixwell, Bazil, Lieut., 232.
Doane, Elisha, Captain, 232.
Dod, John, killed, 162.
Dogan, Michael, dies in prison, 287.
Dogaman, Peter, a prisoner, 178.

Dogs, employed, 102; give notice of the vicinity of Indians, 114, 116, 117; order to dispose of them, 132; in the Florida and other wars, 133.
Doliber, Thomas, 233.
Donahew, David, Capt., 43; exploit, 66; surprised and slain, 75; of Newbury, 77, 82, 199, 229, 233, 284.
Doolittle, Benjamin, 10, 13, 78, 94, 105, 109, 125, 152, 296; Hon. Mark, 11.
Door, Jonathan, a captive, 111.
Dorman, Ephraim, exploit, 93.
Doty, Mons., interpreter, 260, 261.
Douglas, James, Capt., 209.
Douglass, William, cited, 17, 54, 56, 58, 62, 66, 67, 72, 75, 172, 203, 211, 221, 247.
Dover, Allen, attacked, 116.
Downing, John, 176; Robert, 113.
Downs, Gershom, killed, 111.
Doyle, James, dies in captivity, 294.
Drake, Francis, Captain, 295.
Drake, Nathaniel, Captain, 114.
Dresser, Nathaniel, killed, 142.
Drisdell, Eleanor, 244.
Drown, Samuel, wounded, 146.
Drowned Lands, location of, 267.
Dubuque, ———, 31.
Du Chambon, M., a poltroon, 54, 221.
Dudley, Joseph, his war, 13.
Dummer, Jeremiah, cited, 20, 33.
Dummer, William, his war, 14.
Dunbar, Robert, escape of, 90, 281.
Dunham, Jonathan, dies in prison, 284.
Dunn, John, Major, 233.
Duplessis, Sieur, 36, 89.
Duquesnel, Meneville, Gov., 54, 56.
Durel, Philip, Capt., 209, 210.
Duvivier, M., takes Canceau, 23, 54, 183, 192, 199.
Dwight, Jasper, councillor, 195.
Dwight, Joseph, Gen., 132.
Dyer, Reuben, captured, 145.
Dyre, Joseph, complaint of, 233.

EAMES, Nathan, a captive, 119; dies, 283.
Eaton, Cyrus, cited, 22, 80; Ebenezer, killed, 159.
Eden, Daniel, a captive, 178.
Edghill, ———, a captive, 168.

Edwards, Jonathan, 152; Richard, Capt., 212.
Egeremmet, a Penobscot chief, 176.
Eliot, John, cited, 22; Mr., killed, 143.
Ely, Joseph, wounded, 141.
Eneas, a Norridgwok chief, 176.
Epsom, people captured, 149.
Erving, John, 30; Shirley, *ibidem*.
Esparagoosaret, a Penobscot chief, 176.
Estabrook, ———, killed, 132.
Eustis, William, Gov., 31.
Evans, Samuel, dies in prison, 289.

FALAISE, Lieut., exploit, 110.
Fall Town, Bernardston, 96, 137; men killed, 148.
Falmouth attacked, 143, 144.
Farmer, Daniel, taken, 168; John, cited, 215, 277.
Fainsworth, Stephen, 91.
Farnsworth, Samuel, killed, 101.
Fearne, John, at Louisbourg, 234.
Fisher, Josiah, killed, 78.
Fitch, John, and family, carried off, 165.
Flag of truce, discussion on, 128, 129.
Flathead, tribe of Indians, 38.
Folles Avoines. See WILD RICE.
Folsom, George, cited, 128.
Folson, John, Killed, 149.
Forbush, Phinehas, 280; dies, 294.
Fort, Abraham, dies, 292; John, Capt., dies, 87, 288.
Fort Dummer, 101, 109, 153, 156.
Fort Halifax built, 20.
Fort Hinsdale, location, 137.
Fort How, location, 137.
Fort Massachusetts, 104; captured, 117, 118, 146, 159, 160; names of prisoners, 119; French account, 122; fight there, 146; other facts, 253, 254, 259, burnt; 260, 297.
Fort Niagara, location, 52.
Fort Pelham, men at, 137.
Fort St. Frederick, 36; built, 52, 124.
Fort Shirley, 137, 253.
Fort, Southerland, a prisoner, 178, 179.
Fort Western built, 20.
Foster, ———, killed, 143.
Fowle, Daniel, printer, 251.
Fowler, Jeremiah, 92.
Frankland, Henry, Sir, 29.
Frement, Samuel, a captive, 179.

Index. 305

French, Nathan, killed, 163.
French, documents, expeditions, 9; war periods, 13, 14; a great armada sent against New England, 26; barbarism of, 32; their management of the Indians, 33; possessed advantages over the English, 34; their account of expeditions sent against New England, 35–41; their story of wrongs, 41–44; receive early intelligence of the declaration of war, 47; had a better title to New England than the English, 50, 53; run away with the bone, 52; built their forts with English strouds, 53; take Canso, 54; defeated by Donahew, 66; ships taken at Lcuisbourg, 70; losses there, 70; prisoners shipped to France, 71, 72; take Fort Massachusetts, 119–22; an armada sent against New England, 129; great sickness among, 132; bounties for prisoners and scalps, 134; success at Pemaquid, 145, 146; defeat at Fort Massachusetts, 147; besiege it, 254; take and burn it, 260.
Frost, John, killed, 163.
Frousac, Strait, 42.
Fuller, Thomas, saying of, 190.
Furbush, Phinehas. See FORBUSH.

GABARUS BAY. See CHAPEAUROUGE.
Galbaoth, William, dies in prison, 287.
Galissoniere, Count de la, 278.
Ganiengoton, takes scalps to Montreal, 37.
Ganon, M., accusation against, 41.
Gardner, John, a pilot, 234.
Garrish, George, a smith, 234.
Gartrage, Archibald, dies in captivity, 294.
Gatienoudé, an Iroquois, killed, 37.
Gatroup, Mattée, a captive, 178.
Gayton, Pierce, Capt., 183, 184, 234.
George Second, King, 47, 272.
George's Fort, 79, 82, 83, 99, 151.
Gerrish, Samuel, 77.
Gibson, James, Col., 22, 23, 72.
Gillett, Adonijah, killed, 126.
Gilson, Michael, wounded, 109.
Girard, Lacroix, Capt., 222.

Girler, William, a pilot, 235.
Glen, Jacob, Jr., killed, 170.
Goffe, John, Capt., march of, 95; William, a captive, 178.
Goodale, Thomas, killed, 153.
Goodman, Samuel, a captive, 119; dies, 288.
Gordon, Joseph, killed, 128; Pike, a captive, *ibidem*, 281; dies, 284.
Gorham, John, Capt., 42; Col., 58, 129, 173, 235.
Gorhamtown, tragedy at, 90, 283.
Gould, Nathaniel, killed, 153.
Graves, Asahel, killed, 168; Samuel, wounded, 164.
Graville, Aylmer, commissioner of exchange, 172.
Gray, Joseph, dies in captivity, 291.
Great Meadows, surprise at, 77; location, 78, 85.
Green Farms, location, 39.
Green River, garrison, 138.
Gridley, Richard, Col., 69.
Groot, Simon, killed, 98.
Grote, John, dies in prison, 283.
Groton, tragedy at, 156.
Groves, ———, Lieut., 146.
Greely, Philip, killed 116.
Guerrefille, Greenfield? 39.
Gun, Samuel, killed, 164.

HAGADORN, Jonathan, a captive, 87; dies, 286.
Hall, Andrew, 77.
Halliburton, T. C., cited, 67, 191, 266, 267.
Hancock, Thomas, 232.
Hardy, Charles, Sir, 201.
Harry, Indian chief, 176.
Harris, Thomas, 235.
Harrison, W. H., Gen., 260.
Harrytown, location of, 95.
Hart, Ensign, his company surprised, 131.
Hartwell, Edward, Major, 94.
Harvey, Benjamin, killed, 151; Josiah, wounded, 100; Moses, 92.
Hawes, Lieutenant, killed, 145.
Hawke, Edward, Sir, 250.
Hawks, Eleazer, killed, 125; Gershom, wounded, 104; John, Sergeant, wounded, 97; at Fort Massachusetts, 118, 152–5, 277.

Hawley, Lieut., wounded, 171.
Heard, Joseph, killed, 111.
Heaton, Cornet, wounded, 105.
Henderson, John, taken, 153.
Hendrick, expedition into Canada, 135, 148.
Henry Fourth, declares war, 51.
Henry, John, captured, 168.
Hicks, Nathaniel, wounded, 235.
Hills, Daniel, a soldier, 235.
Hilton, Ebenezer, killed, 149; William, taken, *ibidem*.
Hinkley, ——, killed, 144.
Hinsdale's fort, ambush near, 111, 153.
Hitchcock, Nathaniel, a captive, 119, 281; dies, 292.
Hobbs, Humphrey, Capt., 163–5.
Hocquart, M., 76.
Hodgdon, Mrs., killed, 159; Jonathan, *ibidem*.
Holburne, Admiral, 242.
Hollis, Isaac, 160, 161.
Holmes, Abiel, cited, 112.
Holton, Jacob, killed, 94.
Hoosuck Fort. See FORT MASSACHUSETTS.
Hoosuck River, 39; Road, 262.
Hopkins, Captain, 126.
Housatunnuk Indians, 77.
How, Daniel, Jr., taken, 68, 109, 110, 287.
How, Nehemiah, taken, 85, 109; dies, 293.
Howard, John, killed, 162.
Howe, Caleb, 78.
Hoyt, Moses, a soldier, 235.
Hubbard, Zechariah, a captive, 292.
Hunniwell, Roger, wounded, 235.
Hunt, Eliakim, killed, 100.
Huntington, Hezekiah, 97; dies in captivity, 291.
Hutchinson, Eliakim, 29, 31.
Hutchinson, Thomas, on Shirley, 17; Speaker of the General Court, 107; commissioner, 63, 84; portrait, 108; cited, 112; at the Indian treaty, 176; anecdote from, 177.

INDIANS, easily imposed upon, 33; chiefly on the side of the French, 34; numbers, *ibidem*; tribes engaged with the French, 41; contagion spread among, 43; had great ad-

Indians (continued) —
vantages in a war, 41; had causes of complaint, 49; great conference at Albany, 53; St. John tribe, and others, attempt the surprise of Annapolis, 55; some employed as rangers, 58; Mohawks secured by the English, 59; some sent to secure the Eastern Indians, 60, 63; war declared against, 61, 82; some killed near George's Fort, 83; barbarously murdered, 84; conference at Albany, 84; surprise Saratoga, 86; signal repulse at Number Four, 105; attempt Rochester, 110; council at Albany, 113, 114; surprise men at Saratoga, 127, 131; at Sheepscott, 132; attempts to Christianize the Stockbridges, 160; great assembly at Albany, 170; some at New York, 173; condition at the close of the war, 175; a delegation at Boston, 175, 176; treaty at Falmouth, 176; annoyance at Louisbourg, 218, 219; at Fort Massachusetts, 255; enter it, 260; carry their prisoners on their backs, 263; and other ways, 265.
Ingersole, Ensign, 246.
Irish, Stephen, surprised, 103.

JACKSON, William, Capt., 236.
Jebucta. See CHEBUCTO.
Jedoure, murders there, 61.
Jenkins, ——, Capt., 207; Philips, 236.
Jennens, Paul, 147.
Jennings, ——, killed, 166.
Job, Col. (Indian), dies in prison, 83; his wife, 84; son-in-law, 100.
Johnson, Joel, captured, 163; William, 26; Colonel, 138; Mrs., narrative of, 174.
Johnson, Lieut., exploit of, 131.
Jones, Thomas, taken, 95; Captain, 66, 67; dies, 282.
Jonquiere, Jaques, P. de T., 40, 154, 180.
Jordan, Henry, wounded, 236; John, dies, 288.
Jose, Francis, a pilot, 236.
Julien, ——, 31.

Index. 307

KAKECOUTE [Schaghticoke?], 39.
Keene. See UPPER ASHUELOT.
Kellogg, Martin, Captain, 161.
Kelton, Jonathan, armourer, 236.
Kenny, Nathan, wounded, 237.
Kilpatrick, T., Lieut., 151 ; John, killed, *ibidem*.
Kincaid, James, killed, 158.
Kinderhook, attacked, 98, 142, 163.
King Philip's war, dogs used in, 132.
Kinlade, James, a prisoner, 84.
Kinsey, John, 85.
Kinslaw, John, Captain, 237.
Kintigo, a Mohawk, exploit of, 147.
Kiskakon Indians join the French, 41.
Kneeland, Abner, Rev., 174.
Knight, William, captured, 142.
Knowles, Charles, Com., 141, 142, 184, 275.
Knowlton, Joseph, 120 ; Thomas, killed, 118, 258.
Konkapot, Ensign, killed, 146.

LACORNE, M. St. Luc, 262.
Lahontan, Baron, cited, 188.
Lake, Benjamin, captured, 159.
Lake George, its Indian name, 267.
Lake of the Two Mountains, 33, 37, 180.
Lake Sacrament, 36.
Lambert, William, prisoner, 28.
Langdon, Capt., men surprised, 131.
Laplante, Sieur, wounded, 140.
Larman, John, captured, 143, 291.
Lawrence, Charles, General, 201 ; Thomas, 85 ; ——, captured, 168.
Leatherland, Jacob, a soldier, 237.
Le Heve, surprise there, 76.
Leke, Thomas, Captain, 271.
Lescarbot, names an island, 75.
Lewis, Thomas, complaint against, 237, 248.
Lion, Aaron, killed, 100.
Littlefield, ——, 274.
Livingston, William, 17, 66, 142.
Long Creek, man killed at, 103.
Longueil, Chevalier, 153.
Loring, Matthew, capture and death, 148, 293.
Lothrop, Simon, Col., 69.
Loudon, Lord, 25.
Louis XV, declares war, 47.

Louisbourg, expedition, 17 ; origin, 23 ; taken, 67 ; details of the capture, 71, 72, 107 ; strength of, 190 ; siege of, 187–224.
Loutre, M. Le, at Annapolis, 55.
Lovet, Samuel, a captive, 119 ; dies, 287.
Lovett, Joseph Woodward, 229, 237.
Lowell, Abner, wounded, 145.
Lower Ashuelot, affairs of, 96, 115.
Lufkin, John, killed, 116.
Lunenburg, garrison taken, 165–7.
Lydius, John Henry, 87, 180.
Lydle, Leonard, captive, 90 ; married, 283.

McCARTEES, Susanna, dies, 289.
McCoy, Mrs., captivated, 149.
McFaden, James, a soldier, 238.
McFarlane, John, wounded, 127, 178 ; Walter, a captive, returned, 177.
McForney, Samuel, taken, 158.
McGraw, Christopher, a captive, 178.
McKenney, Daniel, wounded, 164 ; wife killed, 93, 94.
McNeer, John, captured, 132, 283.
McQuade, James, killed, 88.
Magawambee, a Norridgewok, 176.
Magra, Thomas, dies in captivity, 288.
Maison Forte, de la, taken, 209, 211, 212.
Mann, Daniel, killed, 162 ; Robert, Capt., 72.
March, ——, Mr., taken, 143 ; John, 238
Marechite, Indian tribe, 55.
Marcy, Joseph, killed, 100.
Mariens, John, killed, 170.
Marin, Mons., defeated, 67, 76, 86.
Marsh, Jacob, chirurgeon, 237.
Martin, Samuel, died in captivity, 291.
Mascareene, Paul, Colonel, 55, 57.
Massachusetts, population of, 34, 35 ; Shirley's services to, 74, 84 ; out of New England, 257.
Materials for history, 8–14.
Mather, Cotton, cited, 13, 33 ; Increase, 248.
Maurepas, Count, 33, 76.
Mayberry, ——, Mr., 150.
Mayhew, Benjamin, 145, 146.
Mejagouche Bay, location, 43.
Melvin, Eleazar, Capt., 103 ; relieves Shattuck's Fort, 137 ; surprise and fight, 161.

Index.

Mihils, John, wounded, 97.
Mickmacks, attack Annapolis, 55; surprise and kill Capt. Donahew and his men, 76; surprise Capt. Rouse, 112.
Mills, John, killed, 148.
Minas, location of, 67, 76.
Missiquecks, number of, 34, 38; join the French, 41.
Mitchell, Ebenezer, killed, 164.
Moffet, Robert, attacked, 96.
Mohawks, held in dread, 58; some go against Crown Point, 124: and Canada, 135, 138; captives, 178.
Mohegans, sickness among, 132.
Mole, Adam, exchanged, 178.
Monckton, Robert, Colonel, 25, 242.
Monteson, M. C. de, exploit, 112.
Moore, Samuel, Col., at Louisbourg, 69.
Morell, ——, Miss, killed, 160.
Morepang, Capt., defeated, 214.
Morris, Col., killed, 83.
Morrison, David, captivated, 114; Hugh, 104.
Morse, Jedediah, cited, 282.
Moulton, Jeremiah, councilor, 195.
Mount Swag, people killed, 149.
Moxas, Lieut. Governor [Col. Morris?], 83.
Murray, James, General, 25.

NAKLOONOS, a Norridgewok chief, 176.
Nason, William, capture and death, 136, 293.
Nasqumbuit, a Norridgewok chief, 276.
Nermon, a Penobscot chief, 176.
Negroes, captured, 87; killed, 95, 96, 98.
Nelson, Temple, 246; John, *ibidem*.
Nevers, Elisha, a soldier, 229, 238.
Newcastle, Duke of, 19, 65, 81.
New England, deplorably situated, 49; population, 35; losses and wrongs, 70.
New England H. and G. Register, 25, 279.
New Hampshire, services, 28; population, 35; in the Louisbourg expedition, 69; French prisoners in, 72.
New Hopkinton, surprised, 92.

New Meadows Neck, one killed there, 144.
New York, offers reward for scalps, 87.
Nichewag, location of? 157.
Nicolson, Joshua, a captive, 179, 180.
Nictumbouit, a Penobscot chief, 176.
Nims, Elisha, killed, 104.
Nipissings, 36; return with scalps, 37-9, 41, 89; location of, 180.
Niverville, Chev. de, 36, 89, 91.
Noble, Arthur, surprised and killed, 136; James, Capt., disgraced, 238.
Norman's kill, people slain, 99.
Norridgewoks, treaty with, 176.
Norris, Isaac, commissioner, 85.
Northampton, man killed, 150.
Norwood, William, dies in captivity, 294.
Northfield, depredations at, 116, 137, 143, 171.
North Yarmouth, depredations at, 116, 159.
Norton, John, marries two captives, 90, 283; chaplain at Fort Massachusetts, 118; letter of, 120; his Redeemed Captive, 251; notice of, 251-3.
Norwood, William, son killed, 98; dies, 113.
Notre Dame, Te Deum at, 57.
Nottingham, men killed at, 149.
Nova Scotia, its importance, 5, 8, 20; key to New England, 51; set off from Cape Breton, 188.
Number Four, attacked, 94; men killed, 100; in distress, 101; again attacked, 105, 114; exposed, 117; brave defense of, 140-2; men surprised, 115.

OBINACKS, number of, 34.
Oequarme Fort [Number Four], 154.
Oglethorp, James, General, 47.
Old Indian Chronicle, 48, 53.
Old Tenor, value of, 62, 88.
Ondcriquegon, drowned land, 267.
Onondagos, former name of, 82.
Ontario, Cadaraqui, 65.
Orange. See ALBANY.
Osgood, Benjamin, captured, 163.
O'Sullivan, ——, Dr., 275, 276.
Oswego, fort built at, 52, 53.

Index. 309

Otis, James, at Indian treaty, 176.
Ottowas, join the French, 41, 82.
Outassago, leads against Saratoga, 36.
Owen, James, killed, 76, 113.

PADENUQUE, James, Indian, 42.
Paine, Capt., at Number Four, 100.
Pais, ——, Mr., 279.
Palatine, a German settlement, 98.
Paper money, value, etc., 17, 62, 88.
Paquage, location of, 117.
Parker, David, wounded, 105; Isaac, captured, 91.
Parsons, Usher, cited, 191.
Particular History, of recent origin, 6, 7.
Peace, proclaimed in Boston, 174.
Pelham Fort, location, 253.
Pemaquid, depredations at, 127, 144, 150.
Penhallow, Samuel, cited, 240, 274.
Penobscots, treaty with, 176.
Pepperrell, William, Gen., 63; Lieut.-General, 69; at Boston, 108; councilor, 195; at Canso, 198; besieges and takes Louisbourg, 187–224.
Pereez, a Norridgewok chief, 176.
Perkins, Moses, captured, 163.
Perrin, Peter, killed, 100.
Perry, John, a captive, 119, 262, 263, 277; Rebecca, dies, 285.
Peters, Obediah, killed, 116.
Petipas, Bartholomew, a prisoner, 43.
Pett, Jacob, killed, 145.
Petty, Joseph, killed, 162.
Philbrook, Job, taken, 158.
Philip Fifth, war with, 47.
Philips, John, a captive, 178.
Philip, King, his war, 132, 246.
Philipson, Philip, a captive, 179.
Phillips, Ebenezer, killed, 114; John, 280, 281.
Phips, Spencer, Gov., 83, 176; William, killed, 77, 78.
Pierce, James, 238; Samuel, wounded, 100.
Pike, Thomas, Lieut., 238.
Pines, Thomas, a soldier, 238, 239.
Pinkham, Zephaniah, a prisoner, 280, 281.
Piper, Henry, a captive, 179, 180.
Piquet, Francis, a priest, 87.
Pitcher, Reuben, captured, 81.

Pitman, John, dies in captivity, 293.
Pitt, William, secretary, 50.
Pixley, Noah, killed, 159.
Place, John, wounds an Indian, 147.
Platter, Lawrence, dies, 282.
Poependal, bloody fight near, 169.
Point de Cheveux (Frederic), 36.
Point Shirley, named, 25.
Poquoig, location of, 157.
Port St. Peter, location of, 43.
Portois, Joseph, 279.
Pote, William, Capt., a prisoner, 279, 280.
Potter, Chandler E., cited, 23, 95, 149.
Poutewatamies, join the French, 41.
Powers, Ephraim, captured, 168.
Pownal, Thomas, Gov., portrait, 24.
Pratt, Amos, a captive, 119; dies, 288.
Preble, Jedediah, Capt., 173; Zebulon, 239.
Price, Ebenezer, cited, 96.
Price, Roger, commissary, 30.
Priest, Eleazer, taken, 155.
Prince Edward's Island, 75.
Prince, Thomas, portrait, 79; history of the Louisbourg expedition, 187–206.
Prindle, William, a captive, 76; dies, 113, 294.
Proctor, ——, Lieut., 83, 114, 142.
Prout, Ebenezer, commissary, 238.
Puans, join the French, 41.
Putnam, Seth, killed, 94, 100.
Pynchon, Charles, physician, 239.

QUACKENBUS, Rachel, a captive, 179; Martha, dies in captivity, 285; Jacob and Isaac, die, 293.

RAMBAULT, Sieur G., 36, 89; taken, 152, 153.
Ramezay, M. de, defeats Colonel Noble, 136, 287, 288.
Rawson, Joseph, killed, 115; Edward, 116.
Ray, Patrick, wounded, 109.
Raymond, Count de, 44.
Raymond, Benjamin, 229, 239.
Read, Jacob, captured, 89; Josiah, dies, 118, 263, 264, 280; dies, 281; John, dies, 283.
Rebellion, southern, 17.
Reddington, Nathaniel, a soldier, 239.

310   Index.

Retaliation, discussed, 133.
Rhode Island, men furnished, 28; population of, 35; in the Louisbourg expedition, 69; other services, 84, 198.
Rice, Ralph, wounded, 164.
Richards, John, a captive, 111.
Richardson, Joseph, killed, 111, 163.
Rice, Hannah, a captive, 276.
Robbins, Williams, killed, 109.
Roberts, Alexander, captured, 116; Robert David, dies, 293.
Rochester, depredations at, 146, 147, 159.
Rogers, Robert, Maj., 92; William, 243.
Rose, Joseph, killed, 168.
Rouse, John, Capt., expedition to St. John, 112; at the capture of the Vigilant, 210; at Louisbourg, 182; biography of, 840-3; on the name, 295.
Rugg, David, killed, 86.
Ruggles, John, Captain, 230, 243.

SABREVOIS, de, Captain, 121.
Saccarappe, depredation at, 142.
Saco, men killed there, 43.
Sadler, John, escapes, 126.
Saint Blein, Sieur, 37, 40.
Saint Francis Indians, 34; a chief killed, 255.
Saint John Indians, war declared against, 61, 64, 82.
Saint John's Island, now Prince Edward's, 75; English surprised there, 113.
Saint Luc, M. de, expedition of, 142.
Saint Pierre, sent against the English, 35.
Samuel, Capt., killed, 83.
Saquish, a chief of Waweenocks, 176.
Sarratoga [Saratoga], depredations suffered, 36, 40, 98, 127, 131, 142, 147; River, 266, 274.
Sartle, Jonathan, taken, 153; Obediah, taken, 101; killed, 174.
Saunders, Thomas, Capt., 80, 135, 176.
Sauteurs, join the French, 41.
Saut St. Louis, 36, 38, 110.
Saumarez, Philip, served with Anson, 154.
Savage, Arthur, of Pemaquid, 104.
Sawwaramet, a Waweenock chief, 176.

Scalps, reward for, 62, 87, 134, 135; brought to Boston, 128.
Scarborough, enemy there, 142.
Schaghticooke, location of, 39.
Schavolani, George, a captive, 292.
Sehenectady, men killed, 169.
Schuyler, John, Col., 98; Captain, 127, 142.
Scofield, Philip, a captive, 110, 131, 287; dies, 288.
Sconce, Andrew, dies in prison, 283.
Scooduck, men killed at, 127.
Scott, Eli, killed, 164; Joseph, 119; Miriam, 266; dies, 285; Moses, 261, 262; Moses, Jr., dies, 287; Stephen, 119, 181; William, 110, 287.
Sedgwick, Theodore, Jr., 17.
Semblin, Sieur, 152.
Sergeant, John, Rev., 59; recommends retaliation, 101; Lieut. ——, killed, 156.
Severance, Samuel, killed, 162.
Shattuck's Fort, enemy appear at, 116; attempt to burn, 136; abandoned, 137.
Sheepscott, people killed, 84, 85, 101, 106, 132.
Sheldon, Eliakim, wounded, 184.
Shepard, Jacob, a captive, 119, 280; dies, 293.
Shirley, William, notice of, 15; eminent services, 16; birth, etc., 18; stupid charges against, *ibidem*; preserves Annapolis, 19; causes forts to be built on the Kennebec, 20; marriage, *ibidem*; appointed Major-General, 21; his conduct triumphantly vindicated, *ibidem*; residence, 25; his remains in King's Chapel, 25; his successors fortunate, 26; Johnson's perfidy to, 26; misrepresented, 28; time of his arrival at Boston, 29; parentage, *ibidem*; his son killed, *ibidem*; portrait accompanying this volume, 30; early foresaw the war, 47; saves Annapolis, 55; declares war against the Eastern Indians, 61; plans the Louisbourg expedition, 67; speech on reimbursement of New England, 73; proceeds to Louisbourg, 80, 81; his anxiety for the

Index.

Shirley, William (continued) —
frontiers, 101 ; recommends sending commissioners to Albany, 113; on the capture of Fort Massachusetts, 123; recommends swivel guns, 128; message respecting the Mokawks, 135; writes the other governors about treating with the Eastern Indians, 175; speeches, 181, 186; dedication to, 187; a principal former and promoter of the Louisbourg expedition, *ibidem;* letter to the Duke of Newcastle, 213-26; careful that New England have full credit for the acquisition, 224.
Shuttleworth, Vincent, wounded, 243.
Simmons, John, attacked, 117.
Simonds, Benjamin, a captive, 119.
Simpson, Elizabeth, killed, 149.
Six Nations, some at Albany, 53, 63, 84, 170.
Skillin, ——, 103.
Sluyck, Tunis, buildings burnt, 98.
Smeed, Captivity, baptised, 264; dies. 291; Daniel, 260 : dies, 290; John, 119; killed, 153, 261 ; Mary, dies, 288.
Smith, John, a captive, 110, 287 ; killed, 145, 146; Richard, 110, 287.
Smith, Thomas, cited, 290.
Smithurst, Capt., lost at sea, 206.
Soosephinia, a Norridgewok chief, 176.
South Fort, 148.
Southerland, James, a prisoner, 279.
Spafford, John, a prisoner, 91.
Spier, David, death of, 243.
Sprong, Cornelius, a captive, 178.
Stacy, Samuel, dies in captivity, 293.
Stanhope, Jonathan, wounded, 105.
Stanley, Nathaniel, commissioner, 85.
Stansbury, Elisha, a captive, 178.
Stanwood, Job, wounded, 243, 244.
Starkee, ——, killed, 144.
Stevens, Arent, commissioner, 85; Charles, killed, 155; Enos, captured, 174; Henry, 163; Phinehas, 95; brave defence of Number Four, 100, 105, 140-2, 168.
Stickney, William, captured, 116.
Stiles, Ezra, cited, 232.
Stockbridge Indians, 59, 160, 161.
Stoddard, John, Col., 63, 84, 132, 134.

Stoddert, B., Lieutenant, 178-80.
Stone Arabia, depredation at, 98.
Storer, ——, Mrs., captive, 276, 277.
Strong, Elisha, a soldier, 244.
Stuart, Edward, the Pretender, 272, 275.
Stubs, Richard, a captive, 127, 281.
Suitzer, Jacob, a captive, 179, 180.
Sullivan, James, cited, 99, 290.
Suncook, depredation at, 158.
Sunderland, John, a captive, 110, 287.
Swanzey, Lower Ashuelot, 96.
Swett, Joseph, shot, 104.

TAINTOR, Benjamin, captured, 104, 110, 287.
Tarrant, Alexander, a soldier, 244.
Tatness, Samuel, a soldier, 244.
Taylor, Isaac, killed, 142; Thomas, captured, 168 ; General Zachery, 113.
Tedder, Christian, dies, 97; dies, 291.
Temple, Robert, marriage, 30.
Terry, John, Captain, 244.
Thanksgiving, for the capture of Louisbourg, 187.
Theganacoeiëssin, Iroquois chief, 36.
Thesaotin, leads a war party, 37, 95.
Thomas, William, surgeon, 244.
Thompson, John, a captive, 178.
Tol, Daniel, killed, 169, 170.
Tomonwilemon, a depredator, 28.
Topsham, depredation at, 80, 144.
Toulouse, Port (Port St. Peter), 43.
Tourmell, M. De, Admiral, 271.
Townsend, Isaac, Admiral, 230.
Toxus, a Norridgewok chief, 176.
Traux, Isaac, missing, 170.
Trayne, Joshua, a soldier, 244, 245.
Treaty, of Breda, 51 ; of Utrecht, 189; with the Eastern Indians, 176, 177.
Trent, Capt., fight at Sarratoga, 142.
Trevanion, John, 250.
Truth will prevail, 26.
Turner, Abner, Captain, 245.
Twichel, Daniel, a soldier, 245.
Tyng, Edward, Capt., relieves Annapolis, 56-8; attends the Governor, 81; letter of, 209-11 ; appointed commodore, 241 ; notice of, 245, 246.

UPPER ASHUELOT, depredations, 93, 94, 99, 167.
Utrecht, treaty of, 189.

VANALSTINE, John, buildings burnt, 142.
Van Antwerp, Daniel, killed, 170.
Vander Bogert, Francis, killed, 170.
Vanderverick's, 264; Gratis, dies in prison, 284.
Van Schaick, Anthony, Capt., 178.
Van Slyk, Adrian, killed, 170.
Van Vorst, Dirk, wounded, 169.
Vans, Hugh, merchant, 232.
Varen, Edward, a captive, 178.
Vaudreuil, M. de Rigaud de, 40; invests Fort Massachusetts, 117; captures it, 118, 258; his losses, 119; Town Major, 121; wounded, 122; paternity, 254; kind to captives, 264.
Vaughan, Samuel, dies, 113, 289; William, 22–4, 202; exploits, 215, 216, 246, 247.
Vedder, Albert John, captured, 170; exchanged, 178.
Verazani, John de, discoveries of, 188.
Vernon, Edward, Admiral, 195.
Vielen, Cornelius, Jr., killed, 170.
Vigilant, frigate, captured, 209.
Villers, George, a soldier, 247.
Volmer, Christian, a captive, 179, 180; J., a captive, *ibidem;* Thomas, 179.
Vort, Simon, a captive, 179.
Vosborough, Peter, a captive, 178.
Vosburgh, Peter, buildings burnt, 98.
Vose, John, killed, 151.
Vroman, John, a captive, 170, 178; Peter, killed, 170.

WALDO, Samuel, General, 69; councillor, 195, 229.
Walker, Nathan, wounded, 164; William, 239, 248; ———, captured, 168.
Wallingford, Ezekiel, killed, 117.
Walter, Nathaniel, translator, 248.
Ward, Edward, Jr., 237, 248.
Wareedeon, a Weweenock chief, 176.
Warren, David, a captive, 119, 280.
Warren, Peter, Commodore, 68, 70, 71, 184, 186; before Louisbourg, 200: captures the Vigilant, 209; services acknowledged, 214.

Washington, George, 21.
Wawawnunk, a Wewenock chief, 176.
Wear's garrison, alarmed, 116.
Webb, Ezekiel, killed, 145.
Weiser, Conradt, interpreter, 85.
Wells, alarmed, 144.
Wells, Ezekiel, wounded, 171; Joshua, killed, 156; Samuel, 84.
Wemp, Ryer, captured, 170.
Wendell, Jacob, at Albany, 63, 84.
Wentworth, Benning, Gov., 23; cooperates with Shirley, 182.
Wentworth, John, killed, 111.
West River, fight there, 162.
Weston, Josiah, supposed killed, 145, 146.
Weweenocks, treaty with, 176.
Whitmore, Edward, General, 201.
Whitefield, George, 13.
Whitney, ———, wounded, 168.
Wild Rice Indians, 41.
Wileman, Tom, depredator, 98.
Willard, Josiah, 95, 111, 112, 152–4.
William Third, King, his war, 13.
Williams, Eunice, 86; Elijah, 146; Ephraim, 171; Israel, 176; Robert, Capt., dies, 292; William, 123, 146.
Williamson, Jonathan, captured, 84, 99, 290; William D., cited, 82, 99.
Willis, William, cited, 114, 279.
Winchell, Jedidiah, killed, 105.
Winchester, depredations at, 115, 117, 143.
Winslow, John, General, 294.
Wiscasset, people killed, 149.
Wolfe, James, General, 201.
Wolcott, Roger, commissioner, 85; General, 195; family of, *ibidem*.
Woodward, William Elliot, 30.
Woodwell, David, a captive, 92; Mary, *ibidem;* dies, 285.
Woolen, Presbury, captured, 158.
Wright, Amasa, wounded, 115; Benjamin, killed, 116; Moses, wounded, 112.
Wyman, Matthew, a captive, 163.
Wynne, Huddlestone, cited, 173.

www.ingramcontent.com/pod-product-compliance
Lightning Source LLC
Chambersburg PA
CBHW052053230426
43671CB00011B/1889